1930

THE WRIGHT BROTHERS

FATHERS OF FLIGHT

When Orville Wright made this flight of twenty miles over the Dayton Cow-Pasture Airport, October 4, 1905, the World believed less in the Airplane than in the Sea Serpent.

The
Wright Brothers

FATHERS OF FLIGHT

By
JOHN R. McMAHON

WITH ILLUSTRATIONS

BOSTON   1930
LITTLE, BROWN, AND COMPANY

ILLUSTRATIONS

7761

ILLUSTRATIONS

THE WRIGHT BROTHERS
FATHERS OF FLIGHT

CHAPTER I

The sky is alive with winged craft. They dart through clouds and slide across the open blue. At night, unseen, they murmur their progress along starry pathways. They wend to distant cities. They cross the oceans, the continents, the North Pole and — lately — the South Pole. They make pictorial map surveys, patrol forests against fire, maneuver in military hosts, bring first aid to regions of disaster, poison insects in field and orchard, carry machine parts to remote mines and a prize cow to a fair, transport people and cash and mail. Cupid also has flown. 'Tis said a kiss improves with altitude.

To-morrow we can see the sky crowded with traffic, needing winged officers to keep the roads clear. At the top leviathan expresses roar along from Chicago to London, from New York to Moscow and from Boston to Pekin. The middle distance is reserved for excursions to Greenland, the South Seas and Patagonia. The broad highway below is occupied by commuters and local travelers on paltry five-hundred-mile runs, salesmen, week-enders, joy-riders, a motley crew with cheap and wabbly equipment who somehow get to their destinations as in the days of reconditioned flivvers. The traffic officer has a task to make some of these people behave, keep on their side of the air and have their tail lamps on at night.

9761

Yet a quarter of a century ago no airplane existed!

Man flew for the first time on December 17, 1903, when Wilbur and Orville Wright launched themselves into the air at Kitty Hawk, North Carolina. They discovered the secret of flight and their principles are embodied in every practical airplane known in the world to-day. They are the immortal pioneers who lifted man from the earth and gave him another dimension to move in with freedom surpassing that of the birds. The airplane has been improved but not essentially changed from the original "flying machine" devised by the brothers Wright.

These are facts accepted by a minority of informed persons. For the public at large the Wrights' title is under a cloud. Indeed, many intelligent folk believe that Professor Langley of the Smithsonian Institution and some clever Frenchmen collaborated to secure the conquest of the air. Langley's attempt at a flying vehicle is on view in the Smithsonian at Washington, District of Columbia. Because of an equivocal label that credited it as the ancestor of aërial navigation, Orville Wright declined to exhibit the real pioneer machine in our national museum and instead sent it to the friendly exile of the Science Museum in London. The English have been more hospitable to the Wrights than their own people — as represented by officials.

It may be asked whether suitable amends were not made at the twenty-fifth anniversary of flight celebrated in connection with the International Civil Aëronautics conference held at Washington in December, 1928.

The answer is there were deficits in the amends and

the program was written by the hand of academic prejudice. There were reservations in behalf of a deceased savant, despite a superficial tone of whole-hearted tribute to the men of Dayton. The details of these reservations ranged from the design of a Wright airplane stamp to the address by the President of the United States. Orville Wright, guest of honor at ceremonies in Dayton, Washington and Kitty Hawk, breathed no faintest word of demur. Indeed he spoke not at all. But he did not see fit to recall the pioneer airplane from its sojourn abroad.

The public finds a mystery in the whole affair. It asks:

"If the Wrights are the true inventors, why are their claims whittled down by government scientists? Why have clever Frenchmen and others obtained credence for partial paternity of Dædalus' dream-come-true? Why, especially, have the Wrights kept a relative silence for years instead of proclaiming their case from the housetops? Why have they not long ago taken the public into their confidence and told their whole story, for the impartial judgment of mankind?"

Some brief answers to these questions may be given in advance of the full explanations.

A main factor in the obscuration of the airplane origin, now removed, has been economic interest — a potent mandate heeded even by writers and editors. The war of ownership has ended with the expiration of patent rights. There is happy peace and good-fellowship on the commercial scene. Perhaps inevitably the actual war has an aftermath of academic strife with learned men exploring the fields of hostility and engaging in mimic combats of their own. It is now a battle of the professors. Their tactics are polite and indirect. At the moment the heaviest battalions seem to be arrayed on the conservative side against the radical supporters of unorthodox genius.

The legal verdict is, ironically, with the radicals. The courts of all countries, including the United States, have in general sustained the Wrights, save on technicalities such as prior disclosure or other points comparable to the failure of a hotel guest to deposit his valuables for safe keeping with the clerk at the desk.

Government scientists are human and those of the Smithsonian were very human in seeking to bask in the fancied glory of a colleague, the ill-fated Langley whose machine crashed in the Potomac River a few days before the historic feat of the Wrights at Kitty Hawk. The scientists were glumly quiet for eleven years until the day when the Langley device, repaired, altered and new-engined, was proved capable of an erratic hop over the waters of a lake. Then they were jubilant, and lauded the late secretary of the Smithsonian as the Columbus of the sky, disregarding the fact that his original machine embodied none of the principles essential to practical flight. The late Doctor Walcott, successor to Langley as head of the Smithsonian, was chiefly responsible for the revival of a museum chimera. Doubtless he was sincere in the belief that an eminent scientist, his friend and colleague, had to be right as against a pair of young "bicycle men" of Dayton, Ohio, who never looked inside a college door. To-day the Smithsonian has a fair-minded and conciliatory head, but the Langley legend and tradition are hard to put down at the national capital.

Professor Langley does deserve our respectful homage in passing, for he valorized the reputed impossible and though he failed, his faith stimulated others to success.

As to the clever Frenchmen and others, they were adapters of the invention proved at Kitty Hawk. They were deft at publicity and colorful feats and at commercializing. Some of them made real contributions to aviation and they added useful refinements, but none was able to dispense with the basic principles discovered by the Wrights or to alter the chief features of the original sky craft. There may be loopholes in patents but not in the laws of nature that govern flight.

The Wrights kept a relative silence and tolerated a partial eclipse, because they were shy by nature and upbringing; they became reticent to protect an invention that half the world laughed at and the other half tried to steal. They had no gift for publicity, shrank from clamor, distrusted the press, came to suspect a large part of their fellow men. It was a natural reaction. They never married. They lived a protected home life with a father and an only sister. They had no knack for business. They received a small fraction of the proceeds of an invention which yielded fortunes to others and has a world value almost incalculable.

It may be argued that patent trespass is a benefit to society, for those who borrowed from the Wrights, going far afield to circumvent prior claims, chanced upon veritable improvements. On the other hand, it is likely that the original inventors, left to themselves, would have inaugurated most or all the betterments devised by their self-appointed collaborators. Assured of peaceful ownership, the Wrights would have early revealed their full knowledge, and thereby have saved the world half a dozen years of costly blundering. The appeal to economy may convince where ethics are dismissed as a superstition out-moded. Let us note too, in passing, that this question, whether it be policy or ethics, concerns society and the whole class of inventors. The experience of the Wrights was far from unique: it was almost typical.

Wilbur, the elder brother, died in 1912. It was a great shock to Orville, who has striven since then to write the chronicle of an epochal achievement, as much to obtain complete honor and justice for that beloved brother's memory as for his own vindication. The task seems too much; it opens wounds, it involves the baring of family intimacies which to a supersensitive character are inviolate.

Aside from fugitive interviews or statements to the press, the inventors have published under their own signatures a total of some dozen items. These consist of technical papers and one magazine article in popular summary of their work, besides another article or two quite brief and topical. Such a record of self-effacement can hardly be matched among their peers.

Although forced by the nature of their invention to become showmen of it before all the world, the Wrights detested a rôle for which they were signally unfitted and retired as soon as possible from the gaudy tumult to the peaceful shelter of their home. Silence became their breastplate and shield.

The American public has a right to view all the evidence that may help to unveil the mystery of the airplane origin and enable it to award due honor to the men of Dayton. Homely details are part of that evidence, often an essential part. The drapes of secrecy do not fit the captains and benefactors of mankind. It was my privilege to study the unpublished documents of the Wright brothers, their diaries, letters and family records, as well as to talk at length with Orville, his father and sister while staying at their home. If the public had the same privilege, it would share my conviction in the utter veracity of the Wrights and their perfect title to stand amid the first scientist-discoverers of all time.

Is it credible that Orville is shy and dislikes the fanfare of renown? The writer met him for the first time in the lobby of a New York hotel. He was a small figure, neatly dressed, wearing a derby hat. One noted that his feet and hands were small. He limped a trifle, as a result of the one air crash of his career. His voice was low, his words pleasant but few, his manner oddly constrained. This man had borne the thunderous acclaim of multitudes in America and Europe, had been received by three kings, an emperor and a president, yet in my inconsequential presence his eyes were cast down and his fingers twiddled a button on the front of his coat! Verily, as the behaviorists now reaffirm, the child is father of the man and a shy, sensitive nature persists into the utmost maturity.

On our trip to his midwestern home, Orville Wright thawed a bit in the Pullman smoking-room — not because, but in spite of tobacco, which he does not use.

He chatted in his mild voice of the baseball score, weather and farm crops. He began a long, quietly humorous tale of his brother Wilbur's scouting trip to Kitty Hawk; how he was almost shipwrecked in a sailboat and saved from starvation by a glass of jelly that thoughtful sister Katharine had packed in his bag. The inventor paused in the narrative and searched his memory.

"Let me see," he murmured. "Was it grape or currant jelly?"

He was bound to be exact in this detail as in every other part of the yarn. He chuckled a little as he happily recalled the kind of jelly that it was. Afterward I heard him discuss with his father the color of a cat that crossed the road in bygone time.

"Orville, it was a black cat," rumbled old Bishop Wright.

"No, Father, I think it was gray with some white streaks."

With such a passion for the exact shades of truth in cats, jelly and else (scientific, after all, and some important events in the Wright chronicle are dated by like seeming triviality), one may understand delay in the production of airplane history by the surviving brother. The flying machine was created in four years but twenty-six years have been too short to narrate its origin.

The guest in the fine new mansion on a hill overlooking Dayton was installed in the host's own room-with-bath at the front of the house. Moreover he was never permitted to follow or walk with the host through any doorway but had to precede. Such Old World or

Southern courtesy almost caused the visitor in his turn to fiddle with his own coat button!

In contrast to the stately, withal genuine, politeness of Orville was the cheerful sociability of Katharine and the amiable gruffness of the old bishop. The household consisted only of this trio with "faithful Carrie" and husband to do all the work — servants treated as friends. There was but one visitor in a week, nor did the Wrights go forth more frequently on errands social or recreative.

There was apparent contradiction between Orville's fine courtesy in personal contact and his indifference to wires and letters from the outside world. Editors and writers vainly coaxed him for statements: "reply collect" was no inducement. Perhaps he held the theory that time answers everything or that silence is a good reply. His sister would be delegated to respond to a few missives from those considered to stand within the circle of friendship. He drove to his city office daily in his own small roadster.

"I never have trouble with my car," he explained one day, "because I never do anything to it. Tinkering a car makes trouble. It is fixed right at the factory in the first place. Better leave it alone. I only give mine gas and oil. It does not use water."

Some time later a home typewriter balked at its task of copying letters and documents pertaining to the birth of the airplane. Orville, forgetting his admonition on cars, essayed to tinker the wayward machine. He toiled at it with screwdriver and pliers for three quarters of an hour. He examined, explored, poked and pushed with serious intensity. Then he gave it up as a hopeless case. I laughed at the thought of the world's premier mechanic thwarted by a little pestiferous device which a youthful repairman was able to adjust in five minutes.

At his office workshop Orville was then working, alone, on an automatic stabilizer for air craft. It was a small but complicated affair with pendulum, mercury in gravity flow and electrical actuation. On a later visit to Dayton, I found the inventor just as interested in a scheme to drive a boat with an air propeller — he was fixing it for a vacation trip in Canada with his favorite nephew, Buster, and thought it would be fun. At his home he also showed me with some pride how he had rigged furnace regulator chains through the floor of the living room, saving a walk to the cellar.

Peter Pan and Orville Wright are related to each other! The latter is perhaps shyer and more sensitive than his fictional counterpart. At the same time he has iron in his soul, an endless tenacity of purpose within a frail body and a delicate nervous system. He is full of gentle humor. Hawthorne and Gelett Burgess are his favorite authors. He likes "The House Of Seven Gables" and equally "The Purple Cow." He used to chuckle with delight over the absurdities of weird inventions as depicted by Rube Goldberg, the cartoonist.

The child is indeed father to the man, emphatically so in the case of the Wright brothers. Their boyhood illumines and makes credible their amazing achievement as men. It is evidential and vital to the history of the airplane. It offers hints to parents, and should delight all who are or once were very young. So I

shall tell every least boyhood tale and anecdote along
with other matter supplied to me by Orville, Katharine and their father, of whom only the inventor now
survives.

The family is of mixed stock — English, Holland
and German-Swiss. The earliest known ancestor,
Samuel Wright, deacon and lay preacher, left Essex,
England, to come to this country and he settled at
Springfield, Massachusetts, in 1636. He had two
ministers and a judge as relatives. The line of descent
runs through James, Samuel, Benoni, Dan I and
Dan II. The latter moved in 1814 to Centerville, Ohio,
now a suburb of Dayton, but then a frontier point
almost in peril of lurking Indians. Here the second
Dan, grandfather to the pioneers of the air, married
in 1818 Catharine Reeder, whose father had been
killed by redskins. Her mother, Margaret, had been the
first white woman in Dayton, which was partly founded
by a brother, Benjamin Van Cleve, after whom one of
the present city hotels is named. The first Van Cleve
was John, who came from Holland to Long Island
about 1650.

The grandmother of the inventors, Catharine Reeder,
was a roguish soul. Her father kept a tavern. She was
pestered by suitors who came from afar and had to
be put up till morning. One night she handed each
arrival a candle and sent him right to bed. The last
suitor was left standing with a candle. He thought he
was favored and waited for her return—in vain. The
man of her choice had a job in a distillery.

"I guess it was a one-horse distillery," judicially

remarked his son, Bishop Wright, recounting to me the family annals in his eighty-seventh year. "A small local plant for making corn liquor. People drank a good deal then and it was usual."

Yet Dan Wright had a change of heart about 1833, for he quit his job and the use of liquor, and would not even sell corn to be made into whisky. He became religious but joined no church. He was a thinker and read what books he could obtain; at the same time he was lazy and transmitted this quality to his son. Thus averred Bishop Wright, heir to the paternal inertia — but his children declared they saw no evidence of such inheritance in his ever active career.

Milton Wright, father of the inventors, was born November 17, 1828, in a log cabin on a farm in Rush County, Indiana. The cabin was "pretty well scutched", having the outside of the logs neatly smoothed with the broadax. It had a fine living room that served also for bedroom, kitchen, bath and what you will. In short, it was a one-room cabin with a good fireplace, albeit smoky until the chimney, which at first ended at the mantel, had been put through the roof. Tallow candles and pitch-pine knots gave light. The farm equipment consisted of one ox with horse harness and a wooden plow with iron-shod point.

At the age of six Milton went to a circus at Clarksburg, three miles away, and eight decades later he gave me a list of the animals present, which is useful as a check on the bishop's memory but not essential to this narrative. — If the reader must know, the animals were an elephant, a gnu, llamas, lions and "the only badger I ever saw." Yes, there was a monkey riding

on a horse, a man who rode two horses at once, and a
clown who, when tickled behind the ear, made a side-
splitting local-pointed jest: "Confound these Clarksburg fleas!"

Milton was converted at eighteen and joined the
United Brethren church, a Protestant sect which was
organized in this country at the beginning of the
nineteenth century, prospered among the German-
Americans of the Middle West and once had about
three hundred thousand adherents. He studied for the
ministry at a little college called Hartsville, in a
town of the same name in Indiana. A fellow student
became his wife and the mother of the inventors. She
was Susan Catharine Koerner, of German-Swiss ex-
traction and was born in Hillsboro, Loudoun County,
Virginia, April 30, 1831. The county is named since
there are two Hillsboros in that State. The natal town
of Susan Wright was only identified a few months before this volume went to press through the discovery
of legal documents, including her father's application
for American citizenship. For this bit of research we
are indebted to Mrs. J. S. Grasty of University, Virginia, who has also initiated the placing of memorials
to the inventors' mother and their sister Katharine.

The young woman would not marry her suitor right
away and accompany him to Oregon as a missionary's
helpmate but — coyly — she consented to write.

A brawny young chap was Milton then, solid and
perhaps a bit slow. Susan, three years younger, had fire
and nimble wits along with rosy cheeks. It is worth
recording that she excelled in the study of mathematics, a basic science which became indispensable to

two of her sons. Her suitor went to his distant post via the Isthmus of Panama (shipping his books of ponderous theology by way of Cape Horn), spent a couple of years as principal of a church school in the Willamette Valley and returned to claim his bride. They were wedded at her father's house in Union County, Indiana, on November 24, 1859. Her father was John Gottlieb Koerner, a wagon maker, born near Schleiz, Germany, who fled to this country from military conscription of the Napoleonic era. Her mother was Catharine Fry, an American of German-Swiss descent. Catharine's father was Philip Fry.

The birthplace of Father Koerner was a small town about twenty miles northwest of Plauen, boasting a palace as well as a cattle market, some cottage industries in toys and else, the burial vaults of princes, and a battlefield where the French and Prussians clashed on October 9, 1806. Quite likely John Gottlieb heard or saw the clash at Schleiz, did not like it at all and was thereby speeded on his way to a peaceful New World. Doubtless he had been an apprentice in a wood-working shop, maybe beginning with toys, and a bayonet seemed to him a harsh wasteful tool compared with a spokeshave or carving chisel. He foreswore allegiance to the King of Saxony on July 11, 1831 in Virginia.

Perhaps the student of heredity can draw conclusions from the mixture of racial strains, dogged, substantial and alert.

Father Koerner had a shop in which he built farm wagons and carriages. It contained a turning lathe operated by foot power, probably the first machine ever seen by two little boys who were awed by it and did not dream they would become expert mechanics themselves. At this time, however, the newly wed Milton and Susan, about to move with a load of furniture to a home in New Salem, Indiana, some twenty miles away, discovered they were short one important item of housekeeping equipment — a rolling pin.

"We have no rolling pin!" wailed the bride.

"Wait!" shouted a relative, dashing into the carriage shop. "Here it is," he announced on his speedy return, "fresh from the turning lathe!" And that sudden rolling pin, neat and smooth, yet gives service in the Wright kitchen.

Orville Wright well recalls Grandpa Koerner who took him, a little tad, between his knees. We can imagine the grizzled old man muttering, "Ja, ja, I could make you a good wagon-builder, yes!"

The parents of the inventors moved around a while, the husband combining school teaching with farming and circuit riding. A "Subscription school" at New Salem yielded an income of twenty-five dollars per month. There was a bit of teaching at Neff's Corners. They stayed two years on a farm near Fairmount, Indiana, which was enlarged to some size in time and remained a family property. Good plowing weather and circuit riding duties did not — unhappily — coincide. The house was a log cabin of three rooms. It had the luxury of a wood stove. The first child was born here on March 17, 1861. He was named Reuchlin after a German theologian. The father picked out the names of all his sons and worked on the theory that Wright, being common, needed an unusual handle. One distinc-

tive handle per child was enough. He was not bigoted
and borrowed the two names which most concern us
from the ranks of churches not his own. Reuchlin became "Roosh" for home use.

Milton became a presiding elder of the United
Brethren and on the death of his father — Dan, who
foreswore the distillery business — took his family to
spend a winter with his mother in Fayette County,
Indiana, where the second child, Lorin, was born November 18, 1862. The name of Lorin was picked off-
hand from a map; it just looked good. There was a
removal to Dublin, Indiana, for a couple of years and
thence to Millville in the same State for a stay of three
years.

Something important happened at Millville, or more
exactly two and a half miles northeast of that hamlet,
within a frame house of five rooms. Wilbur Wright
was born here on April 16, 1867. The co-inventor of
the airplane was named after Wilbur Fiske, a personage in the Methodist Episcopal Church. His family
nickname was Will or Willie. In after years his brother
Orville and sister Katharine often styled him Ullam,
which was owed to a German version of William as
rendered by a customer at the Dayton bicycle shop.

Again the family moved, this time to Hartsville,
where the parents had studied and courted. Now the
father was minister of a church and also taught theology in the college. After a year he left to become
editor of the *Religious Telescope,* a weekly church
organ, at Dayton.

This city is located in a State early famed for oil,
factories and presidents, an approximate rectangle be-

tween the Eastern States and the veritable corn belt, with Lake Erie on the north and the Ohio River for its southern boundary. The city is less than Cleveland and Cincinnati, not to mention three other boastful rivals, in population. It is in the south-western part of the State at the junction of the flood-inclined Miami with minor tributaries, fairly level amid rolling country with an altitude of some seven hundred forty feet. The climate is hot enough for a Zulu in summer but more reasonable in winter. The site was bought from John Cleves Symmes (perhaps the middle name connects with the Wright ancestry) in 1795 and the next year the town was christened in honor of Jonathan Dayton, a revolutionary soldier, member of Congress and Federal Senator. The population in the Wrights' early residence was around thirty-seven thousand with a fair percentage of Germans, fewer Irish and a quota of Negroes. Dayton was strong on churches and religious schools, had a home for soldier veterans and a courthouse carefully modeled after the Parthenon. It was emerging slowly from the phase of cottage industry, small business, rugged and often eccentric individualism.

A small house was bought on Hawthorn Street about a mile and a half from the center of Dayton. This house was the family home for over four decades, save for temporary sojourns elsewhere. Orville Wright was born in this dwelling on August 19, 1871. It was the only home of Wilbur Wright in his manhood and the place where he died. Moreover, within these walls the airplane was largely conceived and created.

It was a little frame structure with wood shingles on

a peak roof, wide clapboards painted white and green shutters at the windows. There was a small porch at the kitchen end. A partial cellar extended under the living room. The new owner raised the back roof so as to have four bedrooms upstairs, and there were three rooms below. No plumbing and no bath. An open well with a wooden pump at the back door was the water supply. Oil lamps gave light, coal stoves heat, and cooking was done with firewood in the kitchen range. The lot was thirty-seven and one-half feet front and one hundred thirty feet deep. The house and lot probably had a total value of fifteen hundred dollars.

A few improvements, including some done by the hands of the inventors, were made in after years.

When I saw this house I felt its pathetic preëminence in a street of meager homes. It was large, compared with a three-room bungalow across the way, and it had style beside the crude effort of some factory worker who had built a dwelling on his own plans in leisure time. But the devout visitor to the old homestead may be inspired by the thought that man can surpass his surroundings. Thus preached the father and so realized the sons. They loved the old house and gladly returned to it after the acclaim of thousands and the greetings of kings. In its physical aspect it was as external to them as their clothes and their numerous badges of honor.

Orville, who arrived following twins who died in infancy, owed his name to Orville Dewey, a Unitarian minister. His familiar title became Orv and Orvy. To his brother Wilbur he was latterly Bubbo, even in letters, while his sister Katharine addressed him as

*Wilbur Wright at 13 — a Consulting
Strategist who derived military lore
from Plutarch.*

*Orville Wright at 8 — General of an
Army, in Junk Business and between-
whiles an Inventor.*

Bubs, Bubo and Little Brother. Such nicknames were spoken in fondness and perhaps expressed a jealous affection within a family circle inclusive and aloof from the world.

The sister and last child — who plays a vital rôle in the historical drama of the airplane — saw daylight on Hawthorn Street on August 19, 1874. It was thought a lucky economy that her birthday coincided with Orville's. Catharine was her name by due inheritance, but the C soon shifted to K through the short form of Kate. A relative bestowed the title of Schwesterchen, or "little sister" in German, which a childish blunder split into two nicknames, Swes and Sterchens. The latter especially became Katharine's appellation in the home and in letters from her famous brothers.

The Reverend Mr. Wright, as church editor, had a salary between one thousand and fifteen hundred dollars a year. This was a good income compared with an annual stipend between two hundred and six hundred dollars in his circuit-riding days. Thanks to his wife's careful housekeeping, it was enough to provide for the family and also to put by something for the future. There was enough plain food on week days and a good dinner on Sundays. Clothes were made over down the line, starting with the retired broadcloth of the minister, so that each child was decently clad.

Wilbur began adventure at a tender age. He fell from a haymow into a barrel. It looked fatal to the scared mother but she hauled him out of the barrel unharmed. Another time there was alarm when the little chap, on his way to Sunday school in charge of two elder brothers, was basely deserted by them on the ground they had to go swimming. Then these naughty elders tried to teach Wilbur how to smoke a grapevine cigar. A lighted match was passed in turn from Reuchlin to Lorin and to Wilbur. It was short when it reached the latter and scorched his fingers.

"Ouch!" shrilled Wilbur, throwing the match in the woodbin, where it started a lively blaze.

Wilbur learned how to deal with the big boys when they misled or abused him.

"If you do that, I'll squall!" was his threat. They well knew that squalling would fetch his mother on the scene.

"I'll squall!" became a family slogan extending into grown-up years.

Wilbur made another infant contribution when he ran crying to his mother: "I've knocked the whole finger-nail off my toe."

Orville was six and his sister three when they paid a joint visit to a neighbor, Ed Sines, who later became Orv's partner in a printing enterprise. A bell rang. The visitors said that was mother's signal and they had to go home. The disgruntled host did not appreciate their obedient retirement and threw a clothesline prop at them.

Mother Wright was "just worshipped" by her children. She had time to play with them while doing all the cooking and housekeeping, making new garments for the minister and remodeling cast-offs for the youngsters, mending, darning, sweeping, washing, even cutting the children's hair with or without a bowl to guide the scissors. At night she listened to the editorials written by her husband for the *Telescope*. He read them aloud to her and took heed of her comment and suggestions for changes. He depended on her to keep his style simple while he availed himself of her fertile and vivid ideas. Doubtless he was influenced by her to become an early advocate of woman suffrage. Long after her passing, Bishop Wright, at eighty-six, marched a mile and a half with his son Orville in a suffrage parade through Dayton.

Sprightly and keen-witted, Susan Wright had an original mind and a knack for invention. She taught herself to design clothes. She made and mended things around the home. She gave an example to her youngsters in self-help, tinkering and creating. A sled was wanted one winter by the two older boys. There was no money to buy it. So the mother built a sled with her own hands and it was as good as a store kind. She was apt with tools and clever with her hands — unlike her husband. Perhaps she inherited deftness and the creative spirit from her father, the German woodworker and carriage maker, and passed on these gifts to sons in whom they were intensified to an illustrious degree.

"Have you heard the latest about that boy Orville?" said one gossiping neighbor to another. "Only seven years old and he and another boy have a little wagon, and they go around picking up bones and sell them to the fertilizer factory."

"Do tell! I wouldn't let my youngster do it. Why, you know a fertilizer factory smells something awful."

"Of course. It's terrible. I hear he finds out which way the wind is blowing and only delivers when it's *to* the factory."

"Mercy! Only, if the wind changed, he might be afflisticated."

The proceeds of the bone traffic went into candy and fishing tackle. Orville lost one good length of fish line owing to his habit of snaring things on land. He tossed a snare into an alley, roping a pig that galloped off with yards of valued fish line.

Making fires was an early passion. Aided by his pal, Ed Sines, he started a blaze against the back fence of the homestead. Three-year-old Katharine ran and tattled to her mother, who put the fire out. It took a long time for Orville to forgive his sister for tattling, and he still likes to make and see fires, the larger the better.

Wilbur once composed a letter to a boy friend in this style:

"Dear Chauncey: Things about here look about here the same as they did when you were about here."

He never finished the letter, being baffled how to continue without dragging in more abouts. The family had another stock joke.

An event which seemed trivial at the time but now appears a signpost on the road of destiny happened when Wilbur was eleven and Orville seven years old. The father went away on a church trip. He thought the boys had been pretty good lately and he would buy them a present. Boughten gifts were somewhat rare in that frugal home. Yet he liked to bring home a few knickknacks for the family. An odd toy caught his eye in the city store. It was expensive, a useless plaything at the price of a shirt, a hymn book or a pair of copper-toed shoes. He hesitated. He examined the foolish gimcrack, was fascinated and yielded to the extravagant urge.

Upon a late autumn evening Father Wright walked into the living room of the Hawthorn Street house with an air mysterious, his hands covering some object.

"What is it, Father? What is it?"

"Something for you boys."

"Let me see it! Please, Father, let me! I said it first!"

"Watch now!"

"O-h-h-h-h!" gasped the awe-stricken youngsters as their father opened his hands and a shiny thing leaped into the air. It soared whirringly across the room, rose higher and smote the ceiling, fluttered a moment as if undecided on its next course and then sank slowly to the floor.

"It's a bat!" shrieked the ecstatic lads.

"A flying bat! Isn't it, Father?"

"No," we may imagine the response. "It is not alive. It is a machine. You see it has two little fans that whirl around because of the pull of this twisted rubber band. The frame is cork and bamboo and the rest is paper. So it is very light. I guess these fans push against the air just as a ship propeller pushes against water. Perhaps there *is* some likeness between this machine and a bat or bird. Anyhow, they both fly. This is a scientific toy. I won't ask you boys to spell its name. It is called a helicopter."

For the next few days the flying bat was put through its paces within the house and out in the yard. It had a strenuous test at the hands of two enthusiastic and ruthless experimenters. They were at it morning, noon

7761

and night. They subjected the motive power to a cruel strain. They racked and tore the fragile device with eager fingers, loudly warning each other against violence.

"I declare, those Wright boys are perfect terrors!" remarked a cross-eyed neighbor, discussing the news of Hawthorn Street with her best friend.

"What have they done now?"

"Why, their father bought them an expensive toy. I hear it cost fifty cents. And in no time at all they tore it all to pieces!"

"What a shame. Minister's sons too."

"That's what I say. I don't see how such destructive little hellions will ever amount to anything! Now my boy — "

Meanwhile Wilbur and Orville Wright had blissful dreams around an experience never to be effaced from memory. That beautiful marvel! That lovely thing that acted like a living creature of the void!

It is a machine. Father said so. The fans go round and round and push the air. They go so fast you can't see them. Faster than a bat's wings. It is a flying bat, like the one that went through the attic window. It might be a bird, the same as those that fly around the chimney. Oh, if I could fly like that!

Destiny smiled on the sleeping lads.

CHAPTER II

The year before the episode of the flying bat Father Wright had become a bishop in the United Brethren church and now, in 1878, his new duties required a temporary family removal to Cedar Rapids, Iowa. This was a town of moderate size in the heart of a rich farming country — the black earth corn belt, renowned for its beef cattle, swine and maize. The name derives from the rapids in the Cedar River, a source of water power that fostered a variety of manufactures. Coe College was established there in 1881. The population included a large number of Bohemians. The cult of Masonry took early root and so did schools of business and institutions of learning by correspondence.

A streak of bad luck pursued the elder brother around this time. About the first of it involved the recovery of Orville from an attack of diphtheria. Wilbur and his small sister Katharine were told they might take the invalid outdoors for a walk. They were so delighted at the restoration of their playmate that they gave him a brisk romp around the yard. It was a plain case of disobedience. The bishop called Wilbur into his study and with more or less citation of texts and proverbs applied the correction of a switch.

Then the lad aimed a stone at a neighbor's pet crow. He was a good shot.

"Honest, I didn't mean to kill it!" we can hear the

affrighted disclaimer. "I just wanted to see how near
I could come without hitting it."

The jinx was with Wilbur when he obtained a job
on a farm but soon lost it. He was not made for such
work. Perhaps he argued with the farmer less con-
vincingly than in earlier years he had done with a
school teacher.

The school scene went something like this:

"Wilbur Wright!"

"Yes, Teacher."

"Wilbur, sometimes I think you are almost stupid.
You are no credit to your father, who is a minister.
You have not solved a simple arithmetic problem correctly. You will stay in after school, and this bright
little girl (pointing) will show you how to find the
correct answer."

Wilbur, however, clung to error. He shortly converted the bright little girl to his own version of arith-
metical solution. The pair marched up to Teacher, who
at length reluctantly conceded that the boy was right.

Some decades later he had an interesting reunion
with his erstwhile small tutor. She had become Mrs.
D. E. Lorenz and greeted Wilbur when he was giving
New York City its first view of the airplane in flight
during the Hudson-Fulton celebration.

Meanwhile Orville was taken by military glamor.
He enlisted an army of small boys of which he was the
general. Wilbur aided with strategy that he derived
from his reading of Plutarch's Lives. He felt it beneath
his dignity at eleven to join the army but he was willing to help with strategic lore of the ancient captains.
Orville was deeply interested in his military career (if

he could have foreseen the part his handiwork would play in a future world war!), and reported its events daily to his mother in the kitchen. At the climax of his enthusiastic report, the curly-haired general would lean forward with his hands on a chair and kick his heels up in the air.

"Tell it again, Orvie!" we can hear the mother say in order to enjoy a repetition of the ecstatic performance.

Orville's army, equipped with putty blowers, laid a notable siege to the woodshed in which the elder brother for once deigned to be the defender. The putty missiles pinged through cracks and hurtled into knotholes. The general shrilled encouragement of his men's deadly marksmanship. But he did not reckon on the strategy of the foe inside, who had pivoted a clothesline prop with cord control so that the stick would sweep the space under the woodshed door. Wilbur's lever, doubtless owed to Archimedes in classic tales, flew under the portcullis and knocked the entire army off its feet.

Around this time Mother Wright estimated the quality of her sons to the following effect:

"Orv is quick, eager and alert — the grass will never grow under his feet — yet his mind will develop and improve until he is fifty. Wilbur is different. He will mature quickly."

There was a camp of real Indians not far from the house at Cedar Rapids. This inspired the boys to join with neighbor playmates in becoming aborigines. They supplied themselves with bows and arrows, feathers and war paint. They learned that a wolf had his den

on a bank of the Cedar River and resolved to attack
the varmint in force. Holding tin-tipped arrows against
the taut strings of their bows, the painted warriors
stealthily approached the den. Chief Wilbur and his
bigger aides tried to smoke out the wolf with burning
paper. Some of the lesser tribesmen stood ready with
stones.

The wolf did not appear and the boys made camp
near by, starting a fire to cook food. Orville, when no
one was looking, measured the girth of the nearest
trees with his arms. He wanted to know which tree he
could climb in an emergency. Unhappily there was
none slim enough for his embrace. As the boys sat
eating, Orville heard a sound, low but menacing. He
did not speak or turn his head, but carefully laid down
a sweet potato and butter knife — then jumped up and
fled to the nearest tree. He had just proved the trees
impossible to climb yet somehow he made altitude on
this one. The other boys rallied to the alarm, seized
their weapons and stood alert.

"Was — it — a *big* one?" panted Orville from his
perch after moments of suspense.

"A big what?" asked Wilbur, who had dropped his
arms and also shinned up a tree.

"Wolf," said Orv, shivering.

" 'Fraidy, that was a dog woofing after cows," announced one of the band, a fact of which the Chief had
been aware.

Wilbur liked to tease his brother and sister. He
plagued the former with a string of words based on
Orville's mispronunciation of Chicago, along with other
faults and episodic fears of dog, hen and cow:

"Chi-see-go — barky dog — picky hen — horny cow — sponky!"

Rattling off this formula of derision while he stood in a doorway, Wilbur would slam the door shut and run, chased by an enraged small brother who picked up missiles on the way. And when an embargo was put on spoken insults, the ingenious elder conveyed detestable meaning by a bent finger and even a certain glance. He made Katharine weep just by crooking his finger at her. She was incapable of Orville's violent defense and could only express indignation with tears.

Wilbur partly atoned for his cruelty by day when, sharing a trundle bed at night with the younger lad, he regaled Orville with the facts and legends of ancient history. He told stories well and his vivid recitals gave the listener a life-long store of mythology. There were also modern tales of pirates-and-blood that thrilled and alarmed the small hearer. Sometimes there was a scuffle in bed. If the mother heard an undue noise upstairs, she would arrive on the scene with a switch, of which a warning motion was usually enough to restore order.

The boys had few whippings. One of these which they protested in after years they did not earn was awarded by the father at Cedar Rapids for the offence of "throwing things" at a passing carriage or wagon. Another chastisement was for "hooking on to bobsleds" — Wilbur, aged twelve, then receiving the last of such discipline from his father. At a later time Orville earned the superfluity of the paternal switch, after his fault had brought him a bee sting; and he vainly sought to escape the meed of full retribution by running through the cellar.

"I governed them," Bishop Wright at eighty-seven assured me, with rumbling brevity. After a moment he resumed, "They were pretty good boys, but mischievous. I had little trouble with them."

A postcard written by Orville to his father, who was away on a trip, was both newsy and concise. It stated (1) Teacher said he was a good boy (2) Water in the back yard was up to the second step (3) The writer set a machine oil can on the stove and the contents — water — shot two feet in the air (4) The cat was dead.

The test with the oil can on the stove was among the first of innumerable experiments made in the kitchen laboratory with the mother's sympathetic approval. Orvie was welcome to be there at any time and to try out all kinds of messy and even dangerous notions. He was not shooed from the kitchen because cooking, baking or other important work was afoot. There he thought out and built many a queer device, played with it until he was tired, and then dropped it, often in the kitchen pump trough. The mother would gently pick up the contraption, perhaps smiling over its absurdity, while seeing in it evidence of constructive talent, and would place it on a shelf for the later use of her son.

"I declare, how M's Wright does coddle her boy Orvie!" we can almost hear a neighbor saying. "Lets him track mud in her kitchen, do anything he pleases in it. I say a kitchen is a kitchen. And it isn't healthy for a boy to be so original, making his own toys and doodads."

Orville was at least normal in his liking for pets. He cherished "Old Mom" and her kittens, along with several chickens. When each child had a pet chicken it was an embarrassing problem to find an unattached bird in the coop to serve for the family dinner.

Fishing was good at Cedar Rapids. And there was plenty of free bait, thanks to a meat-packing plant which discharged its offal into the river by an open chute. The era of industrial economy and salvage of by-products had not arrived in a pioneer land, nor was the protection of water supply a general policy. Doubtless Orville, profiting by his experience in delivering bones to a fertilizer factory at Dayton, was not daunted by a mere packing plant. The boys seized pig livers whizzing down the chute and had bait that was very pleasing to the fish.

If the proverb is true that three moves equal a fire, the family was burned out thrice when it removed in 1881 to Richmond, Indiana. It would seem that a proverb does not always hold. Shifting around was hard on furniture but probably beneficial to the folks. Travel may be educative. The last move was due to Bishop Wright's taking the editorship of a church paper, the *Richmond Star,* and the desire of his wife to be with her widowed eighty-four-year-old mother, Catharine Fry Koerner.

Richmond was a town of fair size, with farm imple‑ ment factories, and a goodly number of Quakers among its population. The newcomers found a friendly atmos‑ phere but somehow had to keep moving, even while dwelling here. They changed their local habitation enough times to raise the total shift score up to an even dozen. The houses were adequate, each being of two‑ story brick with the usual equipment of lightning rods, coal stoves, oil lamps and so on. The yard attached to each house was ample for a lawn, a place to hang up the Monday washing on lines, room for a flower plot and also for a vegetable garden. As to the utilization of such a spacious area — a neighbor observes:

"It seems a sin the Wright family don't use half their back yard. Not a cabbage or a turnip do they grow, only a few posies that the mother tends herself. I can't blame the bishop — he travels half the time and has enough church work. But I say the boys, Wilbur and Orville, might show a little interest in the garden instead of fooling their time away and making their poor father buy all the vegetables for the table. Everybody gardens except the Wrights. What laziness!"

I would fain voice a stern rebuke of this backbiting neighbor. But the indictment has too much truth in it. Neither as boys nor as men did the brothers ever care for the gentle joys of gardening. The love of mother earth was never theirs. They would not soil their hands with earth while unmindful of dust, grime, grease and oil. They approved of foodstuffs in the prepared state or packed in cans. Adam was a gardener — and had poor luck. These lads, though born and bred in America's chief garden — its corn belt — derived from Tubal-Cain, artificer.

The boys were not lazy, as charged. Yet it must be admitted they argued not a little as to whose turn it was to fill the wood box. Out in a shed was the wood-pile along with a sawbuck and bucksaw. The wood had to be cut into lengths to fit the kitchen stove and then carried in. It was a monotonous chore for two young-sters given to schemes and projects. At times they

hated the woodpile. Then they began to discover its
hidden virtues. It had the makings of toys and devices,
it gave practice in the use of tools, and it finally supplied material for an ambitious machine, a turning
lathe, which became an early landmark in their career.

Bishop Wright had more title than income. His sons
had to strike out and earn their own spending money.
Orville at the age of nine embarked in the scrap-iron
trade. He hauled a little wagon through the streets of
Richmond, picked up all the old iron in sight and sold
the cargo at a local junk yard. It was cleaner and nicer,
though more laborious work, than the bone trade. Six-
year-old Katharine was now allowed to assist and received a share of the profits. She was useful too, as on
the occasion when bashfulness prevented the boy from
asking the manager of a chain factory whether he
might have a heap of scrap iron outside and he sent
his sister into the office to make the request.

"Sure, help yourself," we can hear the chuckling
official reply, as he glimpsed Orvie peering through the
door crack.

All the boys of the vicinity used to munch pine tar.
It occurred to Orville at ten that with this substance
as a base he could make a real chewing gum, both for
home use and for sale. He mixed a quantity of pine tar,
sugar and other ingredients in an iron kettle and cooked
the whole upon a fire built in the back yard. Eager to
sample the product before it was quite cool, the maker
filled his mouth and found his jaws clamped together
by the hardening gluey mass. He needed both hands to
tear the stuff out of his mouth and release his jaws.
Moreover, the compound had a frightful taste. Long

afterward Wilbur's scornful mention of "tar chawing gum" had an effect no less than emetic.

In school vacations the brothers and their sister held picnics in the woods. Along with potatoes for baking, other food items and fishing tackle, they carried an original homemade device for a fireplace. This was a fold-up chimney, tin cans fitted to telescope into one another. The chimney made a superior camp fire, and with luck there was a meal of fried fish. On one trip Orville showed courage by voyaging Katharine and himself across a pond on a decrepit raft. He was getting over the fears of his wolf-hunting days.

That he could bear physical pain also was indicated when his left hand was caught by the collapse of a small wagon in which he was coasting down a hill. The index finger was scraped raw. The whimpering lad saw a silver lining, for along with the skin went a row of warts that he had long labored to remove with slip-knots, mullin milk and other youthful treatments.

Barnum's circus came to town in the summer of 1883. Orville was inspired to organize a local show styled "The Great W. J. and M," — that is, Wright, Johnston and Morrow, the two latter being playmates. The father of Johnston, a taxidermist, loaned a variety of stuffed birds and animals ranging from parrots and cranes to a bear. Wilbur did not join the enterprise but gave advice, and as publicity counsel wrote an advance notice for the boys to take to the *Richmond Evening Item*. They were afraid to enter the sanctum but dropped the notice in a box, and it was printed. There was quite a turnout of town folk along the line of march of the parade preceding the show.

Orville and his two colleagues, mounted on high bicycles with wooden wheels and iron tires, led the parade, blowing tin horns as music. Next came the stuffed bear, wabbling on his perch aboard a rickety cart that had once been a Wright family carriage. Small boys hauled the cart. Katharine marched close to the bear and a rabble of youngsters made up the disorderly rear. All was well with the parade until the proprietors of the show saw the multitude of citizens on the route ahead. Then they felt panic, turned their bicycles into a side street and made escape from too much success, followed by the curtsying bear and the shouting rear guard.

Despite the fiasco of the parade, the circus held in a barn that afternoon was well attended and brought good revenue at five cents a head — no adults admitted.

The Wright boys were always queer. They earned their own spending money and made most of their toys. They gathered bones and junk, held a show and made novelties which they sold to the less creative boys of the vicinity. Perhaps they were more ingenious because they had less to work with. It may be that the average boy needs apparatus and material. These lads throve on deprivation. They were short of all aids — except home sympathy.

Stilts of an unusual and lofty style, which Wilbur would reverse to gain more altitude, were built and sold by them at Richmond. They devised a special model of stilts for their sister. She was rarely left out of their plans, having the rôle of junior partner in many enterprises. She had her own share of hickory nuts and walnuts gathered in the autumn woods. The nuts were separated into three piles on the barn floor and only Katharine had the right to make free with another's portion.

The boys went into the manufacture of kites, both for pleasure and profit. The kites were made of tissue paper over a light framework of wood, with tails of knotted rags. Sales were promoted by contests in kite-flying held in fields and open spaces between houses. Somehow the makers generally won in these contests, coaxing their entries to soar higher than any rival. Orville and the chaps of his own age did most of the jockeying with the aërial mounts while the sedate Wilbur, now almost fourteen, acted as trainer.

"Wilbur is always on his back reading and never hears when he is called," we can hear the mother report, a little vexed.

"Oh, well, he has a fair taste," observes the bishop. " 'Ivanhoe', 'Robinson Crusoe', 'Plutarch', not to mention other pretty solid books of history and biography. Reading maketh a full man."

"Orvie is too busy to read," says the mother, smiling. "He is always making another experiment or invention. He flits from one big idea to another. He still drops half-finished toys all over the kitchen while he runs off on a new project. Of course, I still pick them up and save them for him to take up again."

The younger brother was ever in the throes of creative ecstasy. Despite a popular belief to the contrary, he had more initiative than Wilbur. He was the prime mover and originator. He looked first into the unknown. But his visions needed the assay of maturer judgment and the ability of Wilbur to convert them into a practical shape.

They were now reminded by their kite activity of the toy which their father had given them years before. What a thrill it had been to see that shiny marvel leap into the air, rise to the ceiling indoors and even soar to the chimney outside! It was freer and braver than any kite hitched to a string. It had prompted vague dreams and aspirations, thoughts about people sailing above the earth and through the clouds.

"Let's make a flying bat."

"Helicopter," Wilbur doubtless corrected. "All right. It's easy. A couple of screws or revolving fans. A rubber band to give power."

They built several helicopters and were sadly disappointed when they found that the larger the device the less its capacity of flight. They did not know the formula that twice the size requires eight times the power. They were baffled and discouraged by the mystery in the conduct of the toy flyer, and resumed their more profitable work with kites.

Between spasms of creation, Orville tried to become a "chromo" salesman. The job was to ring doorbells and convince people that they needed an ornately colored picture of flowers, fruits and other objects. Although he started at a far end of town where nobody would know him, the young canvasser suffered anguish over the mere task of pulling a doorbell. He patrolled the street for long minutes before he gained courage to ring. Two chromos were sold, doubtless to motherly souls who took pity on the bashful lad with curly hair. Then he resigned the agency.

There was a home tournament of checkers among the older brothers. Wilbur won and observed the remaining contest between Reuchlin and Lorin. He saw that one move would end the struggle, a fact of which the players were unaware. Wilbur fretted internally awhile, then stood in an open doorway for escape from wrath and shouted as he ran:

"Move your king!"

This phrase became a family slogan along with his earlier threat against fraternal abuse; "I'll squall."

At seventeen Wilbur left Richmond High School without graduating. Why? History raises a polite eyebrow and professors shake their heads. Neighbors with diploma-winning sons vowed that it was a pity. They were glad to know that the boy had not quite wasted his time and had a fair record in history, composition, mathematics, chemistry and physics. It seemed he liked history above all and drew from the public library many works on that subject.

Abroad, years later, he astonished persons, perhaps including a king or two, by his knowledge of French chronicles. This was due to his gift of a photographic memory, which his father also had, but not his brother Orville. The latter had an average memory. Wilbur's mind was a storehouse of dates, figures, names, things trifling and important, with every item instantly available for inspection. Such a mind was indeed a great asset to the brothers in their future collaboration.

Some writing talent was shown by Wilbur's high-school essay that he styled, "High School Cyclopedia." He was sociable with his mates to a moderate extent and was briefly attracted by one of the girls — a point

Bishop Milton Wright, Father of the Inventors, about the Age of 50, when he bought for his sons a significant Helicopter Toy.

Susan Koerner Wright, Mother of the Inventors, around her 44th year. They inherited from her deft hands and a creative urge.

John G. Koerner, Maternal Grandfather of the Wright Brothers, a German Carriage-maker, who became an American Citizen and bequeathed talents to the creators of the Airplane.

To be sure, there was religious routine in a bishop's family. There were family prayers of ten or fifteen minutes after the seven o'clock breakfast, joint prayers again at bedtime, grace at all meals, a Sunday school and also a sermon on Sundays — unless the youngsters were let off from the latter service. But the religious exercises did not seem oppressive to the children, and on Sundays the liberal-minded father allowed them to read general books instead of confining them to tracts and piety. Sometimes Katharine and the boys went to a religious "experience meeting." Since there was no church of the United Brethren in Richmond, the family attended a Presbyterian church.

Santa Claus was shocked when he saw no Christmas tree in the Wright home and no stocking hung from the mantel!

"It's this way, Santy," we can hear the bishop parley with the white-whiskered red-robed driver of reindeer. "You are a jolly chap and yet a pagan myth. I can't quite approve of you and your tree. But if you will kindly hand me the presents, I'll put them beside the children's plates on the table before they get up. I know they will be delighted with your gifts."

Santa obliged and the youngsters, up before dawn, shrieked with joy over a find of one orange apiece, hard candy fishes, red-striped peppermint and a small "regular present." Anything that cost a dollar was a memorable "big present," like the wind-up engine that came to Orvie on his eighth or ninth birthday. There was an orthodox Christmas dinner with turkey, cranberry sauce and two kinds of pie. Wilbur and Orville would trade pies to meet their taste, so that the elder doubled on pumpkin and Orville had a glad repetition of mince.

When the youngsters began to earn money, they gave one another birthday and Christmas presents. Orville bestowed many dolls on his sister. At twelve he spent the savings of months on a super-doll priced at two dollars and he could not help telling nine-year-old Katharine on Christmas Eve what was coming to her. At this period he and his sister received an annual stipend of five dollars apiece for washing the family dishes. Each found the gold piece beside the breakfast plate on New Year morning.

All the children helped to some extent with home tasks, for there was no regular servant and only occasional aid by relatives. When the mother fell ill with pleurisy, Wilbur, then fourteen, became the family cook and also did the weekly laundry work with scrubbing board and iron. If he had been unable to hear calls when lost in the pages of a favorite book, he was now keenly alert and caught the least whisper of the invalid. There was a special bond of tenderness between the mother and this her third son. It seemed later that perhaps he foresaw the shadowed future and knew that her apparent recovery left her with an insecure hold on life.

The Wright boys realized at the latter part of the stay at Richmond that their inventions and manufactures called for machinery. They talked it over somewhat in the following vein:

"Will, we need a wood-turning lathe."

"That's a fact, Orv. It would save time and do better work. Mother was just telling about the lathe in Grandpa Koerner's carriage shop.. You remember that story when she and Father were just married, and they were short a rolling pin, so they stopped at the shop and somebody made a rolling pin on the lathe in greased-lightning time."

"Yes, and I remember visiting Grandpa Koerner at his shop. Perhaps Mother could tell us how that lathe was built."

"I know she could, Orv. She's a pretty fine mechanic herself and used to make things for us boys when we were little."

"The trouble is, Will, what to make the lathe out of."

"Well, we still have the woodpile that you and I used to fight over. I saw some long pieces of sugar maple in it this morning. Then we have part of that buggy — the one you had the stuffed bear ride on for your circus parade."

"That ought to do. If we need to buy anything, I have a little money in my bank. Don't you think we ought to make it up to date, with ball bearings like they have in the new bicycles?"

"Good idea, Orv. Let me see. The balls might be commas — little marbles — running between a wooden groove and an iron ring. Where's the ring? I have it! Take it from that old horse bridle!"

The lathe, built in the barn behind the house, was the foremost creation of this period. It stimulated ingenuity, developed knowledge of mechanical principles and promoted craftsmanship. It was more than a plaything, being a full-sized machine with a length of eight feet. The source of power was a foot treadle long enough to accomodate the feet of no less than six boys.

On the day of its test a host of youngsters volunteered for the honor of joining the propulsive battery. We can hear the shrill, excited pleas:

"Aw, Wilbur, let me!"

"Orvie, I was always your friend!"

"Give me a chanst. I bought two kites from you."

"My legs are awful strong — let me run it!"

Under the convulsive kicking of eager feet, the lathe sped into action with a deafening noise. It shivered and shook while the marble ball bearings raced between wood shaft and horse-bridle iron rings with a rattling roar. The din was heightened by the happy clamor of the operators, to an extent which made them oblivious of a rival performance by nature outdoors.

In fact, a cyclone was just then overhead! It tore a skylight off the barn and unroofed a church two blocks distant. The boys kept pumping at the lathe treadle. If they heard an extra sound, they credited themselves with it.

At last Orville saw the barn tip a trifle. And glancing outdoors, he beheld his sister oddly flattened and even pasted by wind pressure against the kitchen door of the house. As he went to the rescue, he doubtless reflected that marble ball bearings were too perishable and that with plain bearings and a few improvements the machine would be entirely successful — which proved to be the case.

If we listen again with attuned ears to the noisy test of a boyish invention in a barn behind a dwelling, we seem to hear an underlying hum like organ point in a fugue, or the surge of leaping waves against cliffs — a majestic sound of man's first winged flight into the immensity of a new sky world.

CHAPTER III

The peregrinations of the Wright family, which had mainly been confined to a limited area in central Indiana, ended with a tenth removal to Dayton as permanent residence in early 1884. The average stay of the pilgrims in each place during a quarter century had been two and a half years. Now there was a short stay in a house on Summit Street before final settlement in the homestead on Hawthorn Street.

The small dwelling of flying-bat memory would have been crowded but that the two elder sons were attending Western College, a church institution, in Iowa. Furthermore the father, while editor of the *Christian Conservator,* published here, traveled not a little, so that the household consisted in effect of the mother with two boys and a sister.

The youngsters had epidemics of indoor sports. Wood carving and engraving was an early attack in the new home. Nightly after supper, at the dining-room table, Wilbur and Orville toiled enthusiastically with the tools of carving and engraving. This was one of the activities which kept them at home evenings and the scene was a pattern of the family life. There was animated chat, considerable litter, a mother who glanced up from her knitting or darning to smile in sympathy on her children's efforts or to act as friendly umpire. The boys turned out some useless things but advanced in the knowledge of tools, and had an interest that obviated street idling. The younger brother surpassed in deftness with chisel and graver. Wilbur built a chair for his ailing mother. It was substantial, albeit its decorative carving was more ambitious in plan than precise in execution.

The boyish indoor amusements were in effect part of a course in draftsmanship and woodworking that became a prime advantage in future creation. Thus they learned to draw plans to scale, and to execute them. There was more wood than metal in the first aircraft and it was well they early learned the difference between ash and oak, pine and maple. This was a profitable home schooling which most of their predecessors in aërial experiment missed. A home workshop does not make every one an inventor yet it develops and edges wits.

There was a joint birthday party for Orville at thirteen and his sister Katharine at ten. The affair was unique as the one birthday party with guests ever held in the Wright family. The feature of the day was a coast down a steep hill aboard a cart that had once been a family buggy. Four wheels, a loose board as seat and a pair of thills: it was decrepit residue of the vehicle that had borne a stuffed bear in Orv's circus parade and had yielded parts for a turning lathe. The guests piled on the loose board. Orville, perched on the front axle, jockeyed the reins tied to the elevated shafts. The venerable cart rattled into full speed. Then the board crashed. A dozen shouting boys and girls were delightfully catapulted down the hillside.

The lad had some pet fowls that he induced to lay

eggs in winter by the expedient of keeping them warm at night beneath a strip of rag carpet. On Christmas Eve, 1884, a chicken thief violated the sanctity of the rag carpet bed. The owner was so grieved on finding the loss the next morning that his three elder brothers rallied to the rescue in their slippers, tracked the marauder through deep snow to his abode — followed by the anxious Orville — and recovered the stolen birds. The owner hailed one of his fowls:

"What! Old Crazy, did they get you too?"

Wilbur took a year's course in the Dayton High School in 1884–1885. Science, mathematics and history were the subjects he now took up. As before at Richmond, he shone on the athletic field and was a leading member of the football team. His academic record seems barren while his athletic activity led to an accident that was not less than fateful. At least, this is a statement of high probability. The accident occurred when he was taking part in a game of shinny on the ice between the high-school team and the sons of officers in the home for veteran soldiers in Dayton. A stick in the hand of an opponent slipped and smote Wilbur on the mouth with such force as to knock out all his front upper teeth. It was a cruel and terrible injury. An army surgeon bandaged the gory face.

"I'll walk home," we can hear the brave lad mumble. "Scare mother if I didn't." He had his way and walked.

Among the effects of the injury were heart and stomach trouble. There followed a long period of delicate health if not semi-invalidism, with a diet confined to liquids, eggs and toast. It seemed to every one that the boy was handicapped for life and none dreamed of the possibility of a great compensation.

A year or so later Wilbur joined the United Brethren church during a local revival service. Orville and Katharine became members somewhat later. There was a split in the sect in 1889, mainly over the issue of secret societies. Bishop Wright took a lone stand against such societies in the church. There was division and an extended legal controversy, in which Wilbur, siding with his father, gave him important aid. Wilbur terminated his connection with the local church while the names of Orville and Katharine, despite their wishes, were kept on the rolls for over two decades. The children ceased going to church for lack of one of their own persuasion.

Orville was fourteen and in the eighth grade of public school — he daily trudged the distance of nearly two miles each way despite a physique slender, delicate and undersized for his years — when he formed a partnership in the printing business. Somewhere he had a store of vitality and surplus energy. The partner was Ed Sines, who had been a neighbor and crony in childhood. The print shop was in the Sines kitchen. The boys had some business correspondence in which they used their firm name and in reply received letters addressed to Messrs. Sines and Wright, which prompted Mrs. Sines to tell them they were a pair of "messers" indeed.

The shop was equipped with a toy press said to resemble an ancient doorlock, a hell-box of junk type presented by a printer, a few wood engravings made by Orville, and some of Mrs. Sines' embroidery stamps, all useful in printing and decorating a catalogue. Some visiting cards were also printed.

Father Wright cheered the struggling partners with a donation of twenty-five pounds of second-hand brevier type at the same time that he prompted Wilbur and Lorin to trade their jointly owned rowboat, which Wilbur had built, for a real press to be presented to Orville. The real press was three by five inches, self-inking, famed as the "Model." When the partners added to this outfit some job type which cost them a dollar apiece (the Miami River flood of May 12, 1886, dates the event) they felt they were genuine all-around printers and were soon emboldened to launch a school paper, styled the *Midget*.

One week they wearied of typesetting and left the fourth page blank save for a diagonal line, "Sines & Wright, Job Printing," whereupon Father Wright suppressed the edition on the ground that it was a slovenly performance.

The revenue of the firm included cash, popcorn and lollipops. Sines wished to eat the edible intake while Wright said it should be sold and added to working capital. The argument was settled by the thrifty partner buying out the other's interest for one dollar, the full amount of his investment in the firm. Then Orville hired Ed to work for wages, a relationship which lasted until the Wrights quit the printing business a dozen years later.

At sixteen Orville decided to create a printing press. He took sticks from the family woodpile — that source of boyish hatred which time transmuted into a magic treasure of the djinn — and shaped them on the turning lathe that had been earlier conjured from a similar stack of kitchen fuel. A junk shop supplied a metal roller which only needed a gravel filling for weight and plugging of the ends with wooden disks. After inking a form of type on its flat bed, a sheet of paper was set in place and subjected to the pressure of the gravel-loaded roller. It worked. But Wilbur cast his eye on the affair and saw how it could be bettered. This was typical of the collaboration between the brothers. The younger, ever full of new eager visions, began projects which were then scrutinized and improved by the elder.

"This press is all right, Orv," we can imagine Wilbur saying. "But it would save work if you didn't have to run up and down with that big roller. Look here, I'll fix a lever to shoot the roller back and forth. Then you just stand and move the lever with one hand."

The elder also helped on a tympanum device and the pair coaxed speed out of the woodpile press, with Orv at the lever and Wilbur inking and feeding.

Wilbur had a job in a grocery store after leaving Dayton High School. A few months of this were enough and he was glad to take up the business end of the church weekly edited by his father. The new business manager of the *Christian Conservator* hired his younger brother and other lads to fold the papers week-ends, while he operated the machine which put the subscribers' addresses on copies.

Orville grumbled at a monotonous task. Good pay, short hours, a pious organ edited by his own father! What was wrong with the boy? Perhaps he needed a dose of that reliable spring tonic, sulphur and molasses. I seem to hear a small peevish voice:

"Folding papers is foolish. Fold, fold, fold! Hands get cramped. No sense to it. Hand work, over and over again. Why do we have to fold 'em by hand, anyway? Wilbur, come here! Say, Will! Let's build a folding machine!"

"Orv, that's an idea!" doubtless responded the business manager.

Again the family woodpile served as lamp of Aladdin or a refined Pandora's Box. It now supplied maple rollers and other items for a mechanical folder.

The new machine was operated by a foot treadle. It was a fearful and wonderful contraption, noisy and rattlesome, balky except to its fond creators, who understood the mystery of its strings and gears. Yet the device had a perfect appetite for the sheets of the religious journal, whirled them through horizontal rollers, clapped them together through vertical rollers, creased them hither and slapped them yonder, then dropped them in a mounting pile of neatly folded copies! It saved labor. It was a victory and a triumph.

If as youths the Wrights were thus able to build a rather considerable and intricate machine out of nothing, we can perhaps understand how in manhood they assembled hacksaw blades and other junk in a bicycle shop to create the world's pioneer device for the correct measurement of air pressure that was a prerequisite to the solution of the flight problem.

When the brothers resolved in the late winter of 1888 to publish a weekly newspaper, they wanted a sizable printing press. I imagine Mrs. Wright looked with dismay on the family woodpile, for the weather was cold. But the press was needed. It was the most ambitious of the inventors' efforts up to this time. A second-hand tombstone served as a flat bed for the press. There was a massive roller and an amplitude of wheels, pinions, pulleys, gears and levers.

"Every part of this press runs at full speed," reported a member of the family. "It is the liveliest thing you ever saw. The racket it makes is terrible."

Its capacity was "at the rate of" fifteen hundred copies an hour, but it got winded in less than an hour, for which reason "at the rate of" joined the family slogans such as "I'll squall" and "Move your king!"

An out-of-town printer came to see the Wright boys' marvel, crawled under it while it was running and tried for hours to fathom the mystery of its operation.

"I know how the perfecting press runs," quoth the puzzled visitor, dusting off his clothes, "but I'll give up if I know how this one runs!"

The brothers whistled, hummed and sang as they toiled together on the construction of their latest masterpiece. Thus they had done over the first boyish feats of invention and so they would do in future when grooming an unheard-of Pegasus for a gallop in the sky. It tokened happy absorption, relief from tedium, solutions of problems, joy of discovery and creation. What did they sing? Perhaps future Homers will ascribe to them heroic ditties and classic lays. The fact is they had no musical gift or training and sang by ear the popular airs of the day along with stray college verses, "Annie Laurie," "Kentucky Home," "Suwanee

River," and so on. Once there had been an attempt at a family glee club, in which Wilbur was first bass and Orville second tenor. The girls who were serenaded at night a few times did not apparently encourage the club to continue.

The *West Side News,* printed on the new press, made its bow to the public in March. The office with plant was a short walk from the home of the owners. Local merchants advertised and the weekly's circulation rose to five hundred copies, which were distributed by small boys. Wilbur was usually editor and Orville business manager, in which rôle the latter borrowed capital from his mother in sums ranging between five dollars and forty dollars. These loans were always repaid.

The home circle had been narrowing, with the father absent half the year on his episcopal tours as Bishop of the Pacific Coast, from 1885 to 1889, and with the two elder sons at college. Now the mother was about to leave on a supreme journey. She came of a family that had lived into eight decades but her days were made short by tuberculosis, of which the proper treatment was then unknown, and perhaps also by pioneer hardships. With housekeeping equipment of water pumped by hand, oil lamps and wood stoves, hand scrubbing board, kitchen as weekly bathroom, home-built beds of chicken feathers and corn husks, she had toiled and struggled, yet had made a home that seemed ideal to her children. She was a skillful housekeeper, keeping everything neat and tidy. Fancy cooking was not hers but she knew the art of providing wholesome fare with plain cake, cookies and doughnuts. The living room had lace curtains and an ingrain carpet, with a tasteful disposition of its few pictures and ornamental objects.

Illness did not quench her cheerful eager spirit. She was consoled by the thought she had given the world two boys who were "special." They were fulfilling early promise and she visioned a high future for them.

Wilbur during the last years nightly carried his mother upstairs to her bedroom. She was able to walk down mornings. There was a close tie between them, together with likeness of tastes and sense of humor. Perhaps inherently the studious Wilbur was more like his scholar sire and the mercurial ecstatic Orville derived especially from the mother.

Susan Koerner Wright died July 4, 1889. She left her sons a rich legacy — skill of hand and eye of her craftsman parent, original minds, the example of her own ability to create and her sympathetic encouragement of their childish and boyish play-steps toward the making of dreams come true. If she could have seen in a magic crystal of the future her sons standing in the White House beside a President of the United States — or striding down a field with the King of Italy — or with their sister in the presence of his Britannic Majesty, Edward VII — Orville smiled upon by an emperor and cheered by a mighty host of whom many sought to touch the edge of his garment — would she have shaken her head or with a startled gasp, weeping, have believed? There is no limit to the hopeful imagination of a mother. She would have believed. And she would have taken more joy in their useful service to the world than in the pomp and glory which attended their success.

With the eldest son married and the next permanently away, the home was reduced to three children and a father often absent. Fifteen-year-old Katharine tried to be a "little mother" to Wilbur who was twenty-two and Orville who was eighteen. The trio became inseparable through the years, unbroken save by death. No one else was as close to the inventors as this sister, their beloved "Sterchens", comrade and perfect confidant. The history of the Wright brothers should read "And Sister." She is vital to the narrative. She was an eyewitness and a participant in historic scenes. Yet it is a baseless fable that she gave her brothers science or knowledge out of her college store.

Chance and trifles loom large in our story. Wilbur's teeth were knocked out in a shinny game, whence an important effect may be deduced. Poor health kept him at home for years, forbidding ventures into the outside world. He did not travel or marry like his elder brothers. He remained in contact with Orville and continued the collaboration on inventive feats. Time equalized the difference in age and experience between them as they came to early manhood. The fraternal partnership, essential to future achievement but once imperilled by age disparity, was now secure. And the bond of union was welded more firmly by death and the care for a sister who tried to become "little mother" of the household.

If the muse of history raised a polite eyebrow because Wilbur did not graduate from high school, let her now lift the other eyebrow! Orville did not graduate when he left Dayton High School in 1889. Thus the brothers did not even finish preparatory schooling.

Methinks I hear laments from the college faculty. Really? Impossible! Surely, you don't mean to say — They did not even finish high school as stated. The Wrights never went to college. Nor did Charles Darwin, James Watt or Thomas Edison. Colleges serve the average. They may be worth nothing to genius.

However, the brothers had no prejudice against academic learning. In fact, Wilbur at one time thought of attending Yale University, for which he might have soon prepared himself.

The owners of the *West Side News* turned it into a daily in the spring of 1890 under the name of the *Item*. A humorous column styled "Predictions by the Weather Prophet" was included among the tasks of Editor Wilbur. The routine advertising was looked after by Ed Sines, erstwhile crony and now print-shop employee, but it took Orville to make big merchants sign on the dotted line. The latter was less bashful than he had been or perhaps more desperate, as he tried to satisfy a daily newspaper's ravenous appetite for cash. That greedy maw took Wilbur's investment of two hundred dollars, which had been hoarded in a wooden box at home, down in a few gulps. The family banker and thrift exponent found nothing for his jest column in this event.

The *Item* luckily died in three months. The relieved owners turned to job printing, for which they had a fair plant. They were quite successful in this field, what with the elder's varied work in the shop and Orville's taste in type and color, besides his speed in composition and his outside activity in soliciting business. All type was hand set in those days. The nimble fingers of

Orville flashed from case to stick in half the time of Ed
Sines or the average compositor: his record was sixteen
thousand brevier ems in ten hours.

Among the output of Wright and Wright, Job Printers, were pamphlets up to one hundred pages, minutes
of the United Brethren church, an advertising booklet
termed "The Snap Shot" for which Wilbur wrote a
new version of "Weather Prophet" humor, and a journal for colored people. The latter was edited by Paul
Lawrence Dunbar, a young Negro who had been Orville's
classmate in high school. Dunbar was given to original
poems which he recited in the print shop. One day he
scribbled on the wall an effort that is doubtless omitted
from the collection which brought fame to the Afro-
American poet. But it has an interesting touch of appreciation if not prophecy:

> Orville Wright is out of sight
> In the printing business.
> No other mind is half so bright
> As his'n is.

The job printers branched out in 1892 with the
addition of a bicycle repair shop to their line. No doubt
they saw profit and were also lured by the idea of
playing with a new machine, the ball-bearing "safety"
with compressed air within rubber tires. "Wright Cycle
Co." was the legend put above the modest shop in a
two-story brick building at Number 1127 West Third
Street. It was the most misleading sign ever raised on a
business, a flagrant violation of Truth in Advertising, a
preposterous understatement. Some cycles were made
and tinkered here, yes. But what else? Let us demand
answer of that mendacious sign which remained blandly

unchanged through the years. Perhaps that sign had a cryptic intention. A cycle is a wheel. It is also a historical era, such as the Wrights inaugurated when they created the airplane in and behind this shop.

Despite two enterprises they found leisure in the fall of 1892 to repair and improve the homestead on Hawthorn Street. They bought the material and were their own masons and carpenters. The principal improvement added to the old frame house a front porch and side porch, neither very wide, with simple wood railings and columns. The neighbors said the boys did a neat job. The house now looked as well as any, on a street where every one worked for a living. It had a bit more style than some of the one-story bungalows across the way.

"If you want your bicycle fixed right, take it to the Wright brothers," was the word passed around Dayton. "They are reliable, and fair in their charges."

The business grew into the sale of new wheels and trade in old ones. In four years the prospering owners had their own model to offer the public, the Van Cleve bicycle, named after one of their ancestors. The machine was not a creation; it was assembled by the brothers from purchased parts. Yet it was first class and up to date, rugged and dependable. About a dozen of these wheels were sold the first year at a price around one hundred dollars. The assembling shop on William Street had good equipment that included an enameling oven. The success of the bicycle business put job printing in the shade and that enterprise was now rented to Ed Sines, who bought it from the Wrights within a couple of years.

"Lilienthal — a German Daedalus — is dead. He had been leaping off roofs and cliffs with self-made wings. The air upheld him on short hops, it is said. But he attempted fate once too often and was killed."

Millions read a news item to this effect in 1896 and the usual comment was: "What a fool!"

The item was taken more seriously by two obscure young men of Dayton.

Orville had typhoid fever at this time. He was looked after jointly by Wilbur, a trained nurse and Katharine, home on summer vacation from Oberlin College. Wilbur was at the house throughout some days as well as every night. The brothers had adjoining bedrooms, each just large enough for a single bed, a washstand and a chair or so. The small rooms were stifling with the humid heat of the corn belt and nothing to insulate the wood shingle roof against the rays of a deadly sun. Ice — perhaps there was a piece wrapped in a blanket. A fan is cooling. I can see Wilbur waving a palm leaf over the fevered patient, keeping it up with monotonous regularity, changing hands to rest muscles, perhaps speculating on a device for an automatic power fan.

"Listen, Orv," we can imagine Wilbur saying one day to his convalescent brother, "you want to catch up on the news while you've been sick. Here is an item from Germany. Lilienthal is dead."

"Lilienthal?"

"Yes, you know — the man who tried to fly with wings. Seems to me we both read about him in a paper or magazine along with the experiments of Maxim and Langley."

"How did it happen?"

"Well, he made some short hops or glides as they call it. But the last time he fell somehow and got killed."

"What a fool!" grumbles public opinion, echoing ghostily from a sultry attic, while a pair of visionary brothers fall into an eager discussion of the flying problem which they had approached before in dreams and curiosity but which now became ennobled with the sacrifice of a pioneer's life. Their minds went back to a helicopter toy and to boyhood play with fascinating kites. Now a man had staked his life on the reality of flight. What difference if he had lost? What though he seemed a fool to the multitude? That the pioneer who failed was a Teuton could not diminish respect in the eyes of these grandsons of a clever German carriage-builder.

"Let's read up on the subject, Orv," the elder doubt-less suggested. "I'll get what there is in the public library and you know Father has a book on bird flight downstairs — 'Animal Mechanism' by a Frenchman, Professor Marey. We'll find out what there is in the whole business."

Yet half an invalid through the autumn, Orville heard his brother read aloud the tenuous documents dealing with flight. They were alone in the house most of the fall and winter, since Katharine was in college and Bishop Wright had church trips to make. A colored woman, Lottie, came in for timely clean-ups, but Wilbur was the main housekeeper and cook, devising dainties for the convalescent among his other tasks. They got along well but were willing to eat in a boarding house when Orville was quite recovered.

Flying then was on a par with spiritism. It had no scientific basis or repute. The literature was meager, though inflated with words and cloudy guesses. Perhaps the lack of substance kept the brothers hungry for more; they tried to find something to put their teeth into, and they now took turns in reading the books aloud on winter evenings at home. After reading, they talked, argued, dreamed, and added cloudy guesses of their own to the fog-enveloped, illusory and haunting topic.

Father and sister, home on visits, observed that the boys were at it again — off on a new enthusiasm which might or might not lead to a minor conquest. Their own view of the matter was yet more modest. They were playing with a fascinating idea, amusing themselves and becoming familiar with a hide-and-seek literature. The idea grew upon them. Perhaps at moments each had a secret vision of adding a tiny footnote to history. The footnote would be in small type. It was several years before they saw how that type might enlarge and come to be the main text of the book of aviation.

The brothers were now in the vigor of early manhood. Wilbur had recovered from the effect of the shinny accident in youth. While not robust, both were wiry and athletic, delicately attuned in mind and body, of nervous temperament yet capable of endurance. They cooperated remarkably in physical as well as mental feats. For example, Wilbur was starter for Orville when the latter competed in amateur bicycle races under auspices of the local Young Men's Christian Association. At the pistol crack, Wilbur shoved and Orville sped five lengths ahead of all rivals. The latter still cherishes his medals of victory in these races.

The brothers were abstemious in their habits, as if awaredly training for a greater contest in which a good physique might not only win but save them from death. They used no liquor, beer or tobacco, which last Orville sampled and quit under the age of twenty. They were sparing of tea and coffee, Wilbur confining himself to a coffee substitute for some years. Parties and dissipations were unknown to them. They went home nights, read, talked and so to bed. There was a certain unavoidable contact with young men of another type among the racers and hangers-on who made the bicycle shop their rendezvous. But also there was an unwritten rule that modified talk and behavior in the Wright shop. The brothers maintained a state of innocence through the years, less by effort and avoidance than by fastidious taste and absorption in their work.

They found enough excitement in applying their wits to the solution of mysteries like that of the bicycle pedal, which had baffled the scientific experts of manufacturers. The pedals were unscrewing, riders complained, although they were designed to tighten in use. The keenly observant Wrights detected the source of trouble and told a thankful manufacturer that friction of the pedal shank against the crank shaft negatived theory and unscrewed the pedal.

They sharpened their wits also on mental tests, so-called mind reading and the doings of spiritist mediums. In a test with ten cards of different colors, five seconds allowed to view them, the average person at the bicycle shop remembered the order of about two colors. Orville scored over ninety per cent. correct. Wilbur began at sixty per cent. and then amazingly made records almost perfect. The secret was his shift of method from a weak visual memory to his strong verbal memory, whereby he disregarded the looks of the colors but registered their names, which he then recited by rote. Orville, on the other hand, had to make a color picture in his mind and reproduced it by sorting out the cards.

In seeming contradiction, Orville could not recall the features of houses on a given square which he had passed daily for four years while Wilbur had a mental register of every pillar and window blind. Doubtless Wilbur had verbalized his architecture or made a mental catalogue of the building features.

The brothers exposed the fallacy of mind reading as to the selection of one out of three objects when the correct article is odd or isolated. They had no trouble in picking a bottle between monkey wrench and hammer, nor a penny placed between two dimes. They knew that a simple mental law of association was responsible for the choice.

Spiritism was popular in Dayton, with several mediums giving public performance. The Wrights challenged the spirits to write a message on a slate which they prepared. They inset a pane of glass on a slate frame with chalk and pencils between, mortised and bradnailed the frame corners, then made a plaster cast of the frame. They offered ten dollars' reward for a message on that slate. The spirits delved for a month and only succeeded in shifting some brads, as shown by reference to the plaster mold. The rigor of scientific method was not lacking in such a test, albeit its devisers had had no benefit of college or laboratory training.

It seemed that the brothers were getting psychic themselves when at the same instant they recalled some event or simultaneously broke forth with the same song. Family and friends shared their astonishment. Were their minds now geared together in harmony that ignored material barriers? Certainly their voices were so much alike that a person in the next room could not always distinguish between them. If the quiet even staccato became extra fast and choppy, like a bit of rapids in a sober low-murmuring brook, it was probably Wilbur.

But they soon exploded the mystery of their attuned minds. It was based on association of ideas with a common memory. For example, if one whistled or sang "Annie Rooney," the other was reminded of the printing press created to the accompaniment of that melody; or mention of the folding machine by one might incite the other to chant "Suwanee River." Certain airs heard on the street revived in both an experience they had shared. Their musical repertory was somewhat enlarged by themes from Schubert and Schumann, brought home by their sister from Oberlin, together with the rollicking college airs. It is natural that the gentle Wrights took to melody, aliment of the peaceful and antidote of wrath. It inspired and soothed. Wilbur was never angry, stated his father. The rest of the family said that the bishop was probably absent on certain occasions.

The brothers were keen scientific sceptics, putting a razor edge on their minds while training their bodies for hazards unforseen.

"How did the Wrights — uneducated — dare attempt what they did?" wails a professor.

But they were highly educated! Their curriculum was as follows:

Bows and arrows, a collapsible chimney, stilts, kites, helicopters and other toys were their grammar and high school course.

The creation of a turning lathe out of a woodpile, an old buggy and marbles for ball bearings, put them through the first year of college.

Making a unique folding machine and original printing presses and solving miscellaneous problems from psychology to unscrewing pedals of a bicycle entitled them to graduate from college.

They were thus prepared and qualified for postgraduate study of the flying problem.

CHAPTER IV

"I hear the Wright boys are going camping this summer," said a citizen of Dayton to a neighbor in the year 1900.

"That so? Making money out of their bicycle business, I guess. Where are they going?"

"Queer place called Kitty Hawk down in North Carolina."

"Why do you suppose they want to go that far?"

"I wonder myself. Wilbur went into a store yesterday and bought a lot of sateen cloth — twenty-five yards of it. Girl says, 'What do you want it for?' He says, 'Well, I want it.' "

"By George, I know! Those Wright boys are real original. They want to start a hunting and fishing camp — charge people money to belong — and that cloth is to make tents and beds."

"That's it," agreed the other.

It was just as well the gossipers did not suspect that the cloth was required for wings on a flying contraption or glider which the Wrights were to test late that summer.

It had taken four years of pondering and minor experiment to create this first man-size model of the future airplane and to test it for the first time in the air.

The Wrights were fortunate in being almost poor

(ABOVE) *The Wright Homestead on Hawthorn Street, Dayton,
where Orville was born and where Wilbur died in 1912.*
(BELOW) *The Brothers' Bicycle Shop and behind it a Work-Shop
where they built Gliders, the Engine for the Airplane of 1903, and
conducted epochal research in Aerodynamics by means of
their Wind Tunnel.*

with little money to spend on experiment. Sir Hiram Maxim was handicapped with two hundred thousand dollars in England, Clement Ader contended with a large government subsidy in France, and Professor Langley of our Smithsonian Institution was encumbered with a fund of seventy thousand dollars or more. These rivals rushed into premature, haphazard, costly and futile experiment with models. The fortunate bicycle men could not afford to do that. They had to build in their minds, think out every step and create a host of imaginary models which in turn they inspected, analyzed, criticized, tore down, rebuilt and finally threw away. It was cheaper — and what is the main point, more productive. This is an age of money and models. The Wrights went back to the ancient method and relied first on their brains.

They staged home battles on imaginary aircraft. It was the agreed duty of each brother to attack, punch and smash with all vigor the other's concept. Orville proposed, Wilbur demurred; Wilbur suggested, Orville swung a destructive blow. They often fought each other to a mental standstill but did not lose their tempers, for their object was a mutual quest of truth. After a fair fight the vanquished was quick to concede victory and to adopt his opponent's viewpoint.

"I like to scrap with Orv," Wilbur used to say, "because I like to scrap with a good scrapper."

Sometimes these idea-boxers chased each other around the ring so fast that at the gong each had reversed his position and stood in the other's corner, which gave them a hearty laugh.

They obtained some new points to fight over in May,

1899, from pamphlets of the Smithsonian Institution, "The Aëronautical Annuals of 1895–1897," compiled by James Means; "Experiments in Aërodynamics" by Professor Langley, published in 1891; articles by Lilienthal and parts of Mouillard's "Empire of the Air" (1881). They had already read Chanute's "Progress in Flying Machines" (1894). It was all a mass of conjecture, dreams, pseudo-science and enthusiasm. But the last item — enthusiasm! — was truly valuable to the Wrights. It kept them going when facts and reason seemed to have nothing to offer.

"Mouillard and Lilienthal, the great missionaries of the flying cause," wrote the brothers afterward, "infected us with their own unquenchable enthusiasm, and transformed idle curiosity into the active zeal of workers."

However, the view that extensive previous research had simplified the task of the Wrights is far from the truth. They did not simply avoid past mistakes and cleverly explore the few remaining avenues of probable success. What had been done was a great confusion. There was a labyrinth of clues with no assurance that any given path led to the center of nature's secret.

The Maxim and Langley group of experimenters believed in power flight, while the school of Lilienthal, Mouillard and Chanute practised on gliding without a motor. The men of Dayton chose the gliding approach to the problem as more sensible and economical while, too, they were fascinated by the notion of flying like birds.

"Balance is the main problem," we can imagine the

brothers agree after long debate. (This in itself was a great conclusion to which few others had attained.) "It's no use to put the center of gravity low or have V-shaped wings — a dihedral angle. That might give automatic stability, yes; but it is like hobbling a race horse. We don't want the animal less sensitive so it bucks and fights the air, but more sensitive so it co-operates with the air like a bird. And it isn't practical to keep balance in the Lilienthal and Chanute style with the rider shifting his weight six ways for Sunday. Half a minute in the air seems to be the limit for such acrobatics."

Let me emphasize here that thirty seconds was the gliding record up to the Wrights' experiments and no man had flown a split second in a power machine. The duration of Lilienthal's brief erratic hops had totaled five hours in five years. The record was indeed dis-couraging: Lilienthal the German and Pilcher the Eng-lishman killed in gliding, then the dismal failure of power apparatus built by Maxim, Phillips and Ader. A period of hope between 1889 and 1897 had been followed by "collapse and despair," and the Wrights began their work in the darkest era of aërial research. Of this time Wilbur later said:

"When we studied the story of loss of life, financial disaster and final failure which had accompanied all attempts to solve the problem of human flight, we understood more clearly than before the immensity and the difficulty of the problem which we had taken up. But as we studied the story of their troubles and con-sidered how and why they failed, we could not help thinking that many of their troubles might have been overcome by the adoption of more adequate methods. We began to study the flight of birds."

"Perhaps the birds can teach us," said the brothers, echoing a thought that has run down the ages from caveman to Da Vinci and our own time. Leonardo Da Vinci, between painting such masterpieces as "Mona Lisa" and "The Last Supper", dreamed of flying.

It is pure but interesting irrelevance to tell what the master painter and varied genius of four centuries ago said and did about flying. He argued that if the eagle can soar, winged man can "make himself lord of the winds . . . the conqueror of space." He observed avian flight and studied the center of gravity of a stuffed bird. He drew angelic wings, not in piety but for the levitation of man, and luckily escaped the Inquisition's fire for such a blasphemous scheme. He built a machine with four wings in the style of a bat, each wing to move forward in turn by means of a crank and piston, operated by the rider's feet — using the power method of the later bicycle. A rudder was to be turned by the head. (In fact, the first Wright airplane was controlled by a hip cradle and one of its successors by a shoulder harness.)

Leonardo did not like his bat and built a new machine in the beautiful form of a swallow. Truth is beauty. The swallow was lovely, and by all the laws of nature and esthetics should have flown right through the enraptured Master's studio window. "My poor dear swallow," we may hear Leonardo coaxing, "be free of the air! Try your delicate wings in the empyrean. Dart in gay zigzags. Come alive, charming bird!" What a pity this creature behaved no better than the ugly sinister bat.

Four decades of failure did not discourage the lofty dreamer, who wrote in his diary: "Man shall fly like a mighty swan."

Ah, the right clue — queen of birds as the pattern instead of noisome bat and insignificant swallow.

And then, like a major prophet slightly dazzled by temporal lures, Da Vinci left us this testament:

"The human bird shall take his first flight, filling the world with amazement, all writings with his fame, and bringing eternal glory to the nest whence he sprang."

The prophecy has been fulfilled. Meanwhile the Wrights pursued their bird study especially on Sunday mornings, when they bicycled to a point on the Miami River some three miles from their home. The spot was known as The Pinnacles because of the Gothic peaks and Oriental minarets carved in sandstone by the rushing water. It was hot summer in the corn belt when birds of prey roved busily over the Miami valley and for some reason favored The Pinnacles as the center of their wheeling reconnaissance. The brothers lay on their backs for hours under the broiling sun and watched the soaring flights of hawks and buzzards overhead. They pedaled home for the noon dinner, discussing what they had seen. At home they observed swallows and other small birds.

"We got plenty of flying fever from watching the birds," Orville told me a decade and a half later, "but we learned nothing about their secret of balance."

In fact, while the airplane wing warp or equivalent

aileron movement is a bird principle, the inventors did not then know it and made an independent discovery without debt to bird or man. Poetry must give way to fact in this matter, however much we may wish to compliment our lovely neighbors of the blue. After watching them for thousands of years, man learned from them hope and aspiration but nothing of tangible value. Indeed, he was rather confused and misled by them into superficial imitations of their infinite variety of shapes and methods.

It was about two years after their warping discovery that the Wrights recognized it as a bird principle in a photograph of seagulls in flight sent to them from France by Captain Louis F. Ferber. It is most doubtful that any other men in the world could have made the identification without knowledge of the principle, or that any one could have purloined the secret directly from the seagulls or their kin. The wing warping of birds is slight, elusive to the keenest vision, and is veiled by the use of other means, as shortening one wing, to maintain balance.

In early June, 1899, the crude germ of the airplane was born in Orville's mind. It was a notion of hinged wings to be moved alternately up and down in order to secure lateral balance. At first glance this was nothing original. Since time began would-be flying machines had copied bird shapes from tail to beak, from bat to eagle and from condor to albatross. Wings had been hinged to obtain propulsion or just because the birds were built that way. The distinct and original object in Orville's plan was to get sidewise balance. However, the brothers agreed the idea was mechanically impractical. They seemed to discard it, yet it remained in the bottom of their minds as a thought both rich and fertile.

Some weeks afterward in late July toward ten o'clock at night, Wilbur was alone in the bicycle store, which was usually kept open evenings to serve the mechanics and factory employees who had no daylight leisure to shop. A customer came in and the talk was like this:

"Say, Wilbur, I want an inner tube for my wheel."

"All right. Here is one."

"Good rubber, eh? Puncture-proof too?"

"No. They all puncture. Show you another if you like."

"Wait till I look this over."

"Go ahead." He was that kind of a salesman.

Idly twisting in his hands the pasteboard box in which the inner tube had been packed, Wilbur talked with the customer. His lean work-scarred fingers gripped the corners of the box and twisted it in opposite directions. Wilbur glanced down, saw what his unconscious fingers were doing. His mind leaped from box to airplane wings! Here was the way to embody Orville's concept of sidewise balance through hinged wings. You can't hinge but you can twist! The effect was the same. What is the price of this tube? One dollar per wing — that is, I mean — Yes, that's the right change. Thanks. A twist is a hinge. Yes, yes, thanks. Good night.

Wilbur closed the shop in haste and strode home to tell his brother of the magic inherent in a pasteboard box. He had to sit up waiting until midnight, for Orville had gone to an entertainment with his sister

Katharine and one of her college friends. At last the younger brother came. Under the gaslight in the living room Wilbur twisted and twisted the precious box of pasteboard, worth half a cent as a container, but untold millions as man's compass toward flight. This was the most pregnant twist in history. It became the warp which in its present-day form of aileron is essential to sidewise balance of all airplanes.

"Will, I'd like to scrap with you on your twist," we can imagine Orville saying, "but it looks right. As you say, it makes my hinge practical. And I guess you're on the right track with those ideas of yours on fore-and-aft balance."

It was a great night which Orville doubtless celebrated with extra vim in his regular good-night trick of going upstairs on all fours, slapping each step with his hands. Perhaps he added the flourish of kicking up his heels as, with hands on a chair, he used to do in boyish ecstasy when reporting an invention to his mother in the kitchen. At twenty-eight he was not quite grown up, and a lot of boy remains in him to this day.

Our narrative has many seemingly inconsequential details, like the reference above to a college friend of Sister Katharine. However, Father Wright wrote in his diary, under date of July 22, 1899, "Hattie Silliman our visitor since Thursday," and this record helped to establish in court the priority of the Wrights in the idea of warping wings. Father Wright began his useful diary habit when he was a missionary teacher in Oregon, suspended it until 1867, then continued the record up to the time of his death.

Although the brothers were now working in the bicycle shop sixteen hours a day — for they opened it to early workingmen customers at six o'clock in the morning and did not close it until ten o'clock at night, taking turns in going home for meals — they found time to test their discovery of the twisted box.

"I then constructed a little model made out of bamboo," stated Wilbur afterwards. It was a tiny biplane glider with thread truss to brace its parts — the first physical embodiment of all the thousand imaginary machines which the brothers had created and cancelled. The next step was to build the first working model, which was also the first crude ancestor of the airplane. It was a box kite or biplane with curved surfaces and open sides, five feet wide and thirteen inches deep. Its ends could be twisted or warped in the air by means of four cords attached to the corners.

Leaving Orville to attend customers at the bicycle shop, Wilbur in early August, 1899, lugged the box kite to Seminary Hill, about a mile from home, for its premier trial. He was escorted by a crew of boys who thought it great fun that a grown-up man — he was thirty-two — should fly a kite and a very queer one just for their benefit. They ran alongside, shouted and called on other lads to see the show. At the hill a host of volunteers wanted to hold the cords but the lean keen-eyed bicycle man, who had once played with kites in partnership with his brother, gave them a friendly smile and said this was a skittish kite that might not behave with everybody.

Wilbur held in each hand a stick with two cords attached and by twisting the sticks he warped the corners of the soaring biplane and thus guided it through the air.

"Say, Mister, it's no good!" shouted the boys, as the flyer ducked erratically from one side to the other.

They shrieked in terror as the big kite made a sudden dive toward them, like a hawk on a flock of chickens, and unable to escape otherwise they threw themselves on their faces.

"It works!" thought Wilbur, grinning cheerfully at the boys.

Among the small witnesses of the experiment were John and Walter Reiniger, and they made an independent report to Orville of the kite's behavior on Seminary Hill.

Orville, his sister and Miss Silliman went with friends on a camping trip north of Dayton in late July or early August. Wilbur stayed in town to look after the bicycle shop but visited camp on Sunday and then, stated the younger brother afterward, "we went off by ourselves a great deal to discuss the experiments with the kite." Meanwhile Katharine possibly told her friend of her own adventures as housekeeper and chef on Hawthorn Street since her graduation from Oberlin the last year. College training had increased her efficiency and had eased the once difficult rôle of "little mother." However, accidents would happen, as when a marvelous peach pie, on its way from baking tin to plate, leaped from the collegiate fingers of the cook and fell on the floor face downward. But the point was that the considerate brothers hardly laughed at all and said with real sympathy:

"Never mind, Sterchens."

Katharine was more than a nominal housekeeper. If her brothers worked sixteen hours a day, she had the task of preparing for them two separate hot meals three times a day. To rise at dawn and spend so much time over a cook stove indicates true devotion and suggests the rare happiness that prevailed in a simple abode.

Despite oddities in the kite's conduct, the Wrights felt they were on their way and the next step was to embody the twisting principle in a man-carrying glider. They had time to plan the glider that winter, owing to the seasonal slack in the bicycle trade. Aside from their own warping device, the construction or shape was that of a biplane as originated by Wenham and developed by Stringfellow and Chanute. This was one of many glider shapes between single and multiple wing types; it was structurally convenient; but none had any more inherent promise of practical flight than the teakettle had promise of becoming a locomotive. Nor were the Wrights indebted to their predecessors for curved surfaces, all of which as used proving to be radically incorrect.

With lateral balance fairly assured, Wilbur suggested a horizontal rudder to obtain fore-and-aft stability as well as to elevate.

A place suitable for gliding experiment would combine steady winds, hills for take-offs and soft ground for landing. The government weather reports showed that suitable winds of sixteen to twenty-five miles an hour would be found along the Atlantic coast. Not knowing whether the other elements of the combination existed in this region, the brothers wrote for information to the Weather Bureau at Washington, D. C. Willis L. Moore, Chief of the Bureau, replied that the place for them was at Kitty Hawk, North Carolina, where a station of the Weather Bureau was maintained.

They planned to go there with a glider the following year.

The machine was to be braced in a modification of the Pratt bridge truss, which was also employed by Chanute. Through spring and summer the brothers toiled at their glider in time stolen from a brisk bicycle trade. Ash ribs were steamed to a curve, struts shaped and fitted with a homemade universal joint, so that wires over pulleys might warp the wing structure. Wilbur shopped for the sateen wing covering. They did not assemble the glider in Dayton, but planned to get some long sticks for the frame at a convenient point near the base of operations.

While Orville stayed to keep shop for a time, Wilbur started for Kitty Hawk around September 1, 1900, taking the materials and a camping outfit. At Norfolk, Virginia, the pioneer found that available spruce sticks were short, eighteen instead of twenty-two feet, so that the area of the glider would have to be reduced from two hundred to one hundred and sixty-five square feet. This was just a foretaste of trials and tribulations galore. It was a day's trip to reach Elizabeth City, North Carolina, sixty miles onward, and there it appeared that no one had ever heard of such a place as Kitty Hawk.

At last Wilbur met an ancient mariner named Israel Perry who knew of the place sought and engaged to take the stranger there by water. Captain Perry owned

a tub of a sailboat and was his own mate and crew.
The course was down the marshy Pasquotank River
and across Albemarle Sound. The tub promptly ran
into the tail end of a hurricane which had just wrecked
Galveston, and had to put back for safety into the
river, anchoring for the night. Wilbur, expecting a
short voyage, had brought no provisions and did not
care for the iron rations of the ancient mariner. He
had a bright idea. Fishing in his valise he drew forth a
glass of jelly (whether grape or currant) which a very
thoughtful sister had slipped in as he was leaving home.
A nuisance before, the jelly was now as a banquet to
a hungry castaway. As an act of politeness and fair
play but sorely against his appetite, Wilbur proffered
the jelly first to the captain, who squinted at the dainty
glass and rumbled:

"I don't know about that. I don't know what that's
made of."

Thus Wilbur was cheered and fortified by the entire
contents of the glass.

The storm raged with increased fury. Wilbur thought
his last night on earth had come. On this solemn occasion he meditated and committed mutiny on the high
seas, or at least high salt water. He deposed the hysterical captain and, landlubber though he was, took command of the gyrating tub. Canvas was lost, the rudder
smashed. But somehow the craft survived and was
brought safely to port.

It took a week to make the six hundred mile trip
from home to the fishing hamlet of Kitty Hawk — a
point on a strip of sand thrown up by the Atlantic for
many a league along the Southern coast, separated from

the mainland by shallow waters of Albemarle and Pimlico Sounds. The strip is one half to three miles wide. Kitty Hawk is on the landward side at one of the wider parts, six miles from historic Roanoke Island, where Sir Walter Raleigh landed an English band in 1585, long before the Pilgrim Fathers arrived at Plymouth Rock. It is about sixty miles north of dreaded Cape Hatteras.

While setting up camp, Wilbur stayed at the home of the local postmaster, William J. Tate. One day there was a bit of dialogue like this:

"May I use your sewing machine, Mrs. Tate?"

"Certainly, Mr. Wright, but can't I — ?"

"Thank you, Mrs. Tate, I can do it myself. Just want to stitch up a pair of wings."

The postmaster's little girls shyly watched and admired the cream-hued sateen stitched into wings by the capable stranger. I suspect they dreamed in secret envy of a better use for that beautiful cloth.

CHAPTER V

Orville joined his brother around September 25 and they hastened to finish assembly of the glider. Trudging through deep sand between their camp near the government life-saving station and the postmaster's house, where they had their meals, was too much of a task. So they moved their site within a quarter mile of the Tate dwelling. There were half a dozen other houses in sight, but in effect the place was as private as a location on the moon. The total population of the hamlet numbered about sixty persons, mostly fisher folk.

A wall tent, twelve by twenty feet, housed the machine, a small work bench and themselves. They had an array of tools between saws, vise and breast drill, and supplies of screws, bolts, tacks, wire, strap iron, not to mention an item which they almost regarded as a panacea for mechanical ills of every sort from slippage to fracture. The reader may have three guesses. Yes, bicycle cement.

"Let's try it!" we can hear the impatient brothers exclaim together, when the glider was winged but yet lacked the front horizontal rudder.

They hurried it incomplete to a sand dune, tied a rope to its nose and with a feverish blessing let Eolus take the steed.

This was the reality of four years' dreams. It rose,

pranced and danced, tugged with vicious and thrilling
power against the arms of its enraptured creators.
What a kite — no, what an air horse for a man to
mount and ride on! Now they had to ride, regardless of
their agreed-on program to proceed slowly like cool
disinterested scientists. They pulled Pegasus to earth
and Wilbur stretched himself on it face downward between wings. It did not seem to mind the passenger.
Orville gradually loosed the rein. It gamboled upwards
with almost as much vigor and steadiness as before.
The man on the ground exulted. It had been his boyhood delight to fly kites and now he was flying a super-
kite with his brother aboard. Science? Pshaw, this was
pure fun, the sport of a lifetime.

Wilbur had another viewpoint and could not share
the enthusiasm of the one below. He repented of his
rashness in wanting to ride a creature so wabbly, skittish and dangerous. He was in the air. Earth seemed far
below. In quick staccato he began to shout:

"Lemme down! Lemme down! *Lemme down!*"

The wind took his voice backward and doubtless
Orville let out a bit more rope, thinking his brother was
cheering and wished to go higher. Then he understood
the purport of the confused summons and hauled Wilbur down from an altitude of something like eight feet.

When the family at Dayton heard of this virgin
flight and listed "Lemme down!" with "I'll squall", "At
the rate of" and other intimate jibes of the home circle,
Wilbur offered a defence.

"I promised Father that I would take care of myself."

"That sounds good," was the retort. "Evidently your

The Wrights' First Glider being flown as a Kite at Kitty Hawk, 1900. Wilbur had the first ride and shouted: "Lemme down! Lemme down!"

promise didn't include the care of Orv, because you let him ride next and he went a good deal higher and had to jump all around that bucking bronco's back to save his neck while you ran pulling it lickety split down hill."

Orville did have a wild ride. It ended with a mild smash from which he rose unscathed. Repairs were soon made and the front elevating rudder was attached. The brothers took turns as jockeys, a halter rope still tied to the steed. Unlike their gliding predecessors, who used a sitting position, they rode in a recumbent face-downward posture, feet hooked over a rear bar as body brace, hips in a tight but movable cradle, elbows in support with hands gripping a bar that moved the elevator rudder ahead. As the hip cradle rocked sidewise, its wire connections warped the flexible wing ends, raising one side while lowering the other, an alternate screw action like twisting and untwisting a pasteboard box.

The glider was tested with varying loads without passengers and put through its paces by cord control of its novel devices. When "lift and drift" were measured, the Wrights were surprised by results very contrary to accepted figures. There was half the head resistance of framing calculated by Chanute and the lifting power was much less than the wing curve should have produced, according to the Lilienthal table of air pressure. They thought perhaps they needed more curve and a cloth more air-tight than sateen. Could Lilienthal and Chanute together be wrong? Well, they would build another machine next year with air-tight cloth and make the wings adjustable to various curves.

Meanwhile they moved camp four miles south to Kill Devil Hill so as to have some real jaunts on their air nag. The sand strip here is about a mile between ocean and sound. Kill Devil Hill, so-called through Indian legend, is the largest of several sand dunes wont to change their shapes and even to move location with urge of Hatteras gales. It was then about a hundred feet high and had a ten-degree slope north-eastward. Seagulls, fishhawks, buzzards and eagles sailed over the sandy desert. Yet hoping poetically to learn something from the birds, the Wrights studied them in action and carefully measured the wing spread — five feet, ten inches — of a fishhawk which they shot.

The second day after arrival at the hill the wind fell to a favorable speed of fourteen miles an hour and they made about a dozen brief glides. Postmaster Tate went along to help launch the machine. He and one of the brothers — the other riding — would hold opposite ends of the glider and run downhill with it against the wind. As the biplane went free, its pilot shimmied his hips to keep sidewise balance and with his hands shifted the forward horizontal fin to maintain a fore-and-aft even keel. It was a pleasant discovery that the pilot did not have to make a two-point landing with his feet but could make a safe stop while recumbent from a speed of twenty miles an hour. Sand flew up under the skids on landing and it was needful to shut eyes.

It had been planned to glide as a boy coasts on a sled, running a bit downhill, then throwing himself upon the sled. But it was found better to have the rider already aboard with two helpers at the wing ends running downhill with the glider and thus launching the machine. Thus the pilot was free to operate the controls at the very start of the flight. In modern gliding without motor the pilot has similar aid in take-offs.

Along with the pursuit of scientific sport there were domestic problems and troubles. Orville as chef had an excellent gasoline stove but found almost nothing suitable to cook on it. The diet of brawny fishermen did not appeal to delicate appetites, perhaps pampered by sisterly care. The worthy postmaster scoured the countryside to obtain edibles for them. It seemed a bright day to the famished pioneers when beefsteak and butter arrived from Elizabeth City. Alas, the steak was only fit to be thrown to the wild fowl. There was hope of salvaging the butter by a process of boiling it. Orville boiled it and soon nothing remained except an odor.

However, their experiments were cheering. The glider went forward against the wind at ten or fifteen miles an hour with reference to the ground while it traveled at twenty-five to thirty miles an hour with allowance for speed of wind. It responded quite well to its novel system of control, keeping equilibrium for a number of seconds in a straightaway flight. It went up or down with the front elevating rudder.

"Although the hours and hours of practice we had hoped to obtain finally dwindled down to about two minutes," said Wilbur afterward, "we were very much pleased with the general results of the trip, for setting out as we did, with almost revolutionary theories on many points, and in an entirely untried form of machine, we considered it quite a point to be able to return without having our pet theories knocked in the head by the hard logic of experience, and our own brains dashed out in the bargain."

They were confirmed in their original ideas that warping of wings was a better system of lateral balance than body-shifting, not to mention the device of automatic stability through V-shaped wings as used in toy flyers; that flying was a good deal a matter of practice; that the recumbent posture was practical, and that the horizontal rudder aided fore-and-aft balance while it permitted steering up and down.

The Wrights did not realize what a great start they had made toward victory. They even doubted that it would be worth while to return to Kitty Hawk the next year and continue their scientific sport. They had had a pleasant, exciting vacation, despite hardships of food, mosquitoes and else. They could not see a cent of profit in their work nor any notable contribution to human knowledge. Being through with the glider, they planned its tidy disposal. They faced it north on top of Kill Devil Hill, weighted it down with sand and departed. It was their notion that the next gale would blow the remains into the Atlantic. But Postmaster Tate, quite agreeing that the machine was no further use to anybody, perceived that it had a certain junk value. He dragged it home as firewood and as sateen dresses for his little girls.

If that relic had been saved, it might be exchangeable to-day for mahogany furniture and a quantity of Paris gowns.

Soon after their return to Dayton on October 26, 1900, the brothers wrote to Octave Chanute, saying they had been doing some gliding and had found some possible errors in his and Lilienthal's air tables. The latter were formulas which gave the pressure of air in motion, or wind, at varying speeds, upon surfaces. The formulas had been supposedly proven by savants long before. They were the essence of the science of aërodynamics and the theoretical basis according to which all gliding machines were designed. It was somewhat presumptuous for a pair of amateurs at the end of their first season's experiment thus to call in question the very arcana of a high and abstruse branch of knowledge.

Chanute, himself the Conan Doyle of a hypothetical aviation science, may have smiled at the presumption of two bicycle men, but he was broad-minded enough to overlook it and to encourage them with words of cheer. He was of French descent but a resident of this country since childhood. He lived in Chicago, and enjoyed high-standing as a civil engineer, being president of the Western Society of Engineers. He had written a history of world wide flying attempts, had planned and tested a variety of aircraft, and welcomed every recruit to the lodge of aërial true believers. Chanute was a credulous and kindly man. He has been miscalled a Father of Aviation. It is enough to say that he was a friendly patron of amateurs. He deserves the affectionate respect of disciples who learned nothing specific from him.

The bicycle business was good and the Wrights decided they could afford another vacation trip to Kitty Hawk the next summer. What about checking those tables of air pressure before planning a new machine? The apparatus used by scientists to register air pressure on surfaces was too complicated and costly. Perhaps a bicycle would help to reveal aërodynamic secrets. Put your testing device in front and pedal for all you are worth, one eye on the whirling telltale and the other — of course — on traffic. A bicycle meets air pressure of ten to thirty miles per hour. It is a perfect auxiliary in experiment and a little brother to the glider itself.

"Hiyi, Mister! Lookit the windmill on a wheel!" jeered the street gamins of Dayton as Wilbur or Orville went by with a whirling wind vane on a rod projecting in front of the handle bars on his bicycle.

"Ha! ha!" chuckled grown-ups. "Does look funny to see a grown man playing with a kid's toy. So solemn about it too. He! he!"

Wilbur one day stood on a street corner watching the conduct of the device as his brother spurted past when a stranger approached and said, "That fellow can run his gizzard out, but he'll never make that thing go up."

The Wrights never learned the identity of this mysterious commentator who divined uncannily the purport of their experiment but whose pessimism proved to be unfounded.

However, the vane on the wheel shed little light on the problem of curves and pressures. The brothers went ahead, planning the new glider on the general lines of the old but with greater lift. The wing curve was increased to one in twelve, in accord with Lilienthal's table, while the area was enlarged to three hundred eight square feet, making the glider about twice the size of all predecessors. The wing span was twenty-two feet, the length with front rudder fourteen feet and the height about six feet. It embodied the last year's device for warping the wings. It was expected that a seventeen-mile wind would support the machine tilted at a three-degree angle.

"I guess the Wright boys are going camping again this summer," said one Hawthorn Street neighbor to another in the late spring of 1901.

"What makes you think so?"

"Wilbur is making a tent-like in the back yard of their house. Anybody who walks by can see him working; so can the folks next door. He uses a sewing machine, fast and clever. His sister Katharine — she teaches now in high school, you know — comes out on the back porch once in a while and I guess tells him what thread to use or something."

But the new teacher of modern languages in Steele High School did not have to instruct her brother in sewing any more than in mathematics, despite legends to that effect. Geometry and physics were never subjects to her taste. She was a good teacher of languages, a rare disciplinarian of unruly youngsters who mistook small stature for weakness, and the sunniest homemaker that ever brothers were blessed with.

Wilbur was absorbed in his "tent-like" job for about a week. He had bought the material himself in a local dry-goods store, which he had hated to enter as a place of frills, perfume and gabble; but once in had proved himself an exacting and even fussy customer. After many questions as to cloth weaves, quality, bleaching and strength, he had ordered a large amount of "Pride of the West" muslin. The back yard lawn was a pleasant work place in the spring sunshine, with robins hopping about; and convenient for laying out the material, cutting and matching the large sections. The cloth was cut at an angle or on the bias, so that its threads would cross the wing frames and act as a brace.

To lessen the hardships of the last year the Wrights planned to have a shed instead of a tent, and to take along enough canned food. A water supply in camp could be had by means of a pitcher pump and a short pipe driven in the sand. They mentioned the water project to Charles Webbert, landlord of their bicycle shop, who was likewise a plumber and furthermore a believer in spiritism.

"I will donate a pump to the cause of science!" exclaimed Mr. Webbert somewhat ambiguously, for he had his own notion as to what the brothers were up to and what invisible collaboration they might secure. Perhaps the donation was a gesture of good will, showing that the tolerant landlord had quite forgotten the episode when his tenants had flouted the mediums with a mortised, brad-nailed and otherwise spirit-proof slate.

Before the Wrights started for Kitty Hawk on July 7, 1901, Octave Chanute dropped into town for a casual visit. He was a short rolypoly figure with gray moustache and wisp of goatee, having a high-pitched voice that remained subdued. His manners were suave and had a genial charm. He was a person as agreeable as his letters had indicated. He was much interested to learn from the Wrights of the gliding advantages at Kitty Hawk and made a proposal to them in the following vein:

"I have a man, E. C. Huffaker, who is building a glider for me in Tennessee. Suppose you let him camp

with you. He'll help to handle your machine and you
help to handle his or my glider. I have another protegé
you might be good enough to take along. He's Doctor
George A. Spratt of Coatesville, Pennsylvania. He is
quite keen, for an amateur, on this flying idea. If you
boys will board the doctor, I'll pay his railroad fare.
You know a medical man is pretty handy in these experiments. I read a joke somewhere that an undertaker
might be useful too. *C'est bon mot, n'est-ce-pas?* Ha,
ha!"

The brothers agreed to the genial Chanute's proposal. They arrived at Kitty Hawk about July tenth
and were joined in a fortnight by Huffaker and the
doctor. A shed of rough lumber was built near Kill
Devil Hill. It was hangar, workshop and home for four
men. The large doors were hinged at the top and when
opened constituted a porch roof of grateful protection
against the sun. There were enough tools and repair
materials. The spiritist's pump with sand-driven pipe
supplied good water. Orville as chief cook presided at
a gasoline stove and laid out a model kitchen with eggs
of numbered sequence in a rack and canned goods —
including dozens of tins of peaches, pears, corn and
tomatoes — assorted mathematically on the shelves.
The camp was perfect except for an hour's trudge
through ankle-deep sand for mail and extra supplies,
and a plague of mosquitoes.

We may imagine the perspiring campers plodding
back from Kitty Hawk village, heavily laden with
watermelons and chickens, maple syrup and bacon,
coffee and butter, losing some of the plunder en route
by leakage and wishing that nature had made water-

melons easier to carry. However, the latter were delicious and cost no more than thirty-five cents a dozen.

The innumerable ferocious mosquitoes amounted to a major problem and indeed almost checkmated science and the progress of the world. A battle against the insects was waged with smudge fires, essences, liniments, a kerosene bath, blankets and netting, yet the vicious enemy came on with undiminished zeal and speared their victims through all defenses. The mosquitoes seemed to be giants in size and still they passed through the finest mesh. It was stifling within the shed, and when cots were placed outdoors amid smudges burning all night, the blanketed campers had an alternative of suffocation or roasting — all except Wilbur whose nose was of a convenient length to obtain fresh air.

"These flyers will never let man fly," quoth a despairing camper.

The brothers found some surcease from the pests by rigging canvas beds for themselves between the ceiling beams of the shed, while they also saved trouble with cots. One of these canvas beds afterward became a place of historical inspiration, for which an Oriental philosopher might give credit to the mosquitoes.

Doctor Spratt was gifted as a story-teller. Huffaker was also agreeable but so absent-minded as to dish-washing and other domestic tasks that the brothers broke camp earlier than they had planned. Chanute made a week's visit, observing the Wright machine; his own partly built glider on which Huffaker was working had been wind-wrecked the night before Chanute's arrival around August 4.

Postmaster Tate and his brother Dan took a hand

with the others in helping to launch the Wright glider. Wilbur was aboard the first trip on July 27 in a thirteen-mile wind down Kill Devil Hill with Orville and Spratt at the corners. The machine quickly nosed to earth. It was evident that the center of gravity was forward of the center of pressure, while it was necessary to have these points coincide. The rider crawled back in repeated trials, inches at a time, until his weight was about a foot to the rear of the first position. Then he sailed off neatly for a distance beyond three hundred feet.

The gallery applauded but the inventors were disappointed. They saw the glider's tendency to nose-dive and to stall backward. The machine of last year had acted better with one quarter the present use of the front rudder, and against this fact there was no consolation in a merely spectacular performance.

Once Wilbur was saved in the nick of time from a perilous stall — loss of motion which preludes a crash — by the warning shout of Orville on the ground: he turned the rudder and hitched his weight a trifle ahead so as to level the machine and make a safe descent.

"Those air tables must be wrong, as we thought last year," agreed the brothers. "The wing curve is too great. We'll truss the ribs and make the curve less."

Pegasus thereby became as well-behaved as last year, ambled three hundred eighty-nine feet over heights and hollows, jogged prettily against a stiff breeze of twenty-seven miles an hour. Chanute was present at some of the flights, took photographs of them and congratulated the brothers on their accomplishment. But they remained dissatisfied. The steed was yet too wild and inefficient for the exacting owners, who measured his pull against a pair of scales and computed factors of area, weight, shape, angle and wind speed with a high degree of mathematical skill. They knew their algebra and trigonometry, although they had never been to college. The lifting capacity of the glider was still less than it should have been. The porosity of the cloth was not to blame. The anemometer or wind gage used at the camp, fell under suspicion. Perhaps the Smeaton formula for wind pressure was a fifth off and Lilienthal's table not more than half right. Perhaps two wings gave less lift than one.

The unpublished diary of the Wright brothers, of which the more pertinent passages are before me as I write, has an entry of some six hundred words under date of July 30, 1901, which weighs the pros and cons of their work up to that time and conveys an undertone of dejection. Four points that were favorable and an equal number of discouraging features were listed. That they were whistling to keep up courage is indicated by an optimistic entry based on the strength of the glider and its escape from damage after about forty landings. The attainment of lateral balance was correctly listed on the good side of the account. To be sure, the all-around performance was improved after this summary record was made, yet the final outlook was far from being hopeful.

The Wrights stopped gliding on August 17, packed their camping outfit and went home.

"When we left Kitty Hawk, at the end of 1901, we doubted that we would ever resume our experiments,"

Wilbur stated later. "Although we had broken the record for distance in gliding, so far as any actual figures had been published, and although Mr. Chanute, who was present part of the time, assured us that our results were better than had ever before been obtained, yet when we looked at the time and the money which we had expended, and considered the progress made and the distance yet to go, we considered our experiments a failure."

More tersely Wilbur at the time said to Orville:

"Man won't be flying for a thousand years!"

The younger brother was more hopeful by nature and perhaps hummed "Wait Till the Clouds Roll By," or cited a text on moving a mountain by faith.

McClure's magazine for September was on the newsstands when the brothers got home and they found in it a cogent discussion of the flying problem by Professor Simon Newcomb, world-famous astronomer and mathematician, who weightily corroborated the temporary despondency of Wilbur. Basing his profound analysis on calculus, logarithms, fluxions, harmonics and whatnot, the eminent savant tried to put a quietus on the vain dreams of bicycle men and other fanatics in these words:

"We may now see the kernel of the difficulty. If we had a metal so rigid and at the same time so light that a sheet of it twenty meters square and a millimeter thick would be as stiff as a board and would not weigh more than a ton, and at the same time so strong that a powerful engine could be built of it with little weight, we might hope for a flying machine which could carry a man. But as the case stands, the first successful flyer will be the handiwork of a watchmaker, and will carry nothing heavier than an insect. . . .

"I have shown that the construction of an aërial vehicle which could carry even a single man from place to place at pleasure requires the discovery of some new metal or some new force."

Perhaps the learned professor was right, in a way. Since no new metal was available, the creation of the airplane within the next two years might be attributed to the discovery of a new force — the elemental genius of Wilbur and Orville Wright.

It is darkest before dawn. If Wilbur had been a seer he would have amended his own discouraged statement:

"Man won't be flying for a thousand years — I mean, Orv, not for about eight hundred and forty-five days."

CHAPTER VI

"The Wright boys want to fly without a gas bag."

"Huh. They certainly can't *without*."

"Guess you're right," agreed the other neighbor. "I was talking with a man in their bicycle shop. He says he advised 'em to put a coat of goose feathers on their machine."

"Would goose feathers be better than chicken?"

"Sure, they're lighter — that's why a goose flies so high."

The Wrights were almost discouraged enough at this time, after two summers of gliding experiment at Kitty Hawk, to catch at straws if not at goose feathers. They did not know that in their discovery of the warping principle they had solved twenty-five per cent. of the flying problem. They were on the straight road to victory but could not see it. Happily, they were pessimistic. Instead of gloating over their record as the world's foremost gliders, they applied themselves to a more searching study of the unknown. They focused their minds on the puzzling incorrectness of the classic air tables.

Octave Chanute, that genial blunderer in the necromantic field of aviation, unwittingly stimulated the Wrights in their quest. As president of the Western Society of Engineers he asked Wilbur to address that body at their Chicago headquarters on the subject of the brothers' aërial experiment. The bicycle men were put on their mettle and perhaps even awed. What an august audience of scientists! All with degrees and titles honorific. . . . Suppose there were hecklers in the audience. Perhaps a mysterious stranger of cliff-like forehead would rise and as he pointed an accusing finger would reveal himself as the Great Cham who had lately thundered excommunication upon flight, with blasting references to insects, watchmakers and a metal as stiff as a board while one twenty-fifth of an inch thick. "In short, Gentlemen, the whole subject is nonsense and the speaker of the evening is peculiarly unfitted to enlighten you upon it. He will only intensify the present darkness of your minds, not to use such a word as hallucination." . . . Be careful. Check up everything. Well, here are the facts, whether the scientists like them or not. Sorry if we have to give President Chanute a little dig too. He means well but here are the facts.

Wilbur scrubbed the grease from his hands, put on his good suit and with a carefully written address in his pocket took the train for Chicago, where he was to speak on September 18, 1901.

The anxious younger brother, between intervals of attending customers at the bicycle shop, rigged a new device of his own to measure air pressure on plane and curved surfaces. It was something different and better than last year's windmill on a wheel, which the brothers had propelled around Dayton to the amusement of grown-ups and the derision of the small fry.

"Oh, pshaw! Lilienthal is right, after all!" I hear Orville mutter in horrified accents, after a hasty check

The Kitty Hawk Camp in 1902. Wilbur Wright standing. Octave Chanute at end of cot (front), then Orville Wright, and A. M. Herring. Chanute encouraged but could not instruct the Wrights.

on the new device of a few figures from the German's air table. "Nearly right, anyhow. I must let Will know in a hurry before he tells those scientists what isn't so!"

Wilbur, astonished and pained by this home work, dutifully squirted water on the fireworks of his Chicago speech. The audience applauded a soggy and safe utterance. On the speaker's return home he sadly agreed with Orville that the address in printed form would have to be made yet soggier and safer. So was it done.

Yet the stubborn Wrights, recanting in public, kept their private suspicion that the classic air tables were moth-eaten and useless. The tables were done in the name of a so-called science, aërodynamics, which was then almost on a par with alchemy and astrology. Savants had labored in this field for decades, erecting a pretentious scaffolding of figures. The French Academy over a century ago issued an imposing array of figures and decimals. The Aëronautical Society of Great Britain later constructed a substantial plus-and-minus edifice. There was a noted Frenchman, Duchemin, who made a neat and logical set of numerals.

The simple-minded Wrights, less gullible than university scholars, saw there was little science in a subject whereon authorities widely disagreed. Indeed there was a fifty per cent. difference of opinion on the basic unit of measurement — the pressure of a mile-an-hour breeze against a one-foot-square plane surface at right angles. There was similar discrepancy as to what the pressure amounted to, when the plane was tilted forward at various angles. Professor Langley, Secretary of the Smithsonian Institution, made costly experiments in this branch of physics, told the world that he had "verified" Duchemin and solemnly announced the discovery of "Langley's Law", which was an aërial application of the something-for-nothing notion.

The scientists attacked the delicate and profound subject of aërodynamics with a host of devices and implements. They even took the temperature and weight of the air, almost put clinical thermometers in their mouths, as they peered at their instruments or wreaked the higher mathematics on pages of figures. They lost themselves in a forest of nonessentials. Like the man in the song who had a chick here and a chick there, they were distracted by a multitude of straying factors, and they made a guesswork allowance for any factors that seemed to be missing. Professor Langley himself thus missed a number of chicks and allotted a percentage to cover the loss. . . .

"We did not owe anything to Langley," Orville Wright assured me, holding in his hands a copy of the thin volume, "Experiments in Aërodynamics." The inventor pointed out the distorted figures and arbitrary guesses that "verified" Duchemin and the feeble basis of facts for the heralded Law of Langley. Mr. Wright did not charge dishonesty but a self-evident credulity and a laxness far from scientific.

Langley deceived every one, including himself. He was a scientific dreamer, to whom aviation is still indebted for a baseless optimism that counteracted Professor Simon Newcomb's can't-be-done ukase and for a while kept the Wrights scouting on an unknown trail.

However, the brothers had to eat humble pie for a time after that Chicago address. They had gone too far; and they had had to retract. Then one morning in the bicycle shop laboratory, checking again those air tables with their homemade apparatus, we may hear glad cries rising above a racket and roar.

"Will, just look at this dial!"

"Orv, that's great!"

"Maybe we're right, after all! I'll bet we are."

"You just tested a few of Lilienthal's figures before and they happened to be nearly right. This shows the table as a whole is moonshine. Hurrah!"

They felt perhaps a greater thrill than when they took their first rides on a glider at Kitty Hawk — not because they had found error in a predecessor but because they had found a sure and accurate method of measuring air pressure on plane and curved surfaces. Perhaps they dimly surmised that they had now converted aërodynamics from a status of near-wizardry to that of legitimate and exact science, and that some day their names might be inscribed on history's roll between those of Faraday and Edison.

Professor Langley and Sir Hiram Maxim had tried to measure air pressure by means of pivoted shapes attached to the end of a revolving arm. It was inherently difficult to register the angles assumed by the shapes at various speeds, despite all sorts of clever electrical apparatus. Centrifugal motion with difference of speed near and far from the center added a number of falsifying factors. The method was hopelessly complicated and full of incalculable errant chicks. The inventor of the Maxim gun was as baffled as the learned Secretary of the Smithsonian.

The Wrights also had fumbled the problem, though briefly, with their whirligig projecting from a bicycle.

Now they were clear-eyed and saw — Orville first — that tested objects should be subjected to equal pressure on all parts, which was not the case when they were revolved around a center, and that measurement of angles should be direct and simple. Instead of moving an object through the air, they would move the air on the object. That is, the test piece would be stationary, except for its angle-reaction through pivots, and would have a current of air driven against it. With such a method they could get the one thing needful — correct angle readings — and could dispense with all the non-essentials of temperature, barometric pressure and else which had confused their predecessors.

Thus was born in a Dayton bicycle shop the world's first wind tunnel, a prime instrument of aërodynamic research now in universal use. It cost the brothers less than fifteen dollars. Savants in Europe and America had vainly spent several hundred thousand dollars on apparatus of the same purpose. There was a homemade metal fan mounted on an emery-wheel shaft, driven by a two-cylinder gas engine which the Wrights had built for shop power. The wind tunnel was of wood, sixteen inches square and eight feet long. Objects were suspended in the air blast and automatically recorded by a gage pointer their angles, according to velocity of the air. Old hacksaw blades and stray bits of galvanized iron contributed to the measuring fixtures.

The apparatus was crude in every way. Its makers knew it and made certain compensations. Orville in the first test had reversed the tunnel and now they improved sensitivity by the simple expedient of jarring the instrument while it was in action. Pounding on the table overcame sticky bearings and gave freedom to the model wings to tell their angular stories.

Over two hundred little wings from three to nine inches in length were tested in the wind tunnel at this time. They were of varied type and surface, and were tried tandem and in multiple combination, as well as singly. A quick, economical and correct answer was obtained to the question of wing number, which alone had confounded previous experimenters. The model wings were cut from sheet metal, bent to desired curves, sometimes doubled for thickness and smoothed with wax. One of the discoveries which most astonished the inventors was the fact that a thick leading edge of wing or strut gave less resistance than a thin edge and that the important thing was to streamline the rear.

The Wrights found the true figures for the center of pressure, or lift, at the various angles of a plane and curved surface. Lilienthal had indeed discovered that this lifting pressure is at a tangent to a forward tilted wing instead of at right angles, as with a plane surface, but his figures were unreliable.

The brothers also established and put into mathematical form as an important law of aërodynamics what had been a surmise on the part of their Kitty Hawk campmate and protegé of Octave Chanute — Doctor George A. Spratt. The doctor who was thought useful to set limbs that might be broken in gliding accidents made an excellent guess when he suggested that the center of pressure under a wing did not keep moving forward toward the front edge but reversed itself at a low angle of wing inclination and shifted toward the rear. While Spratt thought of it first, only the Wrights were able to prove it, and without the hint they would doubtless have made an independent discovery of the fact with their wind tunnel. Similarly others anticipated Newton on the law of gravitation: he consolidated and proved; and none questions that he is master mechanic of the universe — *pace* relativity.

Nevertheless Doctor Spratt deserves honor, which hitherto has been generally withheld, for his contribution to aeronautical science, not only as to the reversal of the center of pressure but also for his vital idea that lift and drift could be measured by a suitable device simultaneously.

The brothers made two principal testing devices, the first to locate center of pressure and the second to find the ratio between lift and drift. Lift is the weight-carrying ability of a wing at a given speed, while drift is its resistance to travel in the line of motion.

To-day the latter term (drift) has been restored to its ordinary dictionary meaning, as getting off one's course, and has been replaced in the technical sense by drag, subdivided into wing drag and structural drag or parasite resistance. The distinction is explained by the fact that while wing resistance is accompanied with useful service in keeping the plane aloft, the body and other structural parts only impede the progress of the craft. Another modern term, "airfoil", is used to include all winglike structures, whether wing, rudder, fin or else.

Drift is used in this narrative in its old sense. Likewise the pioneer meaning of angle of incidence, as being the tilt of a plane to its air stream or line of travel (which may or may not coincide with the angle of plane to horizon) is preserved in these pages. To-day such a varying tilt is called angle of attack, while the former expression is reserved for the fixed angle between wings and body or fuselage of the airplane as built by the manufacturer.

A paradox of lift developed by modern research is that a wing is upheld much less by air pressure beneath than by air suction or partial vacuum above, due to the high-vaulting atmospheric current over the curved top surface. In fact, the suction is two or three times as effective as the pressure. Of course philosophers of the egg-and-chicken school may find a moot point in the interplay of suction and pressure.

Scientists had vainly attempted to measure lift and drift separately and apart from each other. The Wrights recognized lift and drift as Siamese twins, which nature itself had bonded in a permanent union. Instead of a futile effort to separate the pair, the brothers found a way to caliper them together, and at the same time to learn how much work or mischief each twin was doing in a joint effort. Messrs. Lift-and-Drift made a loud protest in the wind tunnel against the revelation of their inner secrets but in the end they had to submit.

"And here goes Langley's Law!" we may hear the brothers exclaim, as their apparatus refuted the Professor's pronunciamento that the greater the aërial speed the less the power required. At best this is a feeble half-truth. Up to a certain low range both airplanes and automobiles take less power to move briskly than to dawdle. Beyond the gait of easy momentum, power must be greatly multiplied to increase speed.

The first wind tunnel of epochal discovery was indeed small and crude compared with the modern tunnel through which an elephant might amble when it is not traversed by a cyclonic blast of air. Its atmosphere could not be compressed, chilled to Arctic temperature, raised to Sahara heat or rarefied to reproduce altitude above the snowy crest of Mount Everest. It lacked the present-day refinements in precision of shapes to be measured and the delicate instruments with which to register results. It was a rough assembly of odds and ends, almost junk in a bicycle shop. Still it was accurate enough to serve its purpose in the creation of the airplane.

"The airplane was a byproduct of the Wrights' supreme discoveries in aërodynamics — a useful application of their first principles of the air," says a pure scientist.

It may be so. The simpler viewpoint is that their achievement in aërodynamics contributed fifty per cent. to their invention of the airplane. Warping, twenty-five per cent., was no laboratory find nor was the last one quarter element of flight.

By February, 1902, or within four months of comparative leisure afforded by the seasonal slackness of the bicycle trade, the amateurs in science had about completed their research and tabulated the main results. In such brief time they canceled the efforts of the world's savants for more than a century and replaced them with genuine knowledge. Merely some figures on a sheet of paper, yet a true chart for the navigation of the unknown. The amateurs sent copies of their figures, or air tables, to Octave Chanute and to Doctor Spratt. No other persons were thus favored, I believe, nor have these tables ever been published.

"What scientist," exclaims a learned critic, "ever withheld important knowledge from the world for a quarter century! Most men hasten to impart discovery, if only to prove they are first, especially in the field of pure science. What is the explanation?"

Perhaps the Wrights are vulnerable to an extent on this charge. In early years they did have reason to withhold their air tables, which were not only pure science but the basis of their practical construction of aircraft.

"The world has all the visible parts of our invention," we may imagine the brothers saying. "It has taken the airplane as far as possible, and we might as well keep for ourselves the invisible part — the air tables. We will keep the pilferers groping and copying instead of handing them a full set of blueprints."

When Orville Wright sold all his financial interest in the airplane in 1915 — three years after the death of his brother Wilbur — he might well have published those tables as one of the steps essential to the attainment of justice for the pioneers.

If the Wrights seemed slightly selfish over their mathematical ewe lamb, the world lost nothing, for it soon helped itself to their air tunnel and thereby was able to produce all the tables it required.

Meanwhile the bicycle men, hardly realizing what they had done, felt a renewal of flying enthusiasm and a keen urge to test their latest discoveries in the air. They had passed the stage of guesswork in devising the size and curve of wings. They were confident that they could now build without recourse to trial and error. They had formulas to design a glider of a size and shape suitable to carry a given load at a certain speed.

"Wilbur must be an expert at the sewing machine by this time," said a neighbor, at sight of that lean mechanic stitching yards of cloth in the back yard of the Hawthorn Street home in the summer of 1902. "He was at it last year and I hear the summer before, down at Kitty Hawk. Some say the boys just go camping and they make their own tents. Others say they are trying to fly. I don't believe they're that foolish."

The wing covering for the third glider was again Pride-of-the-West muslin and as before Wilbur cut it on the bias to get the bracing effect of diagonal threads. He used the best thread and made strong seams. The lawn of clipped grass was a fine place to work, spacious, dappled with sunshine, having every convenience, including a well with pump for drinking water. The buzz of the machine mingled with its operator's cheerful humming or whistling of popular airs. Birds sang in the trees that lined the narrow street. Some of them perched on the board fence at the side of the lawn and cocked quizzical heads at the man at the sewing machine. A worm-digging robin skipped on the wing cloth and seemed disgusted because it could not work through muslin to the sod.

I venture to recreate here a bit of dialogue which doubtless had its scene under the gaslight of the low-ceilinged living room in the frame house.

"Will," remarks Bishop Wright, "I have a church fight on my hands that is wearing me out. The United Brethren are a sect small enough to be peaceful yet we have some terrible rows."

"Wildcats are small too, Father. What's the trouble now?"

"Oh, a lay official has embezzled church funds. They want to whitewash him to save scandal and obviate loss of donations. I want to publish the facts. Now they're attacking me. I don't feel well, and I remember how you helped me in that other church row back in 1889."

"Orv and I will take a hand in this shindy, Father!"

"But you boys want to go to Kitty Hawk early this summer."

"We did plan to, but we can put it off."

"Look here, Will, you and Orvie have been working for years on your flying machine. Now you think it is almost perfect and you want to try it. Perhaps it is a bigger thing than you imagine. The world may be waiting for this invention."

"Let it wait. It has waited a good many thousand years and I guess another year or two won't matter. We'll clean up this church trouble first and fly afterwards. We'll stay home all summer, if necessary."

Wilbur in fact shelved the airplane to aid his father; who for a time was ostensibly deposed from his episcopal office and even the ministry, by the opposing faction. Playing the rôle of expert accountant on the defaulter's books, Wilbur unearthed proof of guilt, and wrote forceful tracts that expounded the situation and disputed the view that whitewashing is a good policy. We may imagine that Wilbur enlivened theology with lessons from aërodynamics and emphasized the thesis that truth pays in religion as well as science. Orville helped also. It was not long before the whitewashing clique surrendered and Bishop Wright celebrated the triumph of rectitude.

This episode has bearing on the character of the inventors, their sense of filial duty and their mental equipoise at a moment of high anticipation. Unlike some other discoverers, the brothers were never fanatical or obsessed. They had a cool vision of relative values.

Since the trip to the North Carolina coast had been delayed, they decided to wait a bit longer for the sake of desirable fall winds. They arrived at Kitty Hawk on August 28. The sandy foundations of their old shed at Kill Devil Hill had sunk and the first task was to lift the building, after which they extended one end to make room for the glider. The machine had a span of thirty-two feet and a depth of five feet. Its wing area was three hundred five square feet. The horizontal front rudder or elevator had fifteen square feet of surface. There was an innovation over their previous craft in the feature of a vertical tail, which was at first twelve square feet in area and was later cut down to half that size. The net weight of the glider was one hundred sixteen and one-half pounds while with an operator aboard — depending on which brother rode — the total weight was two hundred fifty or two hundred sixty pounds. The machine was stanchly built. With a man aboard, it could be upheld by the wing tips.

Chanute and Spratt repeated their last summer's visit to camp. The Chicago engineer also had on the scene an employee, A. M. Herring, to test gliders. If the camp hosts had been embarrassed the last year by absent-mindedness of another Chanute mechanic in regard to dish-washing, they were now soon inclined to think of kitchen slackness as a minor breach of taste. Herring, first employed by Chanute in 1896, had also been employed by Professor Langley, and kept thinking that Washington had a good climate. A man of enterprise, Herring seemed averse to the risks of gliding. When about to ascend in a Chanute machine, he fainted. Doctor Spratt felt his pulse. Afterward, alone with the physician, Herring said:

"I hear them calling you Doctor. Are you an M.D.?"

"Old Man," observed Spratt to himself, as he later recounted, "I know what *you* are thinking."

Chanute had two gliders to be tested, one a biplane and the other a multiple wing affair. Both failed to show any merit and their designer was quite disappointed. It is evident that the so-called Father of Aviation had scant knowledge and small desire to be informed in his mystic hobby. He had seen the Wrights demonstrate their warping principle the previous year and had only been stirred to a verbal enthusiasm. They had sent him a copy of their air tables, but he had ignored the epochal formula of aërodynamic discovery and had designed his pair of gliders according to the principles of hit-and-miss fantasy.

The unpublished diary of the Wrights — which, like their air tables, should have been given to the world long ago — contains some five thousand words on this year's campaign at Kitty Hawk. It is before me. So many words of compact entry and phrasing would seem adequate for a season of six weeks, but in fact a considerable portion of the total record of 1902 has been lost. Wilbur stated afterward that one of the notebooks of this period "was left lying on our desk a few years ago and was evidently thrown in the wastebasket by the maid." Without prejudice to the maid, one is reminded of Newton and his dog Diamond. The portion which remains was written by Orville "on a little vest pocket blankbook . . . and extends to October 17." No extensive record was made during the first two seasons at Kitty Hawk, but for the succeeding quadrennium a minute daily register of field experiment and other events was kept. It became increasingly precise in scientific detail while it included many items of a personal nature.

The substance of some lighter entries made in 1902 is as follows:

Friday, Aug. 29. Kitchen fixed up and sixteen-ft. well driven.

Monday, Sept. 1. Raised building, made beds to last half a year.

Saturday, Sept. 6. Put beds at ceiling. Watched eagle soaring.

Monday, Sept. 8. Began work on glider after shooing away native razorback pigs and ending careers of two mice, one with a gun.

Tuesday, Sept. 9. Put in eight hours apiece on glider.

Wednesday, Sept. 10. Sewing and tacking wings, not a full day.

Friday, Sept. 12. Fixed ribs and wing cloth; tried top surface on hill.

Friday, Sept. 26. Devised a deadly trap for unfortunate but very annoying mouse.

Saturday, Sept. 27. Orville roused from sleep last night by mouse walking across his face. Wilbur suggested covering head, else it might be chewed off as befell one Mona who seemed toothsome to a bear. The impudent mouse, who has eaten corn bread bait, will pay for insulting conduct.

Monday, Oct. 6. Mouse dies a natural death.

Wednesday, Oct. 15. Cold enough for five blankets last night and the shivering inventors had but four! Orville made slingshot to defend camp against intrusive razorbacks.

Friday, Oct. 17. They collected shells and starfishes at the beach for small nephews and nieces, children of their brother Lorin.

While confident of their new lore, the prudent Wrights tested the glider for the first time as a kite. They also wished to know whether it would soar at a small angle and were pleased when it confirmed calculation by floating easefully at an incline of seven degrees.

The next day they began gliding against the wind from the one hundred-foot eminence of Kill Devil Hill. Wilbur was the rider when a gust hit the left wing, causing it to rise. The prone pilot needed to act. He did promptly shimmy his hips to warp the wings, and moved the front elevator with his hands. But he forgot in his excitement that the control system was different from last year's and made the wrong move! The glider reared like an outlaw mustang, slowed and threatened to topple backward. Wilbur had a split second to correct his error. He reversed the rudder and lunged forward to bear with his weight on the high end. Orville below held his breath and then sighed with relief as the glider's nose went down and it planed off to a fair landing.

There was peril of death in these pioneer flights, even with motorless craft and small elevations. The brothers knew that Lilienthal had been killed by a drop of fifty feet and Pilcher by a fall of forty feet. The Americans needed all their athletic ability, which they had early developed in school games, foot races and bicycle races. They had kept themselves in physical trim with senses keen and bodies nimble. Thus they were saved from premature death while they had the essential opportunity, hardly shared by any preceding experimenters except the two named, of testing their science and inspiration in the air. The Wrights could not have invented the airplane without personal ascents, which is not the same as saying that aviation came from acrobatics. But we may conclude that the Chanutes, Langleys, Maxims and others had no chance of success in that they were personally unable to take the air.

While both the Wrights advanced their knowledge through aërial observation, Orville was especially keen to note significant details and to register important signposts in brief but thrilling trips through the atmosphere.

Orville made a long careful record in his diary on September 23, telling how he crashed backward that day from a height of some thirty feet, damaging the glider considerably but not himself. Despite the accident, he and his brother were more than cheerful in view of the machine's general good behavior in control and ability to soar at low angles.

The new feature of a vertical tail — which was rigid — had been added as an aid to lateral balance and to

prevent a tendency of the machine to pivot or turn on
its axis when the wings were warped. Sometimes the
tail seemed thus useful and then again quite the reverse.
The wing tips were shifted to curve like those of a
gull, as in the previous glider. That did not help. They
went back to the tail as the crux of a mysterious problem. Since it was proper and useful in theory, because
of its leverage eight to ten times as effective as any
near wing brake to check unequal speed between right
and left wing with consequent turning, why did that
tail so misbehave? It was an aggravation and a torment.
Sometimes it kept the glider from skidding sidewise.
Then it accentuated skidding, when it was wind-smitten
on the side toward the low slow wing.

The Wrights had the airplane by the tail! It was
well they clung onto it like grim death.

Insomnia is sometimes a disguised blessing. It may
force thought as well as the enumeration of imaginary
sheep.

Orville had the luck to be sleepless on the night of
Thursday, October 2, as he lay on his canvas bed amid
the ceiling beams of the shed at Kitty Hawk, for he
then had the inspiration that the tail should be movable.
He recorded the fact in his diary the next day, using
just twelve words, including mention of his insomnia,
to state this major discovery.

It had come to him in the night that a movable rudder
turned toward the high or fast wing would check its
speed, reduce its undue lift and thereby restore lateral
balance. Turning the rudder right or left would keep
both wings even and the craft level in the lateral plane.
Was this a new idea? It was revolutionary! To be

sure, mariners had used rudders from the dawn of time but for the purpose of steering ships. The object of the aërial rudder was totally different, that is, to maintain sidewise equilibrium in conjunction with warpable or movable wings.

The brothers were used to severe mutual criticism of ideas in the interest of truth, but each was quick to accept the other's genuine find. As Orville had adopted forthwith the amendment to his hinged wings — warping that Wilbur visualized through a twisted pasteboard box — so now the latter instantly accepted the movable vertical rudder. And as usual Wilbur offered an improvement. Since the rudder would have to be turned each time the wings were warped, let rudder and wings be connected with wires so as to operate together. Thus one lever or mechanism would control lateral balance. Another lever would take care of fore-and-aft equilibrium.

Thursday night came inspiration. On Friday its application was discussed, and Saturday afternoon the Wrights were making the new rudder. Orville tells the latter fact in his diary record of October 4, with the statement that foodstuffs were short, which was important to him as housekeeper, especially since Chanute and Herring arrived the next day. There was no butter or bacon, and the canned goods were few. Sunday dinner had to be meager, and it rained. The campers spent Sunday indoors and there was talk until the unusually late hour of ten o'clock.

The improved glider during the next ten days or so made about seven hundred flights with a success unprecedented. It sailed against thirty-five miles an hour

Wilbur Wright in the Glider of 1902 at Kitty Hawk, North Carolina. The air was in fact conquered then. Only an Engine and Propellers were needed to make the Glider an Airplane.

wind and repeatedly covered distances over six hundred feet. It was balanced with ease, guided high and low, right and left. There was no serious attempt to circle or to attain much altitude. The season's total record of flights was eleven hundred.

The Wrights did not know it, but the airplane was virtually complete. The new rudder had added the hitherto lacking twenty-five per cent., which combined with an equal warping value and fifty per cent. of aëro-dynamics, gave mankind dominion of super-terrestrial atmospheric space.

Wilbur and Orville did not see any great future for their vehicle and were far from dreaming that it would some day crowd the sky. They looked on it as a scientific feat of fair dimensions. A motor would make the glider go faster and farther. Before leaving Kitty Hawk this year they began to design a power machine and to draw up a patent application. The patent was not in expectation of money return but to establish a record of priority for the sake of scientific credit.

Chanute saw the Wrights' performance with tempered enthusiasm, as of a critical spiritist who likes to select his photographs of fairies. His own gliders had failed utterly in the hands of his employee, Herring. The Wrights had reason to be surprised, therefore, when the latter told them he would rejoin them at Kitty Hawk the next year with a power machine of his own.

"Guess I'll go home to Chicago by way of Washington," casually announced Herring at camp breakfast on Tuesday, October 14.

Some glances were exchanged around the table. The

speaker had always liked the climate of the capital. Perhaps the brothers smiled wryly as they sensed a too early installment of inventors' recompense.

"Hm, I'll go that way too," said Chanute, who had an uneasy look on his face. He was acquainted with the talents of his employee.

The engineer and his mechanic left camp that day *en route* to Washington. Chanute met and talked with Langley while Herring missed him. A letter sheds light on the situation:

Smithsonian Institution,
Washington, D. C.

October 17, 1902.

DEAR MR. CHANUTE:

I should like very much to get some description of the extraordinary results which you told me were recently obtained by the Wright brothers. I have to-day a letter from Mr. Herring, who was in the city, speaking of some ideas which he would like to submit on the possibility of carrying larger weights for the power, depending chiefly on surfaces of the requisite arrangement, form and curvature. I understand that he has spent the last few weeks with you, and I have inferred that he might have been with you at these Wright trials, and have those in mind in what he writes. I have not, however, felt able to take him again into the Smithsonian service. . . . Very truly yours,

(Signed) S. P. LANGLEY,
Secretary.

It appears that Langley, whatever else may be said of him, was upright and even scrupulous in conduct. But the Professor was willing to obtain information legitimately, for he sent the following wire:

Washington, D. C. Oct. 19, 1902.

Mr. Wright,

Kitty Hawk, N. C.

Mr. Chanute has interested me in your experiments. Is there time to see them? Kindly write me.

S. P. Langley,

Secretary, Smithsonian Institution.

The brothers replied they had broken camp and ended their experiments.

Professor Langley continued eager to partake of the Wrights' knowledge as shown by his letter of December 7, the same year, to Octave Chanute:

I should be glad to hear more of what the Wright brothers have done, and especially of their means of control, which you think better than the Penaud. [An automatic balance device of no value.] I should be very glad to have either of them visit Washington at my expense, to get some of their ideas on this subject, if they are willing to communicate them. I have been spending a great deal of time and money on an apparatus to accurately measure the lift and drift of the wind. [Which the Wrights had done for all time with their wind tunnel!] It is nearing completion, and I should be glad to have you see it.

The evidence given explodes an old myth that Langley was teacher and the Wrights his pupils. In fact, the relation was reversible. Langley could have been and wished to be taught by them, but they politely declined the opportunity. They rejected his overtures, wishing to keep for themselves what little scientific credit they might reap — perhaps tokened by medals and honorary degrees in Latin conferred on the bicycle men for their invention of the airplane.

But long before the soothing syllables of appreciation in a dead language fell on their ears, they heard the ululation of the pack that scents from afar inventive loot.

CHAPTER VII

Phut! Boom! Hut-phut-tut! Bang! Bang!

A dozing policeman sprang from his back-warming chimney prop and swung his club wildly.

Dogs barked, a cat ran, small boys with ear muffs hurrahed, a woman leaned from an upper window screaming "Fire!" and shopkeepers in white aprons ran outdoors in the wintry air after their customers to find out the meaning of the racket.

"What is it? Where is it? Somebody killed! It's dynamite! No, shooting."

" 'Tis a Jesse James hold-up!" quoth the bluecoat, stalking warily toward the alley that led behind the office of the Wright Cycle Company, whence the noise emanated. Bluish smoke drifted from a shed in that alley.

"Mercy, Officer, what can it be? Oh, send for an ambulance!"

"Don't be afraid, folks," proclaimed a pompous citizen. "There is no need for alarm. The Wrights always did make a lot of noise with their homemade gimmicks. This time they're testing their own gas engine."

"Oh, it's a gas engine," repeated several vaguely.

"Bah!" snorted the policeman, disgusted yet relieved. "Well, an engine ain't agin the law, but I will say this one sounds drunk *and* disorderly."

Nobody in the crowd dreamed that the unmuffled barking, coughing and back-firing that regaled their ears was a noise historical — a dissonance which was a prelude to the hum of a myriad motors in the sky — the pristine song of the airplane engine!

It was Lincoln's birthday, February 12, 1903 — not yet become a general holiday — that the engine had its first test. The brothers had sought to buy an engine for the purpose and had written to several manufacturers — in vain. Some of the recipients did not waste postage on a reply.

"Haw, letter from a couple of chaps in Dayton says they want a gas engine for a flying machine! Wastebasket, Miss Jones! Almost funny enough to keep!"

One company did answer, offering to supply an engine of eight "French horsepower."

While the brothers had built a two-cylinder two horsepower gasoline motor for shop power in 1899, they were not too confident that they would succeed with a larger engine. Internal combustion was yet a crude novelty, spark plugs were freaks, self-starters unknown. A while before Christmas, 1902, the Wrights began work on their motor, which was to be four-cylinder in line, placed horizontally, eight horsepower, with a total weight of 200 pounds. Water cooling and magneto ignition were planned.

Orville "prepared the plans of this motor, which was merely an automobile motor simplified and reduced in weight," stated Wilbur afterward. The drawings were turned into wooden patterns outside the shop at an expense of twenty-two dollars. The engine case of aluminum was cast at a local foundry but the machining was mostly done in the bicycle shop by the proprietors and their only employee, Charles E. Taylor. At one time Charley was regarded as a Sancho Panza who served two Don Quixotes. He looked after the bicycle trade when they were at Kitty Hawk, made whatever queer things were required, was utterly loyal and remained through the years as permanent a feature of the Wrights' shop as "faithful Carrie" in their home. They treated him with affectionate familiarity. It is needless to say that Charley was a good mechanic, caught a lot of sparks from his two bosses and had an enviable job.

If the neighbors were scared by the noise of the new motor, its makers were afraid too. The racket was worse than that of their boyhood creation of a turning lathe which had drowned out a cyclone. They noted a demonic engine speed of nine hundred revolutions a minute and did not imagine that twice as much speed would become ordinary. The horsepower was a little better than planned. Charley Taylor was sickened by the smoky exhaust which filled the shed. Another test was made next day when dripping gasoline deprived the bearings of lubricant so that they "froze," breaking the engine body and frame. After repair, the motor spurted to sixteen horsepower for a few seconds but settled to a steady gait of twelve. If the pistons had been glass smooth and the other parts made to correspond, the engine with its four-inch bore and four-inch stroke, would have had almost three times as much power.

"The Wrights flew because of their engine," is an old

bedtime story. "You see, children, internal combustion gave us the automobile and then the airplane."

Children, be assured this is a fable, although repeated as lately as 1928 by an American physicist of world repute.

In the first place, the Wrights established the principles of flight without power and thereby made possible all-day motorless gliding, which promises further gorgeous development in free birdlike travel. Then their motor was much inferior to the engines of their predecessors. It weighed over sixteen pounds per horsepower by the most rigid estimate. Wilbur stated for court record that the weight was twenty pounds per horsepower, including in the total weight, the engine, magneto, radiator, cooling water and "the small can of fuel weighing three or four pounds."

About half a century before, Stringfellow, an Englishman, sought to fly with a steam engine of thirteen pounds per horsepower. In 1893 Sir Hiram Maxim had an eight pounds per horsepower steam engine to push an impressive five-decker craft into the air but the push, totalling several hundred horsepower, was all in vain. About the same time Clement Ader, a Frenchman, failed to quit the ground with a seven pounds per horsepower motor, and an engine equally light did not profit the experimenter Phillips. Professor Langley's engineer, Charles M. Manly, built for his employer a motor weighing less than three pounds per horsepower: it was of the radial type now in vogue and was "years ahead of its time." Incidentally, the modern airplane motor weighs between one and two pounds per horsepower, has between four and twelve cylinders, includes radial and vertical types, and inclines to exclusive air cooling.

"The Wrights flew in spite of their engine," is the correct version of that bedtime story.

Doubtless one reason for the legend has been the theoretical calculation by engineers of the Wrights' motor power, based on bore-and-stroke dimensions and assumed speed, regardless of actual performance. The inventors rarely troubled themselves to correct such errors, after having stated the facts once or twice. They understood that some of the encomiums lavished upon their engine were no more than subtle depreciations of their true achievement in pure and applied aërodynamics.

The next job after the motor was to design propellers. It looked easy. No doubt naval engineers had worked out the theory of marine screws. Take a water screw and adapt it to the air by means of the aërodynamic tables which had been lately made in the bicycle shop laboratory. But the brothers learned with equal surprise and disappointment that there was no help for them in marine screws, which after half a century of use were shaped by rule of thumb instead of science. Even a dozen years after this date, Orville Wright pointed out to me that the steamship *Caronia* of the Cunard Line was then changing its propellers, in the hope that a new style might perhaps yield more push.

Sir Hiram Maxim had got nowhere with his tests of numerous tiny propellers of all kinds of shapes. Professor Langley had mounted an air screw on a flat car which was whisked over a track half a mile long. He obtained a dusty answer.

A marine authority asserted that almost any guess-work screw would be fifty per cent. efficient, and at first the Wrights were inclined to try the recipe. Then they resolved to attack the problem with science. They saw that the blades of a propeller were curved surfaces like those of an airplane wing, although the former moved in a circular instead of straight path through the air. A screw is a wing, yes, but it travels sidewise; at the same time it advances and also kicks the air backward. How can you apply the formula of the wing table to a complicated, ornery, multiple-actioned, logarithmic, mean and mulish pest of a propeller? Archimedes sighed for a fulcrum to support his world-moving lever. The Wrights yearned for a fixed point whence they might begin calculations. We can imagine their fervent cry:

"Give us the angle of incidence at which the screw blades hit the air and we will do the rest!"

Nobody in the world was then donating angles or other useful data on flying, so the brothers buckled down to help themselves. In earlier stages of their invention, they had held long and vigorous debates, each fighting the other's position with all his might, so as to arrive at truth. But no previous debate compared in intensity and duration with the one now begun. As before, Wilbur took the affirmative and Orville had the negative. Then it was Orville's turn to affirm and Wilbur's to refute. Their low staccato voices sounded like muffled machine guns in the low-ceilinged living room of their home and in the little bedrooms upstairs, where they continued to hurl angles, sines, cosines and tangents at each other through the thin partitions.

"Orv, you've stolen my side!" exclaims Wilbur.

"Your side?"

"Yes, my side of the argument!"

"Now, Will — Say, that's a fact!" And with a mutual chuckle that grows into a laugh the fraternal combatants settle themselves to sleep.

The debate was resumed at breakfast, had no pause at noon dinner and at supper found new breath to last through the evening. It excelled the talking record of Congress, for it went on for days, weeks, then entered a count by months! Katharine was at first a fascinated auditor. She hastened home from teaching a high-school class to hear another exhilarating if mystifying set-to in a region of rarefied science. As the days passed, she lost her zeal to listen and stopped coming home early. The brothers were getting tired also. They kept at it hammer-and-tongs, using the hammer unduly, forgetting at moments that the object of the combat was truth. Their nerves became spent. Screws in perpetual motion spun within their throbbing heads.

"If you don't stop arguing, I'll leave home!" cried the exasperated, almost hysterical Katharine one day.

It was a useful sobering shock. They cared more for their sister than for all science. Their fevered minds were cooled by the domestic ultimatum and — presto! — they saw the solution of their problem and knew how to design a propeller according to the formula of the air tables.

A single screw has a gyroscopic effect that tends to hold an airplane on a fixed axis and to resist steering, so it was decided to have two propellers, whirling in opposite directions. Each was made of two lengths of two by four spruce glued together, shaped with a draw-knife and other tools, often calipered to meet the dimensions of the mathematical pattern. The twin blades were eight and a half feet long and six inches in width at the tip. Half a dozen years later the world's copyists were puzzled whether to use one, two, three or four blades on a propeller and had no idea how to obtain the correct pitch.

The Wright screw was fixed to its shaft with a sixteen-inch metal strap, wood screws and a portion of the shop panacea of the inventors — bicycle cement. It stuck for them and they stuck by it to the last aircraft they built. But it was a problem how to connect motor with shaft. Belts and locally obtained chains were a failure. Then an Indianapolis firm supplied a sprocket chain that was satisfactory and was used by the brothers ever afterward. In order to give one propeller a motion in reverse of the other, one chain was made to cross itself like a figure 8. Doubtless this was a crude expedient, as later pointed out by Lilliputians of refined mechanics. The bare chains flapped, rollers were not a success, and finally the chains were cased in metal tubes in which they ran with slight friction. The transmission loss by chain drive, instead of having screws on engine shaft, was figured by the makers at five per cent.

A shop test of engine and transmission with fans substituted for propellers was made in May and showed the first two features satisfactory. Since the motor had more than its expected power, it was planned to increase the total weight of the airplane with its operator from six hundred to seven hundred fifty pounds. The added weight was put into heavier or strengthened parts. It seemed to the pioneers that a machine so massive, five times as heavy as a glider, having the power of a dozen horses or more than one hundred men, would need to be exceedingly strong. So they braced and fortified and had liberal factors of safety beyond the calculated strains on every part. They did their best with wood and common metal, lacking vanadium steel and duralumin. It is noteworthy that no Wright machine, experimental or finished model for the market, ever failed through preventible structural weakness.

Amid these labors Wilbur found time on May 24 to write a letter of some length to Doctor George A. Spratt, discussing aërodynamic problems with geometrical diagrams drawn in illustration. Along with the recondite passages, Wilbur wrote: "It is the experience of both birds and men that a center of gravity about on a line with the surface gives the best results. The buzzard hangs below and pays the penalty of its laziness by its unsteady flight as compared with hawks." The letter concluded with the writer's theory of Lilienthal's last fatal glide, illustrated with six diagrams showing how the center of gravity kept moving forward while the center of pressure moved backward until the machine capsized.

The inventors started on their history-making fourth-year trip to Kitty Hawk on September 23, and arrived two days later at their old camp near Kill Devil Hill. The next day Orville wrote a jocular letter to Dear

Swes — Katharine — saying everything was in fair shape and reviewing the past marvels of Kitty Hawk from a one hundred seven miles per hour wind that had torn away the anemometer cups, to the hordes of mosquitoes that dimmed the sun and lightning that made day out of night. Orville also stated that he had worked about half a day devising a French drip coffee-pot which would obviate the use of eggs for clearing the beverage, a worthwhile endeavor, in view of local egg scarcity. At the end of the amusing missive it occurred to the writer to add that the new camp building was going up, the old glider was ready for practice, and the new machine would be worked on during rainy or windless weather.

Wilbur on October 4 wrote to his father that the new shed, forty-four by sixteen by nine feet, was about finished. There had been two days of first-class gliding last week, with the longest flight lasting forty-three seconds, which was a slight improvement over last year and also a world record. (He did not deign to mention that an American Munchausen of his acquaintance had claimed forty-eight seconds.) Soon, wrote Wilbur, they would raise the record above a minute, for they could now hover almost stationary in a favorable wind. Hovering was a feat beyond all previous experimenters. Wilbur emphasized to his father that there was less danger in gliding than before and all precautions were taken by Orville and himself.

Orville on the same date wrote to Katharine with brief and modest reference to gliding records and flying hopes but with considerable personal and domestic detail. That Sunday's dinner of stewed chicken burned to a frazzle while the brothers were visiting the life-saving station. Money was taking wings; not a dollar left in the camp treasury. There was a queer little bird visitor at the camp kitchen that would have interested the writer's small nephew, Milton. The study of German had been added to the labors of cooking and aërial experiment, and the student could now understand a bit of the German poems he once recited with his sister. A friend had sent a Cincinnati paper with a picture of Langley's machine, and this was the only news of the outside world that had reached them so far.

Another letter of Orville to his sister on October 12 mentions a great storm lasting four days, and how the writer in a twenty-five to thirty-five mile wind whizzed straight up in the air and in bringing down the glider slammed Wilbur on the head and smashed the wings at one end. Also one wing of the new machine was being completed and to this brief reference Orville could not help adding a touch of exultation in a phrase of children who term anything immense or delightful as "whopper" or "wopper."

To his father, on October 15, Orville described how he landed on his brother's head, extolled the beauty of the new machine of which the upper surfaces were now complete, and drew a diagram to indicate wing improvements. He reviewed the current newspaper account of the preliminary failure of the Langley machine at Washington, District of Columbia, observing that its surfaces were apparently quite inefficient and that it lacked all means of control. In contrast, the writer and Wilbur had had much air experience and had fairly solved the control problem: they were more than pleased with what they were doing this year. How were those church affairs in Dayton? Octave Chanute had written that he might not be able to visit camp this year. Orville said he had learned enough French in camp last season to understand letters the brothers received from foreigners and now he was tackling German for an hour each night. The usual bedtime was eight o'clock; now it was nine and with Wilbur long retired, high time to close.

I regret that I must abridge for the reader the voluminous Wright letters and diary records of thousands of words pertaining to their momentous campaign of 1903, a thrilling series of unpublished documents. One of the best letters, full of quips and merry nonsense, decorated with humorous sketches, was written on October 18 by the usually sedate Wilbur to his sister. It tells of a gale that almost wrecked the camp building and sent five vessels ashore along the Atlantic coast, one within sight of Kill Devil Hill. The brothers, abed, feared that the incomplete rocking domicile would crash down on them. Toward four A. M. with the floor partly under water, they hastened to apply interior braces to their structure. The tarpaper roofing began to fly off. Orville donned Wilbur's overcoat and with a ladder went outdoors to mend the imperiled roof. The wind blew him backward some fifty feet, the tails of his coat standing out like wings, as illustrated by the writer's sketch. Wilbur went to the rescue and helped to set up the ladder. As Orville perched on the roof edge with hammer and nails, he was put in chancery by the wind-driven coat being folded tightly over his head. Another sketch illustrated his plight, laughable in retrospect, but serious enough when it happened. Orville himself said afterward that he could hardly drive his hammer against the savage pressure of that gale. Happily, the camp building was saved.

Wilbur's storm letter refers to the airplane, which he thought might be completed about November 1, in the Alice-in-Wonderland style of a small niece who had christened it "the wopper flying machine" and also quotes as apropos that young lady's enthusiastic description of some memorable sight:

"Oh, you ought to have seen it! You ought to have seen it! Great big sing!"

Charley Taylor, that faithful mechanical squire of the knightly Wrights, who now attended to their bicycle shop in Dayton, received much news and banter direct from Kitty Hawk. Orville was the principal source, often cramming several hundred words on a postcard. A festive card of October 20 compares flying-machine prospects with Wall Street reports: stock was quoted at 208 yesterday morning but fell to 110 at noon. This was due to temporary misbehavior of the old glider. In reference to Charley's complaint that he felt unsteady on his legs, Orville advises that he brace his legs with the Pratt truss used on the airplane and here is a little diagram to show how to do it!

Octave Chanute and Doctor Spratt had been invited by the brothers to visit camp about November 5 for the expected trial of the power machine. The doctor came on October 23, Chanute on November 6. It was too cold for the elderly Chanute, who had passed the Biblical limit of three score and ten years, although the anxious hosts stuffed rags in all cracks of their building and kept a roaring wood fire in a stove improvised from an old carbide can. He left camp, shivering, on November 12.

Orville's diary of November 10 quotes Chanute as saying he wanted the brothers to test his machine with oscillating wings; also he wished to buy and perfect the French machine of Clement Ader. This diary record, hitherto unpublished, is enough in itself to cancel the fictitious title of Father-of-Aviation sometimes given to Chanute. At this time he had a copy of the Wrights' air tables and had seen the amazing performance of their last glider which only lacked propellers and power plant to make it the airplane — yet Chanute clung to his old delusions and mystical guesses. He was a cheerful Moses who indefatigably scouted the trail to aviation's Promised Land but could not see it when it lay before his eyes.

The power machine seemed under a spell of bad weather and accidents. There was a lock-out of the sole camp employee, Dan Tate, who "sojered" on his chore of fetching firewood, despite his liberal stipend of a dollar and a quarter a day when the local wage scale was fifty cents. Dan lost a place in history together with his job.

At the first ground test of the airplane, the steel tubing shafts of the propellers twisted out of shape in a few seconds.

"Too bad," we may imagine Doctor Spratt's sympathetic murmur. "Well, you think Charley Taylor can fix them. I think I'll go home — been here two weeks now — though I would like to stay and see the first flight of your ship. On my way home I can express the shafts to Dayton from Norfolk."

"Thanks, Doctor, very good of you," the grateful Wrights doubtless responded to this time-saving offer. The Doctor went with the shafts on November 5. He did the helpful errand and, like Chanute, missed the inaugural of a new era in the third week in December.

Charley Taylor at the bicycle shop brazed the cross arms of the old shafts upon new ones of gas pipe. Meanwhile the brothers practiced sailing with the old glider and hugged the carbide-can stove to keep warm. The new shafts arrived on November 21 and two days later Orville wrote to Charley, saying he had done a bang-up job of brazing and everything. It was fine that the bearings were not hurt. At the test the engine was jerky because two oil-filled cylinders missed fire and in ten seconds both sprockets for the chain drive worked loose. Well, continued Orville, while there is life there is hope. They applied the standard remedy for all mechanical ills, Arnstein's bicycle cement, guaranteed to cure anything between a stopwatch and a threshing machine. Did it work? Why, it just froze those sprockets in place. Also the engine now performed nobly. Stock in the flying machine was soaring.

A line of tribute is due to bicycle cement, which had now gummed the airplane in two places and likewise mended a stopwatch that timed the premier flyer, as intimated in Orville's letter to Charley. The magic substance anchored a loose hand on the stopwatch.

However, a dire and sickening accident befell on November 28. The engine was speeding in its test when — smack — a bit of metal flew off one of the new shafts. *Dunder, blitzen* and *cochon!* as a certain student of languages may have thought but I am sure did not say. Winter was near, two months had been spent in a sandy desert, it was a thousand miles and two weeks' round trip to the home machine shop. A bright school child may ask to-day why they didn't send for new parts by airplane. . . . Perhaps that thought occurred to Wilbur and Orville and made them laugh. They did cheer themselves by whistling and singing a few popular songs as they used to do in bright and dark moments. Song inspired them to ignore trouble and find a way out.

We see a young man of slight but wiry build, a suit-case in each hand, trudging through four miles of ankle-deep sand from a camp shed to the hamlet of Kitty Hawk. He stops often to rest on the lonesome, clogging trail. The suitcases weigh like lead; indeed they contain more metal items than clothes. It is cold, yet he wipes sweat from his brow and at times removes his cap to march bareheaded. He arrives, takes a boat for Elizabeth City, North Carolina, there counts the meager bills in his purse, gets a night's lodging at a cheap hotel, curbs a hearty appetite to save funds, and in the morning buys a railroad ticket for Dayton, Ohio.

"Not a nickel left for carfare," mutters Orville, on arrival at the home town. "Well, I can walk."

He lugged the weighty suitcases a mile and a half to Hawthorn Street, astonishing father and sister with his unheralded appearance.

"Well, I'm here," he stated. It was a fact. Details waited on food.

About a week later, on December 9, Orville was

boarding a train to return to Kitty Hawk with new shafts made of solid steel — something different from tubing and gaspipe, that would withstand the playful spite of whizzing propellers. He bought a newspaper and read something like this:

Washington, D. C. December. 8. The Langley flying machine, which met with a fiasco at its recent trial in October, registered final failure to-day. The ponderous and costly apparatus crashed in the Potomac River at the time of launching from a houseboat. Over $70,000 of government and other funds had been spent on the ill-fated attempt to realize the dubious dreams of Daedalus, Leonardo da Vinci and Darius Green. The wrecked machine was designed by Prof. S. P. Langley, who as Secretary and head of the Smithsonian Institution has been regarded as an eminent scientist. Prof. Langley has worked on the flying problem for many years and is considered an authority on aërodynamics. The fact remains that his airship is wrecked and there is some question at the Capitol why government money was spent on such an enterprise.

Doubtless Orville felt a momentary chill as he read. On the heels of this monumental failure, he and his brother Wilbur — who had not known that Langley was attempting a man-carrying machine until a few weeks before — were aiming to succeed. What chance had a pair of self-taught bicycle men, who had not spent one tenth of seventy thousand dollars in all their aërial experiment, to prove the validity of dubious dreams? Then Orville recovered his poise and smiled. Probably he thought:

"Langley is just a name. It doesn't mean anything. We found from our wind tunnel that his air tables are wrong. Last year Langley telegraphed and wrote, asking for information from Wilbur and me. We did not tell him. We know how to balance and control a glider. When that engine zips along and twirls these new propeller shafts, we'll have a power flying machine."

The Wrights' diary states that Orville arrived in camp on Friday, December 11, and that next day there was an abortive test of the machine on its starting track, a sixty-foot monorail of iron-shod wood. Sunday as usual was a day of rest. At 1:30 Monday afternoon, says the diary, a signal was set for the men of the government life-saving station who were to lend a hand. Five men came and helped carry the machine up Kill Devil Hill and to lay track on a slope of eight degrees, fifty minutes. Two little boys who had trailed the men skedaddled for home and mother at the first cannonading roar of the engine.

The brothers tossed a coin for the first ride and Wilbur won. He climbed in and lay on his stomach. There was trouble with the releasing device. It was corrected. Wilbur shot forward prematurely, Orville clinging to the right wing struts and running alongside as fast as he could go. At forty feet the younger brother had to quit and then snapped his stopwatch. The machine had lifted a bit, six or eight feet from the end of the track. Now at a distance of some sixty feet from the track, it was about fifteen feet above the ground. It lost headway and shortly came down on its left wing, breaking several pieces of the wooden frame, including one skid. The excited Wilbur forgot to stop his engine for some time after landing. The flight lasted three and a half seconds and covered a distance of one hundred and five feet.

"Well, boys, the dingus flies," we may imagine a sun-tanned brawny life-saver saying to his mates in a throaty rumble. "Don't know what use it is. Give me a boat or a buggy for travel."

Only that it might confuse the record and upset the agreed-on fable which is history, I refrain from the assertion that man made his first flight in an airplane on Monday, December 14, 1903. Let us wait patiently for the official date, three days later.

Wilbur sent a short wire to his father, reporting the initial flight; misjudgment had reduced distance; success was certain; don't talk.

The brothers were rightly confident, for they had now proved the last doubtful point — efficiency of propellers. This came up to the figured sixty-six per cent. or a third more than Maxim or Langley had attained.

Tuesday was spent on repairs. These were completed by Wednesday noon and the machine was set on its track in front of the camp for a test on the level. The wind was too light for an attempt. As the brothers awaited a proper breeze, a stranger wandered up from nowhere and said:

"What do you call this thing — flying machine?"

"Yes, it is a flying machine," Wilbur (I believe it was) admitted.

"What're you going to do with it?"

"We expect to fly it when conditions are favorable."

"Well," remarked the stranger, after walking around the machine with eyes of keen appraisal, "I should think that thing might fly — when the *conditions* are favorable."

All the citizens of Kitty Hawk had been informally

invited by the Wrights to view a flight the next day, Thursday, December 17. A few years later crowned heads and throngs of a quarter million folk thrilled over the same marvel, but the virgin voyage of the airplane drew only two spectators. The natives were hardly enough interested to be sceptical. Perhaps the brothers had a shrewd thought to insure privacy by asking everybody to come. The ignorance of the natives seems abysmal until we reflect that the wisest of scientists were then little better informed, regarding the air as a gas but not as a highway.

The inventors themselves, despite proven science and success of their first aërial hop, had moments of passing doubt. They knew; yet who knows anything? They had shaved death with a light glider. Now they would ride a mechanical bird as weighty as a piano, forced through the atmosphere with the thrust of a dozen wild horses. Men had been killed by falling with gliders house-high. A drop of a few feet with the power machine might finish rider and ruin hopes, proving the device a scientific curiosity, too costly for human service.

Thursday was sunless and wintry. A chill wind blew. Ice floes were visible along the shore of Albemarle Sound and some whitecaps on the Atlantic Ocean whose surf drummed the beach half a mile away. The long strip of white sand between ocean and sound was spotted with ice-skimmed gray pools of water. A leaden sky with drifting cloud wrack harmonized with the bleakness of the scene below. At intervals gulls shrieked, eagles and fishhawks soared or darted dizzily to capture prey at a breaker's crest.

The man-made bird on the sand was no match in grace for its rivals overhead. It was much larger. Its cream-colored wings spanned forty feet, with an area of five hundred and ten square feet. There was a twin vertical rudder behind and in front a twin horizontal rudder of forty-eight square feet. A spectator could hardly tell which end went first. The rider would lie on his stomach between the main wings, flanked on his right by the engine and with whizzing propellers behind, using hands and twisting hips in a movable cradle to balance and guide the craft.

Wilbur Wright was thirty-six and Orville thirty-two years old at this time. They were in their physical and mental prime. The height of the elder was five feet, ten and a quarter inches, that of the younger just one and three quarter inches less. Their weight was nearly equal at one hundred and forty-five pounds, which saved trouble in calculating total load for the machine. Their oval faces were smooth shaven. Wilbur had a prominent aquiline nose, firm thin lips with incipient upward lines at the corners, a little baldness at the forehead. Orville's hair was yet thick and curly, brown with a hint of red. Both had grayish-blue eyes, keen, quick and frank. Their voices were alike soft and quiet, similar in tone, Wilbur's more inclined to staccato. They were swift in physical action, deft and nimble.

Athletes of a delicate type, they felt the biting cold of that day and could not withstand it like the hardy natives. They ran indoors frequently to get warm over their carbide-can stove, filled with blazing driftwood. They slapped arms, danced and jumped in the nippy wind outside. They had no sort of flying costume, not very warm ordinary clothes and could not wear over-coats during the virgin flights.

Five persons who came as aids or spectators wit-nessed the airplane debut. They were John T. Daniels, W. S. Dough and A. D. Etheridge of the life-saving station; W. C. Brinkley, a lumber buyer of Manteo; and Johnny Moore of Nag's Head, a sixteen-year-old who stumbled upon more wonder that day than the luckiest Boy Scout has chanced upon since. Johnny's name will never perish. He was there!

At 10:35 A. M. in a north wind blowing twenty-seven miles an hour, Orville boarded the roaring craft for the first ride, rose ten feet or so, scooted uncertainly up and down, owing to a difficult control of the ill-balanced front rudder, and came to earth about a hun-dred feet from the track end. The time was about twelve seconds. This was the first flight of aviation's accepted birthday.

A ship is passing on the tumbling white-capped hori-zon. Let us hail the passengers to have a look through their glasses at a new vehicle that will soon whirl them across the wide Atlantic in a day and night. But they will tell us we are mad . . . Ahoy! Sir Walter Raleigh, returning to civilization from the savage New World — passing this very spot outward bound from Roanoke Island — tell Queen Bess that America may produce something even more remarkable than a narcotic plant.

After minor repairs, Wilbur at 11:20 o'clock made a flight around one hundred and seventy-five feet in length.

Orville had the third trip at 11:40 o'clock, reached

The First Time in History that an Airplane flew — Orville Wright's 12-Second Flight at Kitty Hawk, N. C., December 17, 1903. The distance was about 100 feet. On the same day Wilbur Wright piloted the Virgin Aircraft 852 Feet in 59 Seconds.

an altitude around fourteen feet and about the same distance as his brother. The merit of the lateral control was happily shown when the left wing hit the ground first.

At noon Wilbur embarked on the fourth and last flight. The craft jogged up and down for three or four hundred feet, then the pilot leveled it to a fairly even course. Smoke and flame belched from the open exhaust. Snarling propellers and bellowing cylinders drowned the shouts of the excited spectators. The prolonged explosive tumult reverberated between sand dunes and leaden sky, alarming the loftily soaring eagles, warning them that their exclusive dominion was over and that winged man would soon chase and outstrip them as they now chased and caught lesser birds. On sped the airplane. It was eight hundred feet from the start when it came to a small hummock. Perhaps the ridge caused a down gust or rut in the aërial highway. The craft wavered, began to pitch up and down as at the start, then quickly darted to the sand. Only the front rudder frame was damaged by the sudden landing.

The flight was eight hundred fifty-two feet in distance over the ground and the time was fifty-nine seconds.

A few minutes after the voyage the airplane, which had been carried beside the camp shed, indulged itself in a summersault with the aid of the wind. It was partly smashed. All wrestled to subdue the belated Frankenstein impulse of the plane, and the coast guardsman Daniels, rolling inside the wings in a tangle of chains and engine, narrowly escaped with his life.

When his sons left home that year, Father Wright had given them a dollar with the remark:

"Now let's hear from you when there is any news."

The dollar was a good investment, I was assured by the aged bishop in his Dayton home, for it brought the following result:

THE WESTERN UNION
TELEGRAPH COMPANY
VIA NORFOLK, VA.

176 C KA CS 33 PAID.
KITTY HAWK N C DEC 17
BISHOP M. WRIGHT
7 HAWTHORNE ST
SUCCESS FOUR FLIGHTS THURSDAY MORNING ALL AGAINST TWENTY ONE MILE WIND START-ED FROM LEVEL WITH ENGINE POWER ALONE AVERAGE SPEED THROUGH AIR THIRTY ONE MILES LONGEST 57 SECONDS INFORM PRESS HOME CHRISTMAS. OREVELLE WRIGHT
525P

An operator's error clipped two seconds from the time of flight and the government anemometer at Kitty Hawk made the wind a little brisker than stated in the wire.

CHAPTER VIII

"Wrights Fly at Kitty Hawk — "

"Haw! haw!" quoth John Smith, scanning the news over his morning coffee. "Now bring on the sea serpent."

"Tut! tut!" frowned a scientist. "Just after Professor Langley makes a fool of himself and discredits all science by attempting the impossible, a pair of Ohio quacks — Ridiculous! Absurd!"

Orville's home wire telling of the virgin flight had somehow leaked from the line and brought a glare of fact-and-fancy publicity on the inventors, still in camp. They received telegrams from newspapers and magazines; they were intercepted on the homeward train by a squad of pressmen. The conservative press ignored the news as humbug, while the popular dailies exploited and embellished the item as a freakish fillip to tastes jaded by two-headed calves. A Norfolk, Virginia, correspondent had ill luck trying to peddle the yarn; some editors would not pay thirty cents or so to cover the wire query, much less order a brief dispatch.

The Associated Press man at Dayton, shown Orville's telegram with a family statement prepared by his father and brother Lorin, said:

"Huh! Fifty-seven seconds! If it was fifty-seven minutes it might be worth talking about."

Doubtless the journalist saw no difference between

the airplane and the dirigible balloon, which indeed had made a better record for staying aloft. An airship was an airship.

In some offices the alert sub-editors or desk men improved the meager facts by changing the time in seconds to as many minutes and a horizontal distance of eight hundred and fifty-two feet to the same figure in giddy altitude. The costumes of the ascending brothers were minutely described and they were credited with the exclamation Eureka! if not also Excelsior! Truth need not hide at the bottom of a well, for it is often effectively concealed on a front page.

Wilbur and Orville arrived at Dayton two days before Christmas. The conquerors of the air were awaited by a chariot of honor—an old one-horse surrey. Within the surrey sat prideful Father Wright, beaming Sister Katharine and grinning Brother Lorin. There were no brass bands, confetti or shrieking sirens. The populace reserved its enthusiasm, lacking the cue of kingly interest and the plaudits of European multitudes of a few years later. Perhaps a few small boys cheered. Friendly neighbors forgave the brothers for giving the press a hoax, since it advertised the town and would help them in their legitimate bicycle business. Live and let live. Some of the local folk believed in spirits.

The nag jogged into Hawthorn Street and stopped before a frame house. Home again and what a dinner to celebrate achievement! Broiled porterhouse steak, thick and juicy, was the favorite dish of Wilbur and Orville, and they had also a fine real dessert instead of bread pudding which they always despised yet dutifully ate. It was a joyous day and a happy meal, perhaps as

big a reward as the inventors ever got. At bedtime Orv
pranced upstairs in his boyish trick of hand-slapping
each stair and kicking out his heels. Wilbur as usual
stood on the first landing, leaned over the newel
post decorated by his brother's wood carving, and
chatted in sociable staccato with father and sister
below.

After lights are out we hear a low buzz upstairs and
surmise a plot with Santa Claus whereby Katharine
received the gift of a lifetime — a set of silver forks
and pearl-handled knives. If only fate had left the
family circle unbroken and permitted the mother to
share these joys and triumphs! Susan Wright was more
than an average mother. She endowed, inspired and
largely molded her sons to their undying victory.

Amid the bells of Yule, hark! O-o-o-o-o! Woo-u-h-
woo!

"Hear that, Will," I imagine Orville saying to his
brother.

"Yes. Kind of a wolfish cry," replies Wilbur.

"What is it?"

"The leader of the wolf pack, Orv. I guess all inventors hear it, soon or late. We heard it first at Kitty
Hawk last year, when Chanute's man Herring went to
Washington. Voice sounds familiar. Like same wolf but
with bigger appetite."

In fact before New Year the brothers had a letter
from an individual who confidently nominated himself
for a one-third partnership in the airplane invention.
In later years many others volunteered to become
partners and in effect became so, despite all the efforts
of the Wrights. The self-appointed partners improved

on Omar's advice by taking the cash and not letting the credit go.

The foreign filchers were aided, innocently, by Octave Chanute, who went to Europe in the winter of 1902–1903 to promote the St. Louis Exposition. He told by the way of the remarkable feats of his young friends the Wrights. The elderly Pollyana of the infant aviation had photographs of their glider of 1902 aflight at Kitty Hawk. He gave a lecture in Paris before the Aëro Club of France, showing the photographs and saying he had seen the wonderful doings of that glider himself.

"Ze airplane is no joke!" shouted the enthusiastic auditors, proceeding to organize an airplane section in what had been a balloon club. "Hurrah for les frères Vricht! Let us fly like zem!"

The French were the first to copy the invention. They were quite frank about it, calling their machines "the Wright type." However, they bungled sadly in the absence of a model and air table figures giving the proper curves for wings and screws. Among the ingenious yet baffled French copyists of this early period were Bleriot, Archdeacon, Esnault-Pelterie and the Voisin brothers.

Wilbur Wright in 1912 said:

"As the real secrets of our invention had not yet become public through the publication of the patent, these French imitations resembled the Wright machine only in outward appearance. They did not possess the features of wing-warping and flexible rudder. . . . Consequently, they gave very unsatisfactory results and led the French to question the results which the

Wrights had obtained. . . . But after our patents issued, the foreign makers discovered the real nature of
our invention. At first they tried to find other methods
of obtaining satisfactory results, but when they failed
in this, they began to imitate more and more closely the
Wright invention, so that to-day successful machines
in use abroad all use the patented system of control."

The brothers applied for a patent at Washington
almost nine months before their virgin flight with a
motor, that is, on March 23, 1903. The patent was issued May 22, 1906. These facts refute several legends.
The far-sighted scientists even anticipated motorless
gliding, for their patent included soaring without mechanical power.

The United States Patent Office regarded aviation
and perpetual motion as twin delusions, and did its
best to prevent the Ohio cranks from squandering
money on fees. It rejected the first application and
suggested a working model. ("Ha! ha! *That* generally
stops 'em," chuckles an official.) At first the Wrights
tried to be their own patent lawyers. The patent office
examiner could not understand the object of connect-
ing the rear rudder to wing ropes; it seemed to him "a
mere matter of taste." He could not comprehend the
warping idea without a model. He was uncertain
whether the airplane was to be lifted by means of gas
or belonged in the class of soaring machines or para-
chutes. In reply the brothers referred to Webster's
dictionary for definitions of warp and twist, and sent
as a model, without comic intention, a "little square tube
or cardboard" to "be diagonally compressed at one
end between thumb and finger" — verily the origin of

the warp but seemingly a loutish jest at the expense of obtuse officials. Luckily for the brothers, they ceased trying to be their own attorneys and their lucid specifications were finally transformed by a proper lawyer into a long-winded series of eighteen claims almost wholly unintelligible to a layman.

Wilbur had to explain later for a court record why the patent was obfuscated with phrases like "normally flat aëroplanes," stating that the specifications were written by a patent examiner and a lawyer, neither of whom was familiar with terms proper for a new art. The brothers did supply drawings of curved wings as appear in the patent. "So long as the expressions seemed to carry the general idea, we did not interfere," said Wilbur. Charged by opposing counsel with withholding from the patent application the inventors' "best knowledge," as required by law, Wilbur replied with some heat and perhaps a trace of pardonable exaggeration: "A statement of all the knowledge we possessed regarding the science of aviation would have filled a number of volumes and would have been entirely out of place in a patent specification." The opinion of the court duly upheld the Wrights as to criticism of their patent form.

There is a traditional gulf of misunderstanding between the laity and the bar. While the inventors attributed patent faults to the legal fraternity, one of their own counsel apologetically explained to the court that the brothers erred in relying upon their untechnical skill when making the patent application and intimated that they needed a good lawyer! At this statement we may imagine "my learned brother" across the aisle nodding in cheerful agreement while lay spectators in the courtroom mutter: "Those fellows always stick together."

The patent document was imposing and solemnly promised the monopoly of the airplane to its inventors for seventeen years; but it proved about as protective to the Wrights as a cotton nightshirt to an Arctic explorer. There was a little more substance in the foreign patent garments obtained by the brothers in 1904. If their case were unique it might be considered tragic.

Yet some will hold that Wilbur and Orville were well enough paid by the thrill of scientific discovery and of pioneering the air, and by world-wide acclaim. Kings shook hands with them. What did the airplane cost them? Up to Christmas, 1903, besides their labor, a cash outlay around five thousand dollars. How much profit did they expect on such an investment? Of course, the world, investing nothing, reaped untold millions. But it needed to recoup itself for the half million dollars or more wasted on futile experiment by predecessors of the Wrights.

Katharine did not finance the airplane as by legend. Perhaps Father Wright did. At least the cost of the machine as stated, was what the brothers realized from the sale of a paternal gift to them three years before, of one hundred and sixty acres of land, half of the father's farm near Casey, Iowa. But they had a greater resource in their bicycle business, of which the savings were sufficient — now that they gave it up to spend all their time on the airplane — to keep them going for the next four years. They lived with parsimony so as to make the little hoard last. They now believed they would make some money out of their invention instead of merely scientific credit; but they did not try to discount the future.

A brief statement of the Wrights to the press, which was published in most newspapers of the United States around January 7, 1904, concluded: "When these points had been definitely established, we at once packed our goods and returned home, knowing that the age of the flying machine had come at last." The last phrase struck most readers as high comedy and became a text for witticisms by press humorists. The startling momentous conclusion did not indeed jibe with the preceding staid, matter-of-fact sentences concerning the difficulties of embryonic aviation, wherein the inventors addressed the public in the confidential style of a country editor hinting at events with which his readers were somewhat familiar. If six persons in America understood, sixty millions laughed.

There was a result more or less similar from an address made by Octave Chanute in December, 1903, before the American Association for the Advancement of Science in which he said, "a successful dynamic flying machine seems to have been produced by the Messrs. Wright." Chanute briefly sketched the brothers' work and referred to their power flight at Kitty Hawk, while stating their methods had not been revealed. This paper was published in *Popular Science Monthly*, March, 1904.

To perfect their machine the brothers wanted a flying field near home. Wilbur called on Torrence Huffman, president of a Dayton bank. The conversation went something like this:

"Mr. Huffman, you own an eighty-acre cow pasture

about eight miles east of town — Simms Station on the interurban trolley."

"You're right, Wilbur, and I have some fine cows there. What about it?"

"Orville and I would like to use that field for a little flying."

"Flying? H'm! Read about you boys flying at Kitty Hawk. Would it hurt the cows?"

"No, Mr. Huffman. I can guarantee that. We would be over their heads. At starting and landing, one of us would herd the cows safely out of the way. We would not even scare them, so as to affect their milk."

"All right, Wilbur, you can go as far as you like. Sure, put up a shed. And I won't charge you boys a cent of rent. I always liked your squareness and pluck in the bicycle business. Hope you're not making a mistake in giving it up for this airship experiment or whatever it is."

"Thank you, Mr. Huffman. I appreciate your generosity."

The writer visited the world's premier flying field and marveled that this stretch of uneven black prairie with knee-high grassy hummocks, swampy holes, underbrush and a few trees served the purpose of the aërial pioneers. The field was wire-fenced with extra hazards of boundary trees and a telegraph line on poles along the trolley highway. It was circled at some distance by low hills of smooth contour.

Using some metal parts from the 1903 machine, the Wrights built a new airplane and engine during the winter, and had it ready for a test at the cow pasture on April 22, 1904. The engine was of sixteen horsepower — four horsepower better than that of the Kitty Hawk flyer. It was still a crude power plant, weighing above twelve pounds per horsepower.

Every Dayton newspaper was invited to send a man for the airplane debut at the pasture. A dozen reporters came. Katharine brought some friends, and in all about fifty spectators stared at the tar-paper shed and the queer white-winged contraption that made an unholy noise. Would the airship fly?

"I guess they flew at Kitty Hawk," observed a spectator, "but can they do the same in Ohio? Maybe this air is different and lighter. That's what a neighbor of theirs thinks. Yes, he believes in spirits too. Says if the air didn't help 'em down in North Carolina, maybe the spirits did."

"That's not scientific!" scoffed a reporter with eye-glasses on a black cord. "Air is air. Take it from me, the Wrights have a can of compressed gas stowed somewhere inside the ship. This thing, scientifically speaking, is a dirigible balloon."

"I told you so!" remarked several, when Orville announced, regretfully, that there was not enough wind for a flight that day. He noted the reaction of the audience and did his best to perform. He got aboard and opened full throttle. The machine hopped. It would not fly.

The Wrights apologized and renewed the invitation to all to be present the next day. On this occasion the wind was right but the engine balked. The spectators said it was very interesting and departed with the resolve not to waste further time or carfare. The reporters wrote short items, saying the local men were toiling zealously on their airship and showed a spirit of commendable perseverance.

For the next two years Dayton and the world at large paid no attention to the historic doings in a cow pasture, whereby the conquest of the air was extended and perfected in detail, though not in principle. The basic discovery had been established; progress depended on mechanical betterment and practice in the art of flying. However, the latter was no simple matter. There were endless accidents which broke in turn almost every part of the plane and jolted, bruised and imperiled the lives of the dauntless pioneers. The appointed tamers of a wild air horse, they ignored danger and cheerfully returned to their task after every spill.

At first the machine needed an eleven-mile wind in order to rise. Why not start it with a mechanical push? The inventors made a device to obviate wind assistance, and tried it first on September 7. The plane on a single wheel carriage was shot forward on its monorail track by a pulleyed rope connected with a six-hundred-pound weight which fell sixteen and a half feet from a wooden derrick at the rear. There was a method of tripping the weight. The whole device was fairly obvious, an inconsequential expedient to overcome the early lack of power. Yet in 1909, five years later, it became the basis of grotesque libel on the Fathers of Flight. With their landing skids, the dropped weight was "probably" their main gift to aviation, observed a supposed authority in a 479-page volume purporting to cover the entire field of aëronautics. If libraries ejected all similar fictions, the aviation shelves would abound in gaps.

Incidentally the catapult principle has been revived

in recent years for launching planes from the decks of ships, and may still be found useful for ground and roof take-offs.

As they had done at Kitty Hawk, the brothers made a minute scientific record of all flights at Dayton. A notebook for the record was kept in the plane. The machine at Kitty Hawk had carried three instruments of automatic register: anemometer, stopwatch and engine-turn meter. Now the last was discarded but a second anemometer was kept on terra firma to give wind speed on the ground. The records were kept with meticulous detail, including date, sequence number of flight, initials of the brother who flew, wind observation, distance in feet or meters, speed down to fractions of a second, sometimes the records of two stopwatches on the ground when Charley Taylor and one of the brothers simultaneously timed a flight.

From the voluminous diary-record of 1904 I have transcribed some random extracts of interest. The figures in parentheses show the consecutive number of the flight:

Aug. 13 (28) Wilbur broke previous distance record at Kitty Hawk with 1340 feet in 39¼ seconds.

Aug. 22 (33) Orville made 1432 feet in 36 seconds.

Aug. 24 (39) Gust flung machine over on its nose, smashing rudder frame. Pilot Orville scratched, wrenched and hurt all over.

Sept. 15 (49) Wilbur made first circling flight in history of airplane. It was a half circle, 2288 feet in 59⅗ seconds. Wilbur had another similar flight the same day but a trifle longer and just missed grazing the pasture fence with a wing tip. Charley Taylor kept time on this with Orville, and the two stopwatches differed by a second or so.

Sept. 20 (52) Wilbur flew a full circle with a circumference of 4080 feet in 2 minutes 15⅖ seconds. A. I. Root, editor of a bee journal, was present.

Oct. 1 (62) Orville sailed over cows.

Oct. 14 (70) Wilbur circled over two herds of cows without hurting them, as he had promised Banker Huffman.

Nov. 9 (82) Wilbur went almost four times around the 80-acre field in 5 minutes 4 seconds.

The circles were three fourths of a mile in circumference. The altitude of all flights this year was about ten feet above ground, for the brothers did not wish to take chances with, as Wilbur said, "only one life to spend." He also stated as to this year:

". . . we decided to try a complete circle. At first we did not know just how much movement to give in order to make a circle of a given size. On the first three trials we found that we had started a circle on too large a radius to keep within the boundaries of the small field. . . . On the fourth trial, made on the twentieth of September, a complete circle was made. . . . In order to circle to the left, we moved the cradle slightly to the left, thus turning the tail slightly to the left," the same motion warping the right wing down and the left wing up. After banking, the rudder was turned partly right and the plane kept circling left. The main factor in steering was warping, of which the modern equivalent is the tilting of ailerons. We may note a likeness between airplane and bicycle in that both are balanced and steered by a dual purpose mechanism.

The horizontal cradle of the pioneers became a vertical shoulder yoke with others. The warp became limited to a flexure of the rear marginal wing edges in the Wright machine and was evolved by copyists into flaps or ailerons of varied location. In 1904 the brothers made a device to move the rear rudder, as desired, independently of warping. This was dropped the next year but was afterward restored as a permanent feature. Some mysterious occasional troubles in 1904–1905, signified in part by a perverse tendency of the airplane to impale itself upon a thorn-filled honey locust tree, were found by the brothers to be due to lack of skill in pilotage. There was early difficulty in circling because centrifugal force was added to the normal load of the machine, which had just about enough motor power for a straight flight only. Frequent stalls were due to the slowing up in circling, and many later accidents have occurred for the same reason. The remedy was to tilt the machine forward so as to regain flying speed and lift.

There were some horses as well as cows in the pasture and the pioneers had quite a task to herd the animals out of the way. The livestock soon became used to the airplane and paid no more attention to it than did scores of human beings who saw or heard the machine roaring by. Every twenty minutes a Dayton-Springfield interurban trolley car skirted the flying field, and the passengers could not help seeing the Wright hangar and derrick, often the white-winged mechanical bird at rest and sometimes in the air. True, the inventors usually timed their flights between trips of the trolley car, but they took no other measure to avoid attention. Dozens of farmers working in near-by fields or driving their teams along the boundary high-way beheld the miracle of flight without the slightest curiosity. There were hundreds of other blind spec-tators — passengers on two railroad trunk lines within fair eye-distance of the pasture. Perhaps their optic nerves registered cattle but rejected the white butterfly image as a sign of liver trouble.

The Associated Press man at Dayton, anxious to keep the world informed as to the Wright "airship," called up the brothers on the telephone at intervals and had a chat like this:

"Any news on the airship to-day, Wilbur?"

"No, nothing special."

"You and Orville been flying any to-day?"

"Just about as usual. Couple of flights."

"How far?"

"Halfway down the field."

"Not so much, eh? Well, you be sure and let me know when anything special happens."

"Yes, we'll be glad to do that any time you call up."

Editor Root of *Gleanings in Bee Culture,* a maga-zinelet for apiarists, witnessed the first circular flight on September 20, as told in the diary record, and be-came the first intelligent convert to the airplane. He tried to inform the world that a new vehicle of great possibilities had arrived. He only succeeded in bearing the tidings to the small group of his own bee-keeping readers. He was his own publisher as well as editor, so none could stay him from enlightening his audience on a topic rather loosely connected with bees. It was his privilege, said the editor in his issue of January 1,

1905, "to see the first successful trip of an airship, without a balloon to sustain it, that the world has ever made."

"I told you there was not another machine equal to such a task as I have mentioned *on the face of the earth*," earnestly continued Mr. Root. . . . "In making this last trip of rounding the circle, the machine was kept near the ground, except in making the turns. If you will watch a large bird when it swings around in a circle you will see its wings are tipped up at an incline. This machine must follow the same rule; and to clear the tip of the inside wing it was found necessary to rise to a height of perhaps twenty or twenty-five feet. When the engine is shut off, the apparatus glides very quietly to the ground, and alights on something much like a pair of light sled runners, sliding over the grassy surface perhaps a rod or more."

There were many future uses for the airplane, surmised the editor. Its gentle motion would qualify it to take eggs to market. And with a happy stroke of divination, the writer suggested that the plane might serve to fly over the North Pole! There must be something in bee keeping which develops both the rational and prophetic faculties.

Mr. Root, as kindly as he was intelligent, sent the Wrights a check as a gift to help them. They returned it with thanks. The bee editor also tried to aid by sending a copy of his journal with his eyewitness account to the *Scientific American*. Receipt of the little magazine, so heavily freighted with exclusive scientific news, was acknowledged with thanks, but none of it was deemed worthy of attention. Perhaps the *Scientific*

American felt that it had committed itself to back another air horse in its issue of December 17, 1904, when it published an article with photograph, "Aëroplanes in France and M. Archdeacon's Apparatus." The article said: "M. Archdeacon's aëroplane resembles the Wright (American) aëroplane in its general principles, but contains different modifications in detail which will no doubt make it an improvement over the former." No motor was mentioned; a later issue recorded failure of the apparatus.

If America was asleep, the British Lion heard the drone of the airplane in an Ohio cow pasture and growled:

"I'd better look into this. A thing that flies might be quite annoying in time of war. Talk about my splendid isolation! G-r-rumph!"

In fact, a British army officer, Colonel Capper, who had been at the St. Louis Exposition, was ordered by his superiors to visit Dayton in the fall of 1904 and see what the Wrights had. He spent a day in town, and talked with the brothers. He did not see the machine. Afterward the War Department of the British Government kept in touch with the Wrights for several years, either by letter or perhaps through the casual visits of a florid person with a calabash pipe who "just dropped over from London to shake hands." This friendly chap must have liked Wilbur and Orville a lot to travel seven thousand miles for a handshake. However, it gradually appeared that the British Lion was not keen on getting the airplane for himself but wished to see that it did not fall into the hands of any of his ill-disposed neighbors.

"Uncle Sam has first call on our invention," said the Wrights, in reaction to the British interest.

They offered it to the War Department at Washington. The reply was short, like that of a busy man solicited by a pencil salesman.

The sensitive brothers looked at each other, put the letter aside and continued work on their third power machine, which had its first trial in June, 1905. It weighed, with operator, eight hundred forty-five pounds. The engine was the same as the previous one but improved to deliver twenty horsepower, which gave a speed of better than thirty-eight miles an hour. The wing curve of the new machine was one in twenty while the former model was between one in twenty-five to one in thirty.

At the first trial the plane whizzed prematurely down the track with Orville riding backwards, draped over the front handle. Luckily there was no great hurt or damage. On July 14 a bumpy landing catapulted Orville through a break in the top wing. He must have touched wood going through, for the diary says he was not damaged a bit. In latter August a number of local spectators, including Banker Huffman, witnessed circling flights over the cows and doubtless some of the children present wondered why, as Mother Goose suggests, the cows did not also fly. (A prize milcher has now done so!) On September 6 Orville circled the field four times or toward three miles. The next day the airplane chanced to kill the first bird in the record of mechanical flight.

Since then pilots have had many perilous collisions with birds. Sir Hubert Wilkins, flying in the

Antarctic in 1928–1929, reported that his craft was endangered by dense flocks of wild fowl. But the odds are generally with winged man. In the United States it has been deemed necessary to protect birds by a federal law which prohibits hunting them by airplane. Otherwise, in some seasons and in certain parts of the country, there would be avian massacres.

On September 26 in the presence of Father Wright, Wilbur flew round and round for about eleven miles, only stopping when his fuel was used up. Orville raised the record to twelve miles on September 29 and increased it to fifteen miles on October 3, with quite a gallery present, including the passengers on two interurban trolley cars that went by during the flight. The next day, before a dozen friends and relatives, Orville extended himself to cover about twenty miles in the air.

Wilbur as the elder brother, felt bound to cap the last jaunt and on October 5 before some fifteen persons, including a local reporter, made a circular trip of twenty-four miles in about thirty-nine minutes, which was the airplane distance and duration record for a number of years.

Dayton began to be mildly excited about the show the bicycle men were offering in a pasture. Trolley passengers stared as they went by. Once a car stopped while the general manager of the line ran to the field, asked how that dingus stayed aloft and could he buy stock in it? A commercial traveler on a Big Four train, which passed half a mile from the field (while the Cincinnati, Hamilton and Dayton Railroad line was but three quarters of a mile distant), reported what he saw and was advised by his friends to dilute his liquor. A woman who picked greens near the cow pasture and with a white horse at her wagon peddled them in Dayton, started some kitchen gossip.

One day a farmer, leaving his team on the Springfield pike, walked over to scrutinize the airplane.

"What is that thing?" he inquired.

"It is a flying machine," replied the inventors.

"I don't want to discourage them fellers," said the farmer in an undertone to a fellow spectator "but that there thing can't fly. There ain't enough *to* it."

Then Wilbur started the engine, and at the roar the farmer fled to his team without a backward glance and drove off in haste.

Other farmers driving along the two highways and the residents of several houses within eyesight of the field did not bother much about the vehicle. None who read the items in the Dayton newspapers of the latest flights thought that they were important; a bit curious, yes; if the local boys kept at it, they might some day almost equal the foreign balloon racers.

Katharine Wright tried to get her fellow teachers in Steele High School to visit the field and witness the prime spectacle of the new century, man's conquest of the air after centuries of vain dreaming. The dialogue on the school steps ran like this:

"Girls, let's go out on the trolley this afternoon and see the boys fly. Wilbur said I might bring you all."

"How nice of you, Katharine — "

"All right, we can get the car right away. It's only twenty minutes there."

"It would be just splendid, dear. I'm sure we all want to go — almost any day except this afternoon."

"But the wind to-day is ideal for flying."

"Of course it is, and we're all terribly sorry. We *must* go out there some time with you quite soon. Yes, indeed!"

But the teachers never found time to accept Katharine's reiterated invitations. Perhaps they wished to spare her feelings, knowing that she was gullible and doted upon her eccentric brothers.

There was enough rumor and hazy publicity to warn the Wrights that they should desist from open experiment in order to safeguard their invention. Their patent had not been issued. Europe was keenly interested, pirates were lurking with fifty dollar press bribes and unfounded claims to share partnership. So the pasture hangar was closed and the machine dismantled in the autumn of 1905. The brothers did no more flying until 1908.

In three years, 1903–1905, the creators of the airplane had developed it from the virgin flight of eight hundred fifty-two feet at Kitty Hawk to a circling tour of twenty-four miles at Dayton. During this time no other person in the world had risen from the ground in any sort of heavier-than-air craft.

The *Scientific American* of December 16, 1905, had an editorial article which confirms the surmise that the wastebasket had received the eyewitness account of Bee Editor Root. The article says:

"At the same time the fact remains that the only successful 'flying' that has been done this year (1905), as in previous years, is to be credited to the balloon type. . . . The future of aërial navigation, as we have said, is bound up with the success of the aëroplane, and the most promising results to date were those obtained last year [1904] by the Wright brothers, one of whom made a flight of over half a mile in a power-propelled machine. It is gratifying to know that during the present year they have been carrying on their investigations."

It would appear that the *Scientific American* partly hit the nail on the head, at least in the way of general prophecy. However, the editorial seer had a lapse of intuitive insight when he observed in the same review: "Some extremely interesting and fairly successful experiments have been made in which the actual wings of birds, or aëroplanes built up of birds' feathers, have been employed."

Doubtless the feathery hopes were pinned on data in two articles published within the preceding six months in the same magazine. The first article told of experiments by three Englishmen with winged planes, covered with plumage. They also "used a pair of natural dried wings . . . in conjunction with a small electric motor and a reduction gear to flap them up and down." In a large model the plumed wings were flapped one hundred times per minute. The second article was written with a degree of literary verve. "It has been truly said," declared the author, W. E. Irish, "pluck the feathers from a bird and it can no more fly than a man; properly arrange feathers on a man, and he should soar like a bird." This was at least a happy epigram with a basis of sound logic. Its originality might stand unquestioned, were it not for Carlyle's earlier surmise that man is a two-legged animal or biped without feathers.

Let me hasten to add that the *Scientific American* purged itself of the avian obsession within the next year and in December, 1906, conceded full credit to the Wrights for "the first successful aëroplane." This was at least a twelvemonth before scientists in general had any notion that the atmosphere might become a highway.

The brothers had sent a short report on their work to a ballooning journal in Berlin at the end of 1904, after which the Aëro Club of France asked them to keep it informed of further progress. They complied. Wild excitement was aroused at a meeting of the Aëro Club in Paris by the news that a Yankee had flown twenty-four miles in a heavier-than-air machine. M. Archdeacon, president of the club, wished to advise President Roosevelt by cable to award the Wrights a million francs for their achievement. His enthusiasm for the Wrights was an interregnum between his attempt the previous year to make a glider like theirs and a statement three years later, if we may rely on press report, discounting their accomplishment.

F. S. Lahm, an American member of the club, cabled his brother-in-law, Henry M. Weaver, a business man and resident of Mansfield, Ohio, to investigate the Wrights. It was the writer's pleasure in 1929 to meet Mr. Lahm, hale at eighty-two years, on his way back to Paris after taking an airplane ride in Texas with his son, Brigadier General Frank P. Lahm, U.S.A., a pioneer aviator.

After some delay Mr. Weaver went to Dayton and

executed the commission of his relative, making a report on December 6, 1905, in part as follows:

"At 7 o'clock the following day I was there. I inquired, after a time, whether there was such a firm in the city (the Wright Bros.) but no one could give me any information. There was none in the directory, and no one seemed to know anything about a 'flying machine.' I then went to the telegraph office, since I knew my messages had been delivered, and finally discovered the boy who had delivered the telegrams, and, through him, their street address. Going back to the hotel I found Mr. Orville Wright, the younger of the brothers, awaiting me, and about as much puzzled as I had been over what the cable message and my telegram meant. . . . His very appearance, though, would disarm any suspicion. . . . A young man of about thirty apparently, slight of build and with the face more of a poet than an inventor or promoter. In contour, head and face resembles Edgar Allen Poe. . . .

"We next called on Farmer Stauffer, living half a mile further up the road. He was a typical American farmer with jolly face, and voluble. He rents the farm which includes the field where the flights are made. On October 5 he was cutting corn in the next field east and which is higher ground. When he noticed the aëroplane had started on its flight, he remarked to his helper: 'Well, the boys are at it again,' and kept on cutting corn, at the same time keeping an eye on the great white form rushing about its course. 'I just kept on shocking corn,' he continued, 'until I got down to the fence and the durned thing was still going around. I thought it never would stop.' I asked him how long he thought the flight continued and he replied it seemed to him it was in the air for an hour. . . . I next called at the pleasant home of these discoverers of the only new thing under the sun. They live very quietly with their father who is a clergyman. The elder brother, Wilbur,I found even quieter and less demonstrative than the younger. He looked the scholar and recluse. Neither is married. As Mr. Wright expressed it, they had not the means to support 'a wife and a flying machine too.' "

There was sober truth beneath Wilbur's jest as to the cost of a wife and a plane. The brothers had no income, while they were paying half of the household expenses, sister and father contributing the other half; with Charley Taylor on the payroll, outlay for aërial experiment and several hundred dollars a year for domestic and foreign patents. The patent upkeep increased later to several thousand dollars anually. Yes, the brothers did not remain celibate through coldness or lack of natural affections. Had they not been hemmed by circumstance and provided with a happy continuation of boyhood relationship, they would have doubtless entered upon the usual course of marriage.

Captain Ferber of the French army had been told by Octave Chanute what the latter had seen the brothers accomplish at Kitty Hawk, and now, after the report of their Dayton flights, he rushed enthusiastically to his superiors.

"This American airplane is a great war machine, Messieurs!" exclaimed the captain. "I beg of you, send me across the ocean to buy it pour La France!"

"Eh bien, you wish a junket!" scoffed the French war chiefs.

M. Letellier, editor and owner of the Paris *Journal*, did not laugh at the captain's story. He told the War Department that he would finance a trip to investigate the airplane, and if it turned out to be genuine the French Government would have the machine and the *Journal* would be repaid in public credit.

"Vraiment, zat is a fair gamble!" quoth the Gallic Mars.

A cable buzzed from Paris to Dayton, saying that Arnold Fordyce (private secretary to the editor of *Le Journal*) was taking a fast boat over to see the Wrights.

If the Briton with the calabash pipe had seen the cable he would have snorted and dropped several h's. The plot thickens. A mystery writer is needed to depict excitement at headquarters of international spies. Low music and black-whisker disguises. A repulsive villain chases the airplane through dense forests of maize which make our corn belt resemble the groves of giant sequoias in California. However, the facts surpass movie delirium. It is plain truth that the nations, now and later, reached out with eager fingers to seize the American invention. They finally took it with small thanks to its creators.

Before this the Wrights had given the United States the first chance to acquire the airplane and had been rebuffed. Now they were urged by Octave Chanute, who learned of the foreign overtures on a visit to Dayton, to offer the machine again to Uncle Sam. It was a patriotic duty. Washington bureaucrats would now awaken and appreciate the offer.

Wilbur and Orville thereupon wrote a letter dated October 9, 1905, to the Secretary of War at Washington, renewing their former tender of the airplane and saying they did not want to take it abroad unless obliged to do so. They offered a machine that would fly not less than twenty miles at the rate of thirty miles an hour, and would contract for a machine capable of flying one hundred miles. One or more persons would be carried. The price, not given, would depend on performance of machines.

The reply was as follows:

War Department
Board of Ordnance and Fortification
Washington, D. C. October 16, 1905.

Messrs. Wilbur and Orville Wright,
Dayton, Ohio.
GENTLEMEN:

Your letter of the 9th instant to the Honorable Secretary of War has been referred to this board for action. I have the honor to inform you that, as many requests have been made for financial assistance in the development of designs for flying machines, the Board has found it necessary to decline to make allotments for the experimental development of devices for mechanical flight, and has determined that, before suggestions with that object in view will be considered the device must have been brought to the stage of practical operation without expense to the United States.

Before the question of making a contract with you for the furnishing of a flying machine is considered it will be necessary for you to furnish this Board with the approximate cost of the completed machine, the date upon which it would be delivered, and with such drawings and descriptions thereof as are necessary to enable its construction to be understood and a definite conclusion as to its practicability to be arrived at. Upon receipt of this information, the matter will receive the careful consideration of the Board.

Very respectfully,

(Signed) J. C. BATES,

Major General, General Staff,

President of Board.

The Wrights were mildly indignant, as may be read between the lines of their reply, dated October 19. This missive lies before me and I venture to paraphrase it thus:

"We are not indigent seekers of a subsidy from the government. We ask for no money in advance, pay for our own experiments, and offer a finished product to be paid for only if satisfactory. Like every manufacturer, we must have specifications for our product. Besides, it is essential for us to know whether the government wishes a monopoly of the airplane."

The reply to this follows:

War Department

Board of Ordnance and Fortification

Washington, D. C. October 27, 1905.

Messrs. Wilbur and Orville Wright,

Dayton, Ohio.

GENTLEMEN:

The board of Ordnance and Fortification at its meeting October 24, 1905, took the following action:

The Board then considered letter, dated October 19, 1905, from Wilbur and Orville Wright requesting the requirements prescribed by the Board that a flying machine would have to fulfill before it would be accepted.

It is recommended that the Messrs. Wright be informed

that the Board does not care to formulate any requirements for the performance of a flying machine or take any further action until a machine is produced which by actual operation is shown to be able to produce horizontal flight and to carry an operator.

Very respectfully,
(Signed) F. C. Dickson,
Captain Ordnance Department,
Recorder of the Board.

Our military wiseacres resolved, in effect, that the airplane did not exist although it had flown twenty-four miles in the presence of some fifteen eyewitnesses, and altogether hundreds of persons had surveyed or glimpsed the levitation of man's new vehicle. Thus the American discovery was rejected at home and sent abroad for its early exploitation.

CHAPTER IX

Arnold Fordyce, scout for the leading newspaper of Paris and indirect agent of the French Government, arrived in the Middle West city during Christmas week, 1905. He was a youthful looking person of urbane manner and a fair command of English. If the simple aspect of the inventors' home, and workshop in an alley, and the rustic character of their airport astonished him, he was too polite to show it and too intelligent to be deterred by such external circumstances.

He talked with the brothers in their tiny low-ceilinged office, heated by a natural gas stove of their own handiwork, located above the old bicycle shop. He went forth to interview witnesses. One of these was Mr. Huffman, president of the Fourth National Bank, who stated that he owned the pasture and the cows over which the brothers had flown repeatedly in his presence; it was a curious spectacle; but in frankness Mr. Huffman could not see any practical use whatever to which such a machine could be put. The Frenchman was convinced by the candid banker and hastened to cable for authority to obtain an option on the airplane.

Fordyce wished to secure the exclusive world-right to the device which might or might not have a practical future. The inventors were reluctant to agree although allured by the prospect of retiring from distasteful business and devoting themselves to scientific research. But they did not wish to sell everything at less than fair value, a nice problem in itself. What price airplane? Should it be five or six figures? To-day seven or eight figures would seem reasonable, merely to start discussion.

There was also objection against the granting of world rights in that it would debar the United States from convenient acquisition of an invention made by its citizens. This government had twice rejected the tender of the airplane, yet the brothers now reserved the right to supply it with machines in the future, while they agreed that France should have exclusive control abroad during a specified period. An option was signed and money was deposited through Paris bankers with the house of J. P. Morgan and Company in New York. The Wrights agreed to demonstrate one machine in the presence of army officers in France, whereupon the option money would be theirs; and it was a very tidy sum, all that they desired from the French Government.

New York pressmen talked with Fordyce, homeward bound in early 1906, and a report was published that a native "airship" was to be exported to a foreign country, thus depleting our natural resources. Samuel Cabot of Massachusetts noted this deplorable action and asked the inventors by letter why they had overlooked the prior claims of their own country. They replied with a complete explanation. The scion of New England's most eminent tribe wrote to Senator Henry Cabot Lodge, who in turn wrote to the Secretary of War, who sent a memorandum to the Board of Ordnance and Fortification, who presumably filed the note in its proper place among their archives and paid no further attention to the matter.

When M. Letellier, editor of *Le Journal,* called on the French war chiefs with the airplane option, they repented of their earlier interest and were inclined to withdraw from the transaction. It seemed to their thrifty minds that the price was large for a novelty of which the military value was problematical.

At this time the clouds of the Morocco dispute rose to blacken the European horizon. There was direct controversy between France and Germany over the control of northwestern Africa, and if these two came to a clash all the powers of the Old World would be involved. There was anxiety over the continent and in England. Kaiser Wilhelm was fingering his shining sword and there was much quiet activity in the plants of Krupp and Creusot on opposite sides of the Rhine. A thought occurred to the French chieftains rehearsing strategy as they conned their maps.

"*Voila,* we will need this flying machine for a war scout!" they exclaimed. "It will be our surprise answer to Germany that is making new guns in the Krupp plant. The Yankee trick will give us a six months' advantage. No more red tape, Messieurs! Action! Speed!"

With secrecy and dispatch a military commission of four men was sent to Dayton. It started with full power to act but this was revoked *en route.* The members were Commandant Henri Bonel, of the Engineer Corps; Captain Fournier, military attaché of the French Embassy at Washington; Walter V. R. Berry, legal counselor to that Embassy; and Arnold Fordyce, representing both his government and his newspaper employer. The latter and Bonel crossed the Atlantic while the others had a shorter trip from our capital. Of this group, Commandant Bonel was the avowed sceptic; he had no faith in any kind of a flying device, having been upon the commission which witnessed the failure of the Clement Ader power apparatus. He thought it a waste of time to look for an airplane in the backwoods of America.

The quartet of foreigners found lodgings in the Beckel House. The incurious citizens of Dayton took no notice of the strangers who paid frequent visits at an office above an old bicycle shop and also called at a little frame house on Hawthorn Street. The strangers were dressed like local business men, albeit a connoisseur might have detected a Parisian touch in their garb and a keen eavesdropper might have noted their language as exotic, especially since Bonel talked no English. However, a juvenile Sherlock Holmes recognized Fordyce as a previous visitor and sent the pressmen after him. Fordyce suavely gave an explanation that satisfied curiosity; his mission was to study "water pipes," or the hydraulic system of a beautiful and progressive city.

It did not take long for the commission to become enthusiastic believers in the airplane, and the sceptical Bonel became the most zealous convert of them all. They had not seen the machine but were more than convinced by the photographs of it in flight, by the tales of witnesses and the simple sincerity of the inventors. A price of one million francs was agreed on and a cable was sent to Paris, asking authority to close the bargain.

The Wrights convinced the commission only too well. They found themselves looked on as a pair of Aladdins in league with the djinn, capable of creating airplanes of unlimited capacity. When the brothers drew plans and met desired specifications, the eager Frenchmen wished to add any number of features which they had previously overlooked. The inventors designed a new machine, adding the new features but leaving out some of the old. The foreigners were grieved that anything should be left out and pouted over the explanation that aërodynamic laws forbade the simultaneous embodiment of high speed with great climbing power and large weight-carrying ability. The Frenchmen insisted that the machine was a miracle and should perform accordingly. They wished it to climb briskly to an altitude of one thousand feet. The Wrights had never risen more than one hundred feet and being conservative would not promise the unattained out of hand. When they turned to their air tables to find answer to some of the demands, the commissioners lifted their eyebrows with an expression as if to remark:

"It would be much simpler to say 'Open sesame' and be done with it."

Meanwhile a clique of army men in Paris, which had curtailed the power of the commission, had been working to checkmate its efforts and arranged that its urgent cables for action were ignored. The commission was sadly exercised as the Morocco crisis came to a climax and La Patrie might lose the aircraft of her salvation. Only the inventors remained calm. They knew they had something of value, whether disposed

(ABOVE) *Theodore Roosevelt, former President of the United States, about to ascend at St. Louis, 1910, with Hoxsey, who was afterward killed in a crash.*
(BELOW) *Alfonso, King of Spain, an Eager Pupil of Wilbur Wright at Pau, France, 1909. His Majesty's desire to fly was vetoed by his Queen and Cabinet.*

of now or later. They were not especially keen to see their device turned into a war engine and doubtless believed that its military use would be confined to scouting. While waiting for the cables that did not arrive, the commission paid some social calls at the Hawthorn Street house and chatted pleasantly with Katharine and her father. Invited to dinner when they had a previous engagement, the Frenchmen signified regret with the entire stock of a florist's shop, which filled the back porch of the Wright dwelling.

The war clouds dissipated with the settlement of the Morocco dispute at the Algeciras conference. This brought an incidental victory to the army clique opposed to the airplane, for the commission was recalled from America after three weeks of inconclusive negotiations. Commandant Bonel soon resigned from the French army in protest against intrigue and shabby treatment of his friends, the inventors, as well as himself.

Some two days after the departure of the Frenchmen, a short, ruddy stranger in Bond Street clothes, given to smoking a calabash pipe, called on the brothers and greeted them in something like this fashion:

"Haw, Mr. Wilbur Wright, I believe? And Mr. Orville Wright. Great pleasure and honor, I'm sure. The fame of your achievements has reached me in London, where I stop when not trotting about the earth. So I just dropped over to shake hands with you both. . . . By the by, might I awsk if the French Commission is still about?"

The Wrights were amazed that the genial Briton possessed such a secret of the French War Office as the existence of that commission, known to few persons in the world, and that he so narrowly missed encountering them. But they learned in time not to be surprised either by the uncanny knowledge or sudden hand-shaking visits of the man with the calabash pipe.

When the French commission departed, Orville remarked to his sister:

"Lucky thing we were not tied up with that contract. The engine just broke down to-day and we couldn't have got ready in less than three months."

While the French negotiations were simmering at long distance to a thin end in the late summer of 1906, the inventors busied themselves making a new motor of four cylinders, yielding thirty horsepower. It was to be mounted in the plane vertically instead of horizontally, as in previous designs. An upright engine was better in principle while easier to look after. The bore of the cylinders was enlarged to four and one eighth inches. The engine speed was up to 1495 revolutions a minute, or about half better than that of the Kitty Hawk motor. For several years this design was used to power all their planes.

Meanwhile Europe was doing its best to fly with crude imitations of the American vehicle.

"*Sacré!*" exclaimed one of the copyists at the Aëro Club of France, "the Wright can get up; why can't we?"

Santos-Dumont, an amateur in dirigible ballooning, was the first to make a seeming success with a near-airplane. He devised a T-shaped box-kite affair, added a motor some four times as powerful as the Wrights' first engine, and on November 13, 1906, made a straightaway hop of seven hundred twenty-two feet. The machine had no possibility of real flight, it came three years after the pioneer work at Kitty Hawk, its distance record may be compared with twenty-four miles done in circling flight by the American a year previous. Yet for a long time Santos-Dumont was famed in various quarters, on the strength of his box-kite feat, as one of the creators of the airplane. The legend yet persists in Brazil whereof the erstwhile balloonist is a native son.

Wilbur was once credited with saying what a certain pilot said:

"Give me enough power and I can make a kitchen table fly."

This was apparently the motto of early copyists whose erratic craft behaved like furniture at a spirit seance. There is no question that in still air almost anything resembling a plane will hop for a short distance. Among the foreign imitators, Delagrange and Ferber were killed in early crashes. Delagrange was a sculptor before taking up aviation. Whatever may be said of the ethics of such men, we must concede their personal courage. They rushed into the air with an almost total lack of knowledge of the principles of flight and it is remarkable that the casualties among them were not greater.

Charles R. Flint and Company, New York bankers and promoters, were led by press items to consider the economic aspect of the airplane. A representative of the firm, Ulysses S. Eddy, called on the brothers at their Dayton office on the day after Thanksgiving, 1906.

There was a brief discussion. When the Aëro Club of America held its first exposition in New York the following January, the inventors attended it and they met F. R. Cordley of the banking firm. He was a hard-headed person who nevertheless capitulated to the brothers' sincerity, at the first meeting. Charles R. Flint, returning from a trip abroad, hailed Cordley at the dock: "What! Has the flying machine got you too?" But the head of the firm also became a convert and sent another representative, George H. Nolte, to Dayton. In early 1907 a contract was made by which the Flints became the business agents, on commission, for the airplane in all countries except England and the United States. The brothers felt that they could manage their own affairs in the English-speaking countries.

The relations of the Wrights with the Flint concern are in refreshing and almost startling contrast with their experience with the world of business in general. The banker-promoters neither sought nor took unfair advantage of the inventors. A liberal contract was scrupulously kept. The brothers always had the most pleasant relations with the Flints, regarded them as genuine friends and felt that they stood the test of comparison with all the human beings they ever met from savants to kings.

Around the time that this business arrangement was made, the Aëro Club of America launched a subscription among its members to pay the inventors one hundred thousand dollars for their patent rights in the United States, which would then be turned over to the government or released to our home public. This was intended as a deed of patriotism and of useful honor to the men of Dayton. There were over two hundred members of the club, including a dozen or more million-aires. At the end of six months the subscription list registered about eleven thousand dollars and the Wrights were informed that lack of interest had made the project a failure. Perhaps they were cheered a bit by the knowledge that their old friend, Octave Chanute, who had no surplus wealth, had written down his name for a major contribution of five hundred dollars.

Chanute was generous even though he never grasped the full extent of the Wrights' achievement. His state of mind now and later may be gaged from his letter of November 20, 1908, to Secretary Walcott of the Smithsonian Institution, apropos the suggested resurrection of the Langley machine. "I believe that it would be desirable to make the test," wrote Chanute, "in order to demonstrate that the Langley machine was competent to fly and might have put our government in possession of a type of flying machine, which, although inferior to that of the Wrights, might have been evolved into an effective scouting instrument."

Chanute's early rôle was to encourage the brothers and stimulate them to vital research, then his blundering friendship gave Europe its first clues for the imitation of the airplane, and finally his muddled complaisance aligned him with those who sought to discredit the Wrights by the refurbishment of a museum relic.

The sceptical penury of the Aëro Club is explained by the twilight of aviation knowledge then occupied by our leading scientists and experimenters. The club published a book, "Navigating the Air," 1907, which bears out this statement. Among the contents is a paper written not long before by Alexander Graham Bell. The inventor of the telephone thought that the true solution of the flight problem would be found in his system of tetrahedral kites, which was an arrangement of cells somewhat in the style of a beehive and calculated to ravish the heart of a mathematician. While conceding that the Wrights had a successful flying machine, Doctor Bell felt that it had a dangerous speed at thirty-seven miles an hour. "Accidents will happen, sooner or later, and the chances are largely in favor of the first accident being the last experiment." It would be prudent for the present to experiment in safety with something like a tetrahedral kite.

In the same volume John P. Holland, submarine inventor, offered a scheme for wings to be worked by the aviator's arms. The apparatus would be strapped on a man's back, and ball bearings would lighten the fatigue of moving the four oarlike wings through the air. The article was illustrated with diagrams showing winged man on earth and in the sky. A contribution of more learned authority was made by Professor William H. Pickering, a distinguished astronomer of Harvard University. The professor had made a study of aërodynamics, had tested propellers and as far back as 1903 had built a laboratory device to demonstrate levitation. There were air fans moved by electric motors. Says Pickering:

"A small white rabbit, weighing one pound, was next placed in the basket and sent aloft. In this position he was photographed; . . . The total lift of the machine with this power was found to be 4.5 pounds.

It is believed that this is the first time that a living animal was ever carried up and maintained in the air by a purely mechanical flying machine."

The rabbit was lifted (a foot or two) the same year that the Wrights flew at Kitty Hawk. It will be recalled that Professor Simon Newcomb, another famous astronomer, held that man required a new metal or new force in order to fly. It seems there was a fatal fascination between astronomy and aviation, like that between the Knight of La Mancha and the windmills. Professor David Todd, astronomer of Amherst College, entered the lists in the volume cited but prudently confined himself to a means of safe landing for a hypothetical future aircraft.

President Roosevelt saw a brief note on the Wright machine in the *Scientific American* in the spring of 1907. He sent it on to Secretary of War Taft with the endorsement, "Investigate." Mr. Taft added his own "Investigate", and passed the item on to the Board of Ordnance and Fortification. The Board swallowed once or twice, hemmed, frowned over the records of two previous snubs administered to the inventors, then wrote to them asking:

"What price airplane?"

"To Uncle Sam — now — $100,000," replied the brothers in effect. They had read Monte Cristo and doubtless chuckled as they applied the Count's schedule of food-and-drink prices to a foe in captivity.

The dignified Board did not get the point, answering that the sum stated exceeded all funds available. Some months later, when the noise of the Wrights' activities in Europe had reached our capital, the Board became nervous over the situation. It decided to approach the inventors again but with new tactics. A polite and cordial letter was sent, saying the War Department earnestly desired the airplane but just did not have one hundred thousand dollars to buy it with. The brothers replied from London that money would be no obstacle; they would supply a plane on satisfactory terms.

An agent of the Flints abroad, Hart O. Berg, soon found a prospective customer for the airplane in M. Deutsch, oil magnate and patron of ballooning in France. The magnate obtained an understanding with the French Minister of War that the government would purchase a number of machines, and there was prospect of a large market on the rest of the continent. Wilbur was summoned to Paris in June, 1907, to conclude the transaction. The airplane seemed to have golden wings. Three quarters of a million dollars was to be paid for the European rights in the invention. A contract was drawn by legal talent and every one concerned was ready to sign. We may imagine that Wilbur mentally composed a cable to Orville:

"Come on over. Bring Swes and Father. We're through with business for the rest of our lives, but we'll have the whoppingest laboratory. . . . Yes, it's $750,-000! . . ."

At this moment some one who knew what was afoot met his friend Arnold Fordyce in the street and remarked that the French Government was to purchase the Yankee invention after all. Fordyce ran with the tidings to his chief. In turn, M. Letellier hastened to the Minister of War, informing him that his predecessor had made a strict agreement, in view of the original discovery of the Wrights by *Le Journal,* whereby the newspaper should take part in all negotiations for the airplane and should receive credit for it. The seeming intrigue and veritable uproar alarmed M. Deutsch. Wilbur did not send the exultant cable.

Orville joined his brother at the French capital in late July, bringing with him a new airplane and Charley Taylor, their mechanic. The machine was put in bond at the customhouse in Havre and was not removed until the next year. There is reason to think that some customhouses are less secure repositories than safe deposit vaults.

Editor Letellier had the best of intentions and personally inaugurated a new project for the sale of the airplane to the French Government. He assured the Minister of War that the foreign vehicle was the only one worth having, since it had flown at least twenty-four miles while the homemade imitations of La Patrie were barely able to rise from the ground. The price was fixed at one million francs, the same amount that had been agreed on at Dayton the previous year. Everything went smoothly for a time. Then the army engineers began to sand the bearings of requirements for a trial machine. It gradually transpired that Captain Ferber, once a warm champion of the Wrights, who had indeed started the first mission of discovery to the wilds of Ohio, now had a notion that he could build a flyer equal to theirs, saving cash and fame for himself and his nation.

Awaiting the outcome of tedious negotiations the brothers stayed for a time at the Hotel Meurice and then removed to a less conspicuous hostelry, the Palais

Quai D'Orsay. They spent a good deal of time in visiting historical spots and also in studying the artistic treasures housed within the Louvre. The former was perhaps more to Wilbur's taste, because of his early familiarity with French history gained through assiduous reading. Orville preferred painting to statuary and cared especially for the works of the Dutch school.

Doubtless the Wrights stood for a long time before one painting in the Louvre. Mona Lisa gazed benignantly upon them. One imagines that in the hushed silence the enigmatic smiling lips parted a trifle and a voice, mute for four centuries, spoke; " 'Man shall fly like a mighty swan.' . . . 'The human bird shall take his first flight . . . bringing eternal glory to the nest whence he sprang.' . . . Brothers, you have fulfilled my prophecy. I, Leonardo da Vinci, give you hail and welcome!"

The inventors had a problem in communicating with the native folk. The elder brother did not know the French language, the younger could read it but was unable to follow the swift rush of syllables as spoken. As their minds had collaborated before on other things, they now joined forces for a unique and triumphant solution of the language problem. On the street or in a restaurant Wilbur used his verbal memory, shown years before in a color-card test, to capture the quick jargon which meant nothing to him and to dole out the words slowly for Orville to translate at leisure. This procedure furnished a little amusement, while at the same time it obviated the services of a guide.

The employers spent some time with Charley Taylor,

who was becoming homesick at a near-by hotel. The trio found recreation in the then popular game of diabolo at the Tuileries Gardens. Both children and adults enjoyed the sport of whipping a wooden spool into the air and catching it on a string between two sticks. Orville's expertness at the game brought him some newspaper attention. The brothers were pleased to see the authentic American game of baseball, which they always favored, played by some young compatriots in the Tuileries Gardens. A professional beggar who asserted that he was an American haunted the playground and at length Wilbur did not wait to be solicited but approached the mendicant on sight with a copper coin as a contribution to a countryman in distress.

Although their simple habits were unchanged, despite the prospect of a million francs, the Wrights foresaw that they might need ceremonious costume. For the first time in their lives they acquired evening dress suits and silk hats. It was an ordeal for them to wear such garments and they donned them as rarely as possible.

At last the budget committee of the War Department met to act on the airplane proposal. The expectant Wrights awaited the decision in their hotel room. The door was flung open by an excited man who was known to them. He slammed the door, hesitated and stammered, then exclaimed:

"It is all right! It is all right! Everything is going through. The French Government buys the Wright machine for one million francs. But — there is one little thing to be done."

The brothers said nothing and calmly waited for the embarrassed spokesman to continue:

"You will get your million francs all right. No trouble about that. It is just that it is necessary to make a change in the wording of the contract, so that you ask one million two hundred and fifty thousand francs. Then it will go through this afternoon. And you will get your million francs."

Wilbur and Orville kept looking at the speaker. They did not exchange a glance between themselves. They acted as if they were deaf or did not understand. They might well have asked questions or requested a few moments to consider the matter in privacy. They were in need of money. So far, four years after their invention, it had yielded them no profit. Indeed, it had swallowed all their savings and lately had put them in debt to their sister, who had mortgaged the Hawthorn Street home, then owned by her, in order to aid them. A million francs — $200,000 — would wipe out the mortgage and every other care and give independence for a lifetime of delightful, absorbing exploration in fields of knowledge yet unknown.

"Orville and I have no objection" — Wilbur is speaking in quiet staccato without consulting his brother even to the extent of a glance — "to the terms. That is, with the understanding that the contract names the man who gets the two hundred and fifty thousand francs and states his position on the budget committee." There was no change in tone or expression as Wilbur concluded.

The provincial Yankees lost their million francs.

Soon afterward they wrote to the Minister of War,

offering to demonstrate their machine without expense to the government. They requested a single favor, that the authorities would safeguard the airplane from piracy. This was not a gratuitous suggestion nor an ironic affront. After the Santos-Dumont performance, Delagrange had hopped. Henry Farman was adding ailerons to a Voisin machine which the builders themselves would not thus equip as being a violation of the Wrights' warping principle, and he made a straightaway flight of half a mile in October, 1907.

The Minister of War did not answer the letter of the inventors. . . . And the measurements of the Wright plane in bond at Havre were revealed by customs officials the following year.

Wilbur was on his way to St. Petersburg in August, thinking optimistically that rubles might contain less alloy than francs, when he found another opening at Berlin.

"Our gracious Kaiser makes us pay much money for his pet Zeppelin airships," said the industrial magnates of the Reich. "This American flying machine is cheap. If we back it, we prove our patriotic loyalty and save much cash!"

"Unfortunately for you gentlemen," grunted high officials of the War Department, "this so-called flying machine is a fraud. It cannot be. Nothing heavier than air will in the air travel."

Orville visited London to consider a flight at the Franco-British Exhibition but found a lack of suitable physical conditions. He then joined his brother in Berlin and labored with the military sceptics, who would not risk signing any document in regard to a

probable hoax. However, they agreed that seeing was
believing and if the brothers actually flew a machine
in their presence, the Imperial German Government
would do business. Wilbur soon started for home. Orville remained at Paris for a month, arranging for the
construction of half a dozen airplane motors of the
Wright type for future use.

Wilbur in the late fall of 1907 conferred with our
War Department upon the building of an airplane for
this government. Red tape required that a vehicle
unique — "Item: One (1) heavier-than-air flying machine" — should be subjected to public bidding as with
saddles, horse feed and potatoes. The comedy was mitigated or heightened by an official request that the
Wrights should lay down their own specifications. There
were twenty-two bidders who offered machines at all
prices between five hundred dollars and ten million dollars. One candidate piously inscribed his bid in German,
"All things are possible through God." The provision
of a forfeit caused withdrawal of all but two rivals of
the Wrights, neither of whom had ever built any sort of
machine: one asked a thousand dollars and the other
twenty thousand dollars. The latter bidder was A. M.
Herring. "It is known that Herring never intended to
build a plane," stated the magazine *Popular Aviation*
in its issue of December, 1928, "even if he had possessed sufficient knowledge to do so. His plan was to
underbid the Wrights, capture the contract and then
sublet it to the brothers. . . ." However, the contract
was awarded to the Wrights at their figure, $25,000.

At this time Alexander Graham Bell put behind him
the siren call of the tetrahedral kite and made a prac-

tical approach to aviation in alliance with Glenn H. Curtiss and others. Mr. Curtiss had been a motor-cycle racer, then a builder of gas engines, and in 1907 had sought to sell to the Wrights a motor for their plane.

The following correspondence, which later interested a Federal court, explains itself:

The Aërial Experiment Association.
Alexander Graham Bell, Chairman.
G. H. Curtiss, Director of Experiments.
F. W. Baldwin, Chief Engineer.
J. A. D. McCurdy, Treasurer.
T. Selfridge, Secretary.

Headquarters:
Hammondsport, N. Y.,
Jan. 15, 1908.

The Messrs. O. and W. Wright,
Dayton, Ohio.
GENTLEMEN:

I am taking the liberty of writing you and asking your advice on certain points connected with gliding experiments, or rather glider construction, which we started here last Monday.

Will you kindly tell me what results you obtained on the travel of the center of pressure both on aërocurves and aëroplanes?

Also what is a good, efficient method of constructing the ribs of the surfaces so that they will be light and yet strong enough to maintain their curvature under ordinary conditions, and a good means of fastening them to the cloth and upper lateral cords of the frame?

I hope I am not imposing too much by asking you these questions.

Very respectfully,
T. SELFRIDGE
1st Lieut., 5th Field Artillery.

Wilbur Wright   Cable Address:
   Orville Wright   Wrights, Dayton
    Wright Brothers
   1127 W. Third Street
   Dayton, Ohio.

                                   January 18, 1908.

Lieutenant T. Selfridge,
   Hammondsport, N. Y.

DEAR SIR:

We have your letter of the 15th inst. You will find much of the information you desire in the addresses of our Mr. Wilbur Wright before the Western Society of Engineers, published in the Journals of the Society of December, 1901, and August, 1903.

The travel of the center of pressure on aëroplanes is from the center at 90 degrees, towards the front edge as the angle becomes smaller. The center of pressure on a curved surface is approximately at its center at 90 degrees, moves forward as the angle is decreased until a critical angle is reached, after which it reverses, and moves toward the rear edge. The critical angle varies for different shaped curves, but is generally reached at some angle between 12 and 18 degrees. With the angles used in gliding flight the travel will be between the center of the surface and a point one-third back from the front edge.

The methods of construction used in our gliders are fully described in an article by Mr. Chanute in the "Revue de Science" in 1903 (we do not remember the month) and in the specifications of our United States patent No. 821, 393.

                            Very truly yours,
                                WRIGHT BROTHERS

The ribs of our gliders were made of second growth ash, steamed and bent to shape.

Hammondsport, N. Y.
Jan. 22nd, 1908.

The Messrs. Wright,
1127 W. 3rd St.,
Dayton, Ohio.

GENTLEMEN:

Yours of the 18th instant received, for which many thanks. I have been able to obtain a copy of your patent and shall endeavor to secure the other references you mention.

Yours,
T. SELFRIDGE
1st. Lt. 5th F. A.

Wilbur Wright   Cable Address:
    Orville Wright   Wrights, Dayton.
      Wright Brothers
1127 W. Third Street
    Dayton, Ohio.

Mr. G. H. Curtiss,
    Hammondsport, New York.

July 20th, 1908.

DEAR MR. CURTISS:

I learn from the Scientific American that your "June Bug" has movable surfaces at the tips of the wings, adjustable to different angles on the right and left sides for maintaining the lateral balance. In our letter to Lieutenant Selfridge of January 18th, replying to his of the 15th, in which he asked for information on the construction of flyers, we referred him to several publications containing descriptions of the structural features of our machines, and to our U. S. Patent No. 821, 393. We did not intend, of course, to give permission to use the patented features of our machine for exhibitions or in a commercial way.

This patent broadly covers the combination of sustaining surfaces to the right and left of the center of a flying machine adjustable to different angles, with vertical surfaces adjustable to correct inequalities in the horizontal resistances of the differently adjusted wings. Claim 14 of our patent No. 821, 393, specifically covers the combination which we are informed you are using. We believe it will be very difficult to develop a successful machine without the use of some of the features covered in this patent.

The commercial part of our business is taking so much of our time that we have not been able to undertake public exhibitions. If it is your desire to enter the exhibition business, we would be glad to take up the matter of a license to operate under our patents for that purpose.

Please give to Capt. Baldwin my best wishes for his success in the coming government tests.

Sincerely yours,
ORVILLE WRIGHT.

G. H. Curtiss,   L. D. Mason,
    President.   Sec'y and Treas.

Established 1901—Incorporated 1905.

World's Record   Diamond Medal
One Mile, 26 2–5 Sec.   National Endurance
Ormond Beach, Fla.   Run, 1907

Curtiss
Motor Cycles
Motors and Accessories

Gold Medal   Curtiss Motors
Highest Award   Adopted by Leading
Lewis & Clark Exposition   Aëronauts and U. S.
Portland, Ore.   War Dept.

Cable Address:
    "Curtiss," Hammondsport.

Hammondsport, N. Y.
Mr. Orville Wright,   July 24, 1908.
    Dayton, Ohio.

DEAR MR. WRIGHT:

I have your letter of the 20th. Reply has been delayed in the rush of getting Mr. Baldwin's dirigible airship to Washington.

Contrary to newspaper reports, I do not expect to do anything in the way of exhibitions. My flights here have been in connection with the Aërial Experiment Association's work. I have referred the matter of the patents to the Secretary of the Association.

Wishing you the best of success at Fort Myer, I am,

Yours very truly,

G. H. CURTISS.

G. H. C-6

The remarkable success of the Hammondsport group in advancing from the kindergarten elements of gliding to the creation of a power-driven airplane within five months caused some persons to believe that an independent discovery of the secret of flight, eclipsing the Wrights' in celerity of results, had been achieved.

This opinion was not shared by judges of the United States district and circuit courts.

Fortune began to smile on the harassed inventors this year after many lean seasons and the defeat of many dazzling hopes. Millions of francs had floated and fluttered before their eyes, danced and coquetted within hand's reach, then utterly vanished. But now there was a prospect of authentic money from our government. And around the time that contract was made, Flint and Company reported to the brothers that their patent rights in France had been sold to a syndicate headed by the once-affrighted oil magnate, M. Deutsch. The syndicate included Lazare Weiller, who directed a taxicab company in Paris; M. Bernheim, shipbuilder; and the Astra Company.

The Wrights were to receive the sum of one hundred thousand dollars; thirty-five thousand dollars in cash and the balance in stock. The terms required a flight of one hour, the carrying of a passenger and the instruction of three pupils in the art of flying. One-half the cash payment would be made on the conclusion of the hour flight and the other half when the pupils had been taught.

At these tidings we may believe that the dinner menu at a house on Hawthorn Street comprised nothing less than a thick and juicy porterhouse steak. There was also a genuine dessert rather than a masquerade of bread in pudding, and plenty of fragrant coffee.

It was decided that Orville would attend to the home contract and Wilbur would go abroad, using for the European flights the machine which was still in the customhouse at Havre. A new plane was needed for the agreement with the United States Government, and this was planned and built during the early spring. Some changes were required in the design in order to provide for the novel feature of carrying a passenger and to make possible extended flights. The former horizontal posture of the hip-cradled operator would not be feasible. The pilot would have to be seated upright and would use a new system of control. None of these changes was fundamental or difficult.

The brothers had not flown for two years and a half and they needed practice, especially in view of the altered control. About the first of May they went to Kitty Hawk, taking as a practice machine their 1905 plane, now arranged for two persons and with controls suitable for a sitting position.

It was high time for the inventors to show the world

what they could do. The ranks of the copyists were
rapidly being augmented. Bleriot, Farman, Ferber,
Santos-Dumont and Esnault-Pelterie were actively
hopeful; and in that month Delagrange hopped toward
eight miles at Rome, being crowned by the press as
another pioneer of the air.

CHAPTER X

The Wrights established themselves at Kitty Hawk in the old camp building which had hatched the airplane four and a half years before. The structure, if in need of some repair, was more true to its site than near-by Kill Devil Hill which had somewhat shifted its sandy base. There was no change in the rugged friendly natives and life guards. The invigorating salt breezes blew in from the restless Atlantic and overhead were shrieking gulls, circling fishhawks and high-soaring eagles. It was a joy to return to the austere yet beautiful scene where the dreams of youth had been so incredibly realized. Orville resumed with enthusiasm his old rôle of cook, with a nice eye for the arrangement of tinned food on shelves and a turn for useful expedients, as in the devising of a French drip coffee-pot. And say what you will, no elegancies of a foreign chef could compare with the dishes that he set upon the table.

"Annie Laurie," "Suwanee River" and Schumann's "Traumerei" were sung, whistled and hummed by the happy brothers as they assembled their machine and fitted it with twin seats and the new system of control. The old tunes stimulated a common memory and with many a chuckle they recalled in unison the first and second printing press, the wonderful folding machine

Edward VII of England visited Pau, France, in 1909 to see the American "Flying Machine." His Majesty stands behind the starting derrick, which was then used to launch the Airplane.

and the boyhood triumph of the turning lathe. With so much cheerful reminiscence one may wonder that any work was accomplished.

The new control system had certain arbitrary features, as that the lever for lateral balance was to be moved fore-and-aft instead of sidewise, as one might expect. The arrangement was thought desirable because the seated pilot could more easily push and pull in a forward line than exert his strength sidewise. Orville saw that a good deal of practice was needed for such an arbitrary, not to say abnormal, system. He prudently suggested some ground practice with the machine on its track, the pilot tilting its wings with the front and rear movement of the lever. Wilbur scoffed. All he needed was "mental practice", of which he gave a demonstration while sitting up in bed. With closed eyes, Wilbur moved an imaginary lever back and forth, murmuring:

"Down right — Up left — Down this way — Up that way."

It seemed that he was right. On May 13 each brother flew in a complete circle and there was no trouble with the new control or the upright position. The next day Orville ascended with Charley Furnas, whom the brothers had brought from Dayton as their mechanic. This was the first time in authentic history, May 14, 1908, that two persons rode in an airplane. A slight and unverified priority, no distance given and the time "a few seconds," has been claimed by French copyists. The Wrights' diary actually credits Wilbur as being the first to go up with Furnas on this day, but the hop was almost too brief to count. Orville took his passenger a distance of two and a half miles in three minutes and forty seconds.

Wilbur then took a solo flight of over four miles and starting on his second wide circle had a chance to test "mental practice" to the full. It seemed to Orville, watching him through field glasses, that Wilbur was like a rabbit in a corner, securely fenced, dodging from side to side to find an exit. The lever was pulled the wrong way and there was a minor crash. When the bruised pilot emerged from the machine he had to endure an additional penalty of pointed comment by his younger brother. A scratch on the nose was Wilbur's chief damage. He deserved all the language, especially as he had taken his time to crawl out of the machine, while Orville was running up to it, instead of abiding by the rule that the victim of a crash should forthwith jump up as proof that he was not hurt.

There was an enemy lurking at a distance of a mile or so from the once deserted flying field, in a jungle of stunted trees and bushes with a fauna of ticks, chiggers and mocassin snakes. This hidden foe was armed with field glasses and cameras, made its bivouac at the town of Manteo on Roanoke Island, was ferried across every morning to Nag's Head and reached its front-line trenches after walking some miles through the deep sand. The obliging ferryman told the inventors all about it. It is hard to identify this hidden crew with the champions of liberty extolled by Milton in his defence of a free press. The newspaper men, unwittingly and without the slightest malicious intention, were the world's spies, seeking to capture the secrets of the inventors and to make them available to the copyists of every land.

But the Wrights were amused rather than outraged. They did not ask their friends, the life guards, as they might have done, to clear the landscape. They asked no questions of a well-dressed stranger who dropped into camp from nowhere but entertained him with small talk about the weather and asked him to tarry for lunch. This man happened to be Arthur Ruhl, with whom the brothers' subsequent relations were entirely friendly. Among the others in distant attendance were James H. Hare, a colleague of Ruhl's on *Collier's Weekly;* a correspondent of the London *Daily Mail;* a Norfolk, Virginia, reporter and Byron R. Newton of the New York *Herald,* later Collector of the Port at New York. Newton's employer, James Gordon Bennett, had commanded:

"Show up those fakirs — the Wright Brothers!"

No doubt Bennett, who lived in Paris and edited by cable, was piqued that a French newspaper, *Le Journal,* had discovered the inventors long before the *Herald* knew anything of them.

This was a difficult assignment for Newton, as also for Hare, a veteran war photographer who had kept cool amid scenes of carnage but was so amazed when the unearthly white-winged bird lifted from the sand at the foot of Kill Devil Hill and roared past him over-head, that he forgot to click the shutter of his aimed camera.

Soon after the Kitty Hawk tests Farman challenged the Wrights to a flying contest, Delagrange had words of patronage for the inventors and M. Ernest

Archdeacon was quoted in the New York *Herald*: " . . . the brothers Wright, being Americans, are essentially business men. For some years they have been experimenting with an aëroplane, and have obtained certain results. What these results are, I am not prepared to say. In fact, it is upon this point that I believe the Wrights have bluffed."

On his way back to Dayton to complete the new machine for the government, Orville scouted the test grounds at and around Fort Myer, Virginia. This suburb of the national capital had few merits as an airport. A hazardous course was laid out amid barracks, carlines, telegraph poles, ravines and wooded hills with no clear or level spots to provide for emergency landing. With small power and scant altitude, an embarrassed plane would have no chance to glide to safety. Probably a modern pilot with equal equipment would decline to accept the risk. The inventor knew the peril and calmly staked his life on the outcome.

There was a home worry in the illness by typhoid fever of Orville's nephew and favorite playmate, Milton. He gave the boy a good deal of personal care, and had a fresh anxiety when it was reported that Wilbur's arm, scalded by the bursting of an engine pipe at Le Mans, was threatened with gangrene. Amid these troubles it was something in the nature of comic relief to glance at the newspaper headlines which registered the plans of an ambitious rival. A. M. Herring was informing the public that his own airplane would fly from New York to Chicago and that it excelled the Wright machine in various ways, being, for example, so compact that it could be carried in two suit cases.

The first formal public flight of the Wright machine in America was made at Fort Myer on September 4, 1908. It was a brief test. When Orville stayed up four minutes the next day, "the crowd went crazy." They had reason to be crazier on September 10, when Orville flew almost an hour in the morning and in the afternoon circled the parade grounds at an altitude of one hundred and twenty feet for one hour and five minutes. The latter was a world record, since Wilbur in France was having motor trouble and no copyist had been aloft more than half an hour. The same day Orville gave Lieutenant F. P. Lahm — afterward brigadier general — a short passenger trip, and was warmly congratulated by Secretary of War Wright, General Miles and other officials. The reader will recall a reference to Mr. Lahm, senior, hale at eighty-two years. It may now be said that he impressed upon the writer that his son was the first passenger in public of the co-inventor of the airplane.

Another record was broken on September 11, with a flight of one hour and ten minutes, not to mention a pair of aërial figure eights. The following day Orville had as passenger Major George O. Squier, Acting Chief Signal Officer, for a tour of some nine minutes. On the same day a solo flight made a new world's record of an hour and fourteen minutes at an altitude of two hundred and fifty feet.

Instead of the special garb of fur-lined jackets and goggled helmets affected by pilots of the time, despite the meager extent of their aërial excursions, the inventor wore an ordinary business suit with cap. The latter was lost at intervals. A detail of costume was noted by a little girl on terra firma, who exclaimed:

"Look, Mamma. Mr. Wright wears tan shoes!"

A woman spectator did not feel that the mere circling of a new vehicle overhead was worthy of her attention and stated:

"Well, if that's all he's going to do, I'm going home."

With Lieutenant T. Selfridge, assigned as passenger at his own request to the War Department, Orville on the late afternoon of September 17 embarked on the one disastrous flight of his career. That his mind was adversely affected and made inattentive by having as companion a man lately connected with a group that sought to rival the invention of the airplane, is a conjecture with scant support. If the pilot was preoccupied, he laughed with his passenger at the moment of ascent, and the mishap was due to a defect in material that, probably, no inspection could have revealed. The machine overcame a bad start and began to rise in ascending spirals.

The pilot heard an ominous tap-tapping through the whine of propellers and roar of the engine. He glanced back and saw that control of the vertical rudder was gone. A cracked propeller blade had snapped the rudder wire. The machine was on the bank of its fourth circle, one hundred and fifty feet up, when it wavered for a plunge. Orville lived hours in part seconds. He sought to balance by warping alone, and did by lightning-swift action level the craft for a down glide. But he had only seventy-five feet left, and moreover the front rudder was now defective.

"Give me twenty feet more!" implored the anguished brain of the world's prime aviator, a credit conceded by his brother and only rival.

"Oh! Oh!" cried Selfridge, grasping a strut at the last fatal dive.

As he lay on the ground with broken ribs and fractured left leg, Orville was acutely conscious, saw his mortally injured companion arising on hands and knees, noted the horror of the spectators and heard their sympathetic cries. He spoke:

"Tell my sister I'm all right."

He was sleepless through four days and nights of torment, aware of everything that had happened at every moment since that tap-tapping sound, without relief of fainting. The army officer died within a few hours.

On the day of the accident Katharine ended her career as a school teacher and hastened to Washington. At this time the family fortunes were at nadir. All savings were gone and the home mortgaged. Bishop Wright had retired from the active ministry three years before. Debt and misfortunes coincided. Wilbur had been delayed in concluding the French agreement and now there was indefinite postponement of any receipts from the United States Government. Loans were offered by friends, notably twenty-five thousand dollars by a scientific admirer after the catastrophe at Fort Myer, but these offers were declined with thanks.

At the military hospital Katharine ignored the tears in her brother's eyes and hailed him:

"Hello! Orv, the children want to know when you are coming home to help them make candy."

It had been his Sunday afternoon diversion to make candy for Lorin's youngsters.

At last her soothing presence brought a little rest. He had said:

"Sterchens, how do you go to sleep?"

She gave him family news and read to him from his favored author, "The House of Seven Gables." Katharine did wonders but not alone. Four days after the accident, Wilbur, on September 21, in France, made a world record flight exceeding an hour and a half, and stepping from his plane at dusk, almost frozen in thin clothes, said:

"This will cheer Orville up a bit."

It did. With the sister's solace, it calmed the torments and brought the first sleep in ninety-six hours. Wilbur's feat across the ocean was a direct message of fraternal love and it was also triumphant proof to the world, quelling criticism, that the disaster at Fort Myer did not imply futility of the airplane or impair the future of aërial transport. Besides this tribute and testimonial, Wilbur, fulfilling in part the French contract, cheered his recuperating brother by cabling home several thousand dollars.

The patient was in the hospital for seven weeks and emerged with a permanent slight limp and a seat of intermittent neuritic pain. While he lay abed in the military institution, persons other than the merely curious were allowed to examine his wrecked machine. Havre and Washington. . . .

While preparing to fly at Le Mans, Wilbur toiled for some weeks in the automobile factory of Leon Bollee, a plump and jolly chap who became an intimate friend of the lean, grave American, despite a total lack of verbal communication between the pair. M. Bollee was not dumb. He merely knew no English as Wilbur knew no French. They conversed a little by signs and more by an interchange of long affectionate glances. There was a mysterious affinity between them.

Joseph Brandreth, in the London *Daily Mail* of August 17, thus pictured the inventor at Le Mans:

"The man who walked out of the rough wooden shed to meet me wore a cloth cap and was in his shirt sleeves. I noticed that his shirt was of a deep green color such as I do not remember ever to have seen before. . . . There was something strange about the tall, gaunt figure. The face was remarkable, the head suggested that of a bird, and the features, dominated by a long, prominent nose, that heightened the birdlike effect, were long and bony. A weird half smile played about the well-shaven chin and puckered lips, and the skin was deeply tanned with wind and sun. From behind the grayish blue depths of his eyes there seemed to shine something of the light of the sun. From the first few moments of my conversation with him I judged Wilbur Wright to be a fanatic — a fanatic of flight, and I had no longer any doubt that he had accomplished all he claimed to have done. He seemed born to fly."

The same writer quoted Leon Bollee as follows:

"I believe him to be a marvel of inventive genius. I have watched him and studied his machine, and I am convinced that his aëroplane, in spite of many crude little points in it, is the most perfect implement of flight known at the present time. Mr. Wright makes the mistake of wishing to do everything himself, and will not listen to any suggestion which would save him endless trouble and make his flights easier. Let me give you an example. He has no ball bearings on his propeller shafts. I pointed out to him that if he used these instead of the old-fashioned bearings, that require an excessive amount of oiling, he would run less risk of overheating, but he would have none of them. Do you know why? Simply because he was unable to make them himself! He would not have those we make. . . . While in the works he worked away at the apparatus from 6 A. M. till nightfall. He would come in with the staff, and when the factory whistle blew, he would immediately drop whatever he had in hand, take off his overalls and go out to dinner with the men. He does not smoke, he never drinks, he eats sparingly, and the ordinary recreations of life do not appeal to him. Such is the man. He is never in a hurry; he will not allow anybody to touch his machine or handle so much as a piece of wire; he even refuses to allow his mechanic to pour oil into his reservoir. In his opinion they don't do it in a correct way."

The English writer continued:

"During the long hours of waiting I watched Mr. Wright in his shed. In the corner of the shed was his 'room.' This consisted of a low packing case from which the top had been removed. Resting on the edge of the packing case was a narrow truckle bed. Nailed to the side of the shed was a piece of looking glass, and close by a camp wash stand. This, together with a cabin trunk, a small petrol cooking stove — he cooked his own breakfast — and a camp stool, comprised the whole furniture. He takes his baths from a hose pipe attached to the wall. He sleeps practically under the wings of his aëroplane. Early in the day he starts to work, whistling the while, and paying no attention to Mr. Berg's [Hart O. Berg of Flint & Co., agents for the Wrights on the continent] requests that he shall come out and be introduced to this and that distinguished visitor. 'Yes,' he says, 'By and by, as soon as I have finished this' — and this generally requires about an hour. He lives in the shed with his two mechanics — a stolid Englishman from Birmingham and a wide-awake, cheerful looking Frenchman, Fleury, who keeps a sharp watch for 'spies.' . . . That his phlegmatic appearance and cold manner belie his real nature I discovered on the occasion of his first flight. When the great white bird rose high into the air and made evolutions with the ease of a ship at sea, there was a feeling of indescribable emotion among the small crowd of onlookers. We somehow felt we had done Wilbur Wright a great wrong in ever doubting his ability to fly. We rushed out and cheered. We felt that at least the dawn of the flying age had come, and we grasped Wilbur's hands with fervent admiration. I saw that his face lighted up and flushed with pleasure, and by his handshake I knew that beneath the outward mask of coldness the man was full of vibrating nerve."

The French were captivated by the magical feats of the air-riding Yankee and intrigued by his austere personality. He kept the Sabbath, avoided women (it was said that one resentful daughter of Eve stole through a sentry line and gimleted a peephole in his hangar), abstained from tobacco, wine and even choice food. What a man! Poets extolled him as a mediæval knight. The peasants, viewing Wilbur and his craft with awe, made pilgrimages to Le Mans as though it were a shrine. Hawkers on the streets of Paris sold picture postcards and statuettes of the American, including portrayals of him as a Billikin in flight. There was a vain effort of patriots to stem popular enthusiasm. The patriots wished to resurrect the machine of Clement Ader — the Langley of France — but the Minister of War had that relic inaccessible to examination and, *hélas!* it could not be used to a good end. When Wilbur, who ignored all detraction, kept making new records, patriots and imitators conceded that the foreigner was "a trifle advanced in dexterity."

Gelett Burgess, the American author of works both grave and gay, called on Wilbur in response to the latter's note:

"I will be glad to meet the man whose book I have read over more times than any other in the world."

"May I ask which that is?" inquired Burgess in conversation, expecting that one of his serious philosophical works would be named.

"The Goop Book," replied Wilbur, quite sincerely, and the humorist was discomfited.

Some persons would regard it as apropos to mention the award at this time of two medals to the Wrights by Baron d' Estournelles Constant on behalf of his universal peace society, in that the airplane was an implement of peace. But the Baron may prove to be finally right. The martial uses of air transport may become an episode of early civilization.

At Auvours field, a few miles distant from Le Mans, Wilbur celebrated the last day of the year 1908 by a world record flight of two hours and twenty minutes, with a distance of seventy-seven miles, at the same time winning the Michelin trophy and prize of four thousand dollars. He had previously taken up a number of passengers in turn and had made an altitude record of three hundred and forty feet. At this date the time performance of the nearest rival among copyists was given as three quarters of an hour.

Austere and taciturn as he was to the public, Wilbur wrote home with gay freedom, telling Katharine of his gold medals "about the size of a small can," surmising that being home again she would be "getting something decent to eat," and citing, apropos of coming birthdays, a sixteen-year-old sister's outbreak of "boo-hoo-hoo" because every one in the family was growing old. There were boo-hoos due because Pop would be eighty in a week, besides others mentioned. Was Orville really doing as well as represented? The writer was "awfully tired" of the long absence from home. Lord Northcliffe's *Daily Mail* had privately suggested a Channel flight with twelve thousand five-hundred dollars guaranteed and as much more in prospect: weather and landing conditions had to be considered. Milan also offered four thousand dollars and gate receipts. There was a Paris dinner in honor of French air pilots at which most of the applause went to Wilbur, who was present, and he tried to be "as decent as" he "knew how to act" under the circumstances. He had ever been on friendly terms with three of the copyists, giving their names; four of them were unfriendly. At the dinner Wilbur's table partner was Madam Armengand and owing to lack of a common language their conversation was like the dialogue between a Scotsman and a Venezuelan on board ship last year. It went thus: Scot: "Paris." Venez. "Paree." — S. "Rome." V. "Roma." — S. "Mälta." V. "Mältá." — S. "Mădrid." V. "Madreed."

There was a request to spend twenty-five dollars for Christmas presents, a reference to substantial gifts to Reuchlin and Lorin, and a suggestion that Orville might care to go "halvers" on a tidy cash gift to Sines, boyhood crony and later print-shop employee. Orville and sister were not the only important persons solicited to authorship, since the writer had received two hundred fifty dollars for a two-page article in a London magazine and was offered a franc a word by a French newspaper. This would be a good time for Katharine to take a year's rest from her beloved "Old Stub" (Dayton High School in familiar parlance) and come to Europe as "social manager" for her brothers, at a better salary than the six dollars a day stipend for academic tasks.

As writers, the brothers were dry and impersonal in their few technical papers, although Wilbur had sprightly passages in his addresses before the Western Society of Engineers. A lengthy stateliness marked their one jointly written magazine article. They became entirely at ease in their diaries and home letters. Here they were simple and natural, vivid and humorous, graphic, even witty. They wrote better letters than many a collegian or even a professional author. They lacked neither words nor pungent idiom nor — especially — ideas when conversing on paper with their kin. Their modest and generous characters shine through the home-written pages. Delightful are the affectionate teasings and ever boyish play with family slogans and points of familiar jest. It would be difficult to find a boast or a harsh word about others in all their correspondence. However, if the brothers never felt keen resentment, whether expressed or not, they would have been incredibly beyond the human.

Wilbur's handwriting tended to be angular and indicated a compromise between scrawling haste and an impulse to careful strokes. It was usually legible. Orville wrote more neatly and in smaller letters, well adapted to a diary, perhaps because diary keeping was his especial task. The punctuation of both was simple, in accord with their usual style of brief sentences, and accurate because of their early training in printing and press work.

Katharine accepted the position of "social manager" to her brothers in Europe, and perhaps having an intuition of kings ahead, paid due attention to the question of wardrobe. She equipped herself with two Dayton-made evening gowns, one old rose and the other black, planning to wear them in alternation. The trains were moderate and high necks became low. There was also a domestic tailored suit, and two more of the same kind were obtained later in Paris. One American hat was reinforced with two of Parisian make. By way of jewelry, she had the solitaire diamond ring which had been Orville's present upon her graduation from Oberlin College. This ring fulfilled the need of ornamental accessories.

At three o'clock in the morning in early January, 1909, there was a joyous rendezvous of brothers and sister at Paris. The silent Wrights sat up talking at their hotel until dawn and they talked enough during the next few days, largely on home concerns. Wilbur soon left for Pau in order to teach air pupils for the French Wright company, leaving his brother and sister to do a little shopping and sight-seeing at the capital. When the latter proceeded to join Wilbur on January 16 they found themselves in a railroad accident in which two persons were killed.

Pau had many attractions and it gave the Wrights the most pleasant experience that they ever had. It was a winter resort in southern France, nestling amid the Pyrenees near the Spanish border, with quaint old houses and a variety of royal monuments besides the chateau in which Henri IV was born. The population was about thirty-five thousand. It was stated with some cynicism that the warm hospitality of Pau to the airplane was based on the fact that the tourist trade had declined since King Edward VII had ceased his visits, and it was hoped that the new vehicle would revive prosperity. In any event, Pau supplied a flying field, built a hangar, policed the grounds and would not permit the Wrights to mention the subject of a hotel bill. There was even a French chef who only required words of praise as recompense for his efforts. While appreciative, Orville delicately gave him hints on the art of washing dishes. This was at the aviators' living quarters in the field shed which Orville shared with his brother, leaving Katharine at the hotel. The camp life with luxuries rapidly mended Orville's health, and he

aided his brother with the machine though not under-
taking to fly himself.

The field was an unfenced grassy plain, quite level
and unlimited in size, at a distance of several miles
from town. Flights were made chiefly in the early
morning and late afternoon, when the wind did not exceed a speed of eight or ten miles an hour. The air pupils were on the field at six o'clock in the morning. In
those days the perennial question of every aviator was,
"How is the wind?" Moistened fingers were held up to
tell the direction of the breeze; flags and vanes were
carefully observed. There was an anemometer here to
settle doubt. The altitude of flights in teaching did not
usually exceed one hundred feet and was often considerably less.

Wilbur gave an unprecedented course in pilotage of
a new vehicle. There were no text books on the subject,
no theories of instruction to go by, no medical examination to sift out the physically unfit, and none of the
later elaborate devices used in ground school to test the
pupils' senses in upside down positions and give him
safe practice. Professor and pupil exchanged a few remarks — Wilbur was no voluble lecturer — then rose
in the air and took their chances. Yet no one was hurt
in the three dozen teaching trips made here. The honor
of being the world's first flyers taught by the Wrights
was shared by Count Charles de Lambert, an experimental scientist and incidentally the champion pigeon
shot of France; Paul Tissandier, a daring automobilist
and sportsman; and Captain Girardville of the French
army. The brothers considered De Lambert their best
friend abroad and were delighted by the favors of his

six-year-old daughter who termed Wilbur "*My* Mister Wright" and Orville "Best Orville."

As an interlude between more exciting things Katharine and Orville had a two hours' balloon trip, sailed sixteen miles and landed at the edge of the mountains. For some reason the European press, which had been filled with the doings of the Americans, did not connect this excursion with the interesting fable that a Grand Duke of Russia had asked the hand of Katharine. Her duties as social manager, together with daily conversational lessons in French, kept her quite busy.

The King of Spain arrived in February. He had sent word in advance, requesting an exhibition flight on Sunday. It is an axiom that a royal request is a command. But the Americans, whose father was a minister, thought of another command they had been accustomed to observe— "I never asked them not to fly on Sunday," stated Bishop Wright afterward — and they politely replied that they would be pleased to entertain His Majesty on any week day. The King changed his schedule to suit while the populace brought out their flags, and the French and Spanish secret service men toiled for a week to segregate all persons who might be anarchists of the militant school. His Majesty was to stay at the Wrights' hotel. Katharine debated whether old rose or black would be suitable for the first evening.

Alfonso unexpectedly romped into the hotel dining room, followed by suite and bodyguard, upon a Friday night. Katharine was flustered, not being attired in either of her evening costumes, but she fortunately escaped the royal eye.

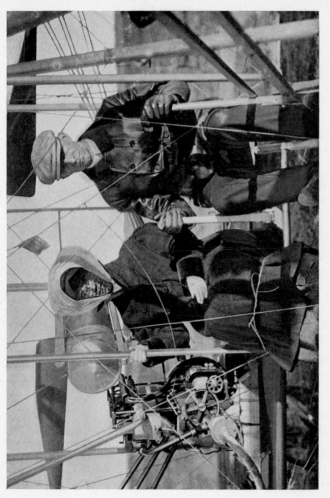

Wilbur Wright taking his sister, Katharine, for an air ride in the presence of the King of England at Pau, France, 1909. It was a complete and delightful surprise plotted by her fond brothers.

At the field early next morning the scene was somewhat as follows:

"Your Majesty, may I present the Wright brothers."

"This is an honor and pleasure!" exclaimed Alfonso, smiling, as he shook hands vigorously with Wilbur and Orville. "What a marvelous invention your airplane is! I have looked forward to seeing this miracle for a long time."

The brothers smiled politely and bowed a trifle.

"I would ask the great privilege of a trip in the air," continued the young monarch, "except for one thing — "

"What is that, Your Majesty?" delicately prompted a courtier.

"My Queen and Cabinet made me promise not to do it!" said Alfonso with a rueful laugh, in which the little group of notables present discreetly joined. "Yet they say a King can do as he likes."

The Spanish ruler asked for Katharine. At that moment she was taking her first lessons in the art of curtsying, in a secluded part of the field at the hands of Lady Northcliffe, who had volunteered to instruct her in this essential mode of greeting royalty. Although Katharine had become quite adept after half a dozen practice curtsies, she decided on approach to the King to be natural. She gave a friendly hand to the monarch, who responded with beaming smiles and compliments and told again his regret at not being able to take a trip in the air. He spoke fluent English and was a most agreeable personage.

As Wilbur landed from an interesting flight, including a few ups and downs, circles and a sudden reap-

pearance after being lost to view behind a clump of
trees, the excited young King ran and jumped over obstacles to reach the machine. Seated in it beside the
inventor he volleyed scores of questions with enthusiastic vivacity and showed that he understood a good
deal of the problem involved in aviation. Quiz and general talk lasted for an hour, after which the Wrights
were invited to luncheon with the King at the hotel.

"I would like to have my equerry taken in the air,"
observed Alfonso casually at the luncheon table.

This was another royal command which the brothers
had to parry without benefit of etiquette book or course
in official diplomacy. Every one on the continent wished
an air ride. Wilbur and Orville, self-taught diplomats,
said nothing in reply but smiled their best at the King
of Spain and at each other, as though delighted by a
gracious compliment not to be taken in earnest. Alfonso accepted the situation with good humor. Wilbur
did finally attempt to take up a Spanish officer, but an
accident to the launching gear terminated the effort.
When leaving town the next morning Alfonso espied
Orville and his sister effacing themselves in the hotel
court and he shook hands with them and raised his hat
in a parting salute.

The airplane was still launched at this time by a
derrick weight, which was hauled to the top by rope
before each flight. The rope was common and the
weight cast iron, yet since these objects were essential
to the miracle of flight they became endowed with a
peculiar sanctity. There was a keen competition among
the high and mighty of Europe, assembled at Pau, for
the honor of pulling on the rope and thus performing

a menial chore. Those who were not allowed to heave
felt it a privilege to put their hands on the rope. Among
those who participated in the complete hauling ceremony were Arthur Balfour, who had been Prime Minister of England; Lord Northcliffe, proprietor of many
newspapers; and the Duke of Manchester. Half a
dozen years before at Kitty Hawk the inventors had
paid a man a dollar and a quarter per day for exerting
his muscle on the virgin flyer.

Some of the worshipful notables envied the job of
the Wright mechanic at Pau who solemnly prepared
the plane for each ascent by walking up to it from behind and giving the tail a brisk wiggle. It was agreed
that the wiggle was an essential detail, but being a simple
ple act should not have been monopolized by a selfish
mechanic.

"Where's the Comtesse de Lambert?" said Wilbur
one evening, as twilight began to fall from the crests
of the near-by Pyrenees.

"Mr. Wilbur wants *me?* He cannot want me but
for *one* thing!" exclaimed the moist-eyed Countess ec-
statically, returning to the field. She had not told any
one of her dearest wish, now to be fulfilled.

The silent American, who had been politely deaf to
a monarch's command, smiled at his friend's wife and
deftly tucked her into the seat. As the plane came back
to earth she was speechless with delight.

Wilbur next treated his sister to her first jaunt in the
sky and despite all her familiarity with the machine,
going back to the days when it was a dream subject
debated by her brothers in the home living room, she
had the thrilling emotions of a novice undergoing a

marvelous adventure. A little dazed and bewildered when the roaring craft left earth below and mounted through layers of velvet dusk to regions of upper light and purer air, she was fearless because Wilbur was beside her.

Among the multitude who wished to fly was an American magnate who came from Paris to Pau by special train, confident that his desire would be gratified without delay. But the inventors did not choose to regard him as different from all the other candidates. He did not go up.

At news that the King of England was coming, a host of his loyal subjects besieged the Wrights with letters, wires, telephone calls and personal visits. There were hundreds of messages, including those from baronets, lords, earls and other personages of the first rank. Many of these distinguished suitors had no desire to hazard their lives by a trip aloft. They merely regarded the airplane as a social elevator and wished to be accorded their proper places in the royal picture, without which the ceremonies would be incomplete. In contrast, some English aristocrats were natural and friendly, and sought to be helpful. A person of the latter sort identified herself to Katharine after meeting her, with the following signature to a note:

"Mary . . . — six feet two."

King Edward VII arrived on March 17, motoring with his suite from Biarritz. The inventors and their sister were presented to him at the field. Katharine shook hands with His Majesty, who spoke pleasantly. He was a stout figure with a pointed white beard, passing into age and weariness. He wore a derby hat and a light-colored overcoat. The brothers explained their vehicle to the King, who listened with courtesy but did not seem to have much interest in mechanical details. He failed to observe the take-off of the plane, being just then absorbed in conversation with one of his party.

Wilbur made the flight in the royal presence and on landing said to his sister:

"Sterchens, don't you want to climb in?"

Katharine replied she couldn't because of her large hat, whereupon Orville, smiling, stepped forward with cap and veil as prearranged with his brother. Thus the delighted Katharine had her second and most gorgeous flight before His Britannic Majesty and over the heads of peasants strewn along the countryside in gay Mardi Gras costume.

"See, a woman flies also!" cried the peasants, waving hands and bright headdresses.

But the occupants of the magic car floating through the lucent air toward the snow-capped mountains soon forgot the lesser spectacle below and felt only the sublime beauty of nature as seen from the eagle's vantage. A man who had mastered the air looked at his passenger, playmate of childhood and woman he loved best, and nodded meaningly toward the sparkling Pyrenees as though to agree that life had been perfected and the last goal attained.

Leaving Pau with regret, Orville and Katharine went ahead to Paris, where there were duties in supervision of new planes and motors as well as a little more shopping and sight-seeing. Wilbur arrived a week later, spent an equal time with them and then left for Rome to arrange flights and fulfill a contract for the sale of a machine to the Italian Government. The sister and younger brother arrived in Rome on Good Friday and Wilbur took them to a hotel opposite the Barberini Palace. It was a cold rendezvous for the trio, who kept on their overcoats and wraps in Katharine's room. The hotel advertised "Central Heating." Wilbur commented, "Guess what we want is local heating."

He was soon fortunate enough to be installed in a little house with garden near the flying field. This was due to the kindness of the Contessa di Celleri who owned the cottage which adjoined her villa. She had not met Wilbur but divined his precise needs. There were flowers and breakfasts and a standing invitation to dine at the villa if he wished but without the slightest obligation to do anything, except at his pleasure. Wilbur usually had luncheon and dinner with Italian officers at their mess and he reported to his kin that in a short time he devoured "forty-seven miles of macaroni."

It was arranged before the others arrived that Wilbur should be presented to the King of Italy at the palace by Lloyd Griscom, the American Ambassador.

"Three bows will be suitable for the occasion," advised Mr. Griscom in a note.

"I didn't know," commented Wilbur later, "whether it meant to wear one under the chin and one under each ear, or whether it meant to make three of them to the King at the presentation."

Assuming that obeisances rather than triple neckties were required, Wilbur started to perform before Victor Emmanuel at the palace.

The tall, lanky American tilted once. He was half-way on the second bend when the short little monarch pushed him cheerfully into a chair, and taking a seat himself, began to talk in plain English, asking questions and making simple but pointed comments. There were no frills on His Majesty. While he showed less enthusiasm than the effervescent Alfonso of Spain, he had more interest in the airplane than the King of England.

The airport was on the Campagna within view of the Roman monuments and an aqueduct of the Cæsars and massive ruins of antiquity that made a bewildering setting for the newest creation of man. Azure hills and sky were the same as they had been when the imperial legions marched hence to the four corners of the known world. And had those legions seen this white-winged bird rising from the ground and soaring into luminous heights of violet and gold, would they have fled in terror or hailed it as a Phoenix, beneficent envoy of the immortal gods?

CHAPTER XI

When the Wrights were talking with the King of Italy on the air field, a little lame boy stood in the crowd outside, gazing wistfully through the cordon of soldiers that encircled the resplendent scene.

"Dad, I wish I could get close up!" exclaimed the twelve-year-old American, stretching his twisted leg to rise on tiptoes.

"Afraid we can't, son," replied the father. "Those soldiers won't let even counts, dukes or millionaires pass through the line."

"Oh, dad, I would love to see the machine and — Maybe if you wrote a letter to Miss Wright — "

"Probably it won't work, but I'll try it," said the father, unable to resist the entreaty in the shining eyes.

The letter was written. Then to the amazement and jealous wonder of all beholders, the military barrier impassable to the mighty opened to admit a frail boy who limped his way to the hangar.

"Ah, he must be a prince — perhaps the crippled Czarevitch," murmured a spectator.

Wilbur and Orville indeed received their small compatriot as if he were a prince. They shook hands with him. They smiled and acted as if they had known him a long time. They took him inside the hangar and showed him everything about their machine that was more wonderful than the flying carpet in the Arabian Nights.

Orville and Katharine were presented to Victor Emmanuel at the field soon after six o'clock in the morning. Katharine was amused and not displeased that the King had a livelier interest in the airplane than in her. His Majesty wore a military uniform without decorations and had a small folding camera strapped over his shoulder. He took a number of pictures of the plane on the ground and during its evolutions in two ascents made by the elder brother. There is a photograph which shows the monarch trotting across the field between Wilbur and Orville.

Besides teaching pilotage to two officers of the Italian army, Wilbur took aloft as passengers Ambassador Griscom and the former premier of Italy, Sonnino. The American banker, J. P. Morgan, Senior, was among the cosmopolitan host who craned their necks to watch the performance of the new vehicle. The Mayor of Rome entertained the brothers and their sister at a palace, where they had to march through endless stately halls of marble columns and rich tapestry with an imposing escort of liveried flunkeys who bowed from the waist to an extreme angle. The Americans liked it better when they went sight-seeing by themselves on their day off, Sunday, the elder brother playing the guide on the basis of his boyhood reading of history. As lovers of Hawthorne, they enjoyed a view of the sculptured Marble Faun in the Capitoline Museum through which they were taken by Mayor Nathan and the curator.

Upon the last day in Rome, Wilbur asked the Contessa di Celleri, who had provided him with the garden cottage, whether she would care to have a ride. She demurred; it was too much for him to do. He replied:

"You have done *everything* to make me comfortable and nothing to make me uncomfortable."

The beaming Contessa yielded and had a most delightful trip.

The travelers were in Paris on the first of May. Katharine had her hair artfully arranged by a *friseur* and to her dismay the bill was twenty-five dollars.

"Never mind, Swes," we may imagine the brothers consoling her. "It's worth the price, even though it couldn't happen in Dayton. It looks very well." . . . Although Will and Orv had been cutting each other's hair in camp between the visits of kings, as they had done in earlier days at Kitty Hawk.

There was a brief visit to Le Mans, where the Aëro Club of Sarthe made presentation of a bronze statue by Louis Carvin, showing the winged muse of aviation above the figures of the American inventors who are perched at the edge of a chasm, gazing upon an eagle in flight. This beautiful work, about a quarter life size, later adorned a hall within the new home in Dayton.

London acclaimed the Wrights as conquering heroes. They were received by Lord Haldane, War Minister, in his office. The Aëronautical Society dined and medalled them. At the Royal Aëro Club dinner the brothers sat between Prince Francis of Teck and Ambassador Whitelaw Reid with their sister close by. There was a toastmaster in red and gold braid with a voice stentorian. At intervals he rose and shouted:

"May it please your Excellency, your Serene Highness, my lords, ladies and gentlemen, the toast is to His Majesty the King." (Clink, clink. Every one: The King! The King!)

"May it please . . . the toast is to Her Majesty the Queen." (Same details. The Queen! The Queen!)

Another to the Prince of Wales, ditto to Parliament, then —

"May it please . . . see that your glasses are charged *to the bumpers; the toast is to the brothers* WILBUR and ORVILLE WRIGHT and-Miss-Wright!" (Business as above, but deafening cheers and clinking glasses sounded like a catastrophe.)

Wilbur spoke for three minutes and Orville managed to utter thanks in three sentences, while the Ambassador made a long fitting speech.

A week later New York endorsed the foreign attitude, and the Aëro Club of America, lukewarm to the inventors two years before, gave them a luncheon. There was likewise a great reception in the home city, an open carriage with flowers, drawn by white horses, to meet the distinguished citizens instead of an old surrey drawn by a single nag as when they returned from Kitty Hawk six years before, ignored as eccentric bicycle men who thought they could fly. The simple dwelling in Hawthorn Street was smothered with flags and paper lanterns for night illumination.

President Taft received the brothers and Katharine at the White House in early June, to present a pair of gold medals, showing busts of the inventors, their machine and the dates of the first hour flight made by Orville at Fort Myer and Wilbur in France. The Aëro Club of America had awarded the medals. President

Taft spoke with pleasant humor and there was an address by Herbert Parsons, Member of Congress.

Back at work in the old alley shop, to build an airplane for the government in place of the one wrecked with Orville the year before, the brothers were interrupted by a two-day medal festival on June 17–18. They received three sets of medals, given by the city of Dayton, the State of Ohio and the Congress of the United States. The latter was authorized by a resolution of Congress, March 4, 1909. It bore the figure of an angel with torch, the words "Shall mount up with wings as eagles" and a further inscription.

If the Wrights had had an astute business manager (they had none) he would have scrutinized all medals in advance and returned them for correction of dates and legends. The gold in them was eighteen carat, the diamonds which adorned some of them were genuine, the art was excellent; but the inscriptions and dates were in effect counterfeit, withholding rightful credit from the inventors, giving rise to future misapprehension and trouble. The modest brothers, when they read their medals did not know what to do about it. Doubtless they felt it was ungrateful to look a gift horse in the mouth. For us to ignore the facts in the matter is to miss an important point in the history of the Wrights and to remain puzzled over its seeming contradictions. One of the medals they could have most dispensed with was the Langley gold medal for aëronautics awarded by the Smithsonian Institution.

No doubt some of the tokens of honor were mislabeled through ignorance and inadvertence, others, apparently, by intent.

Let us glance over the inscriptions upon a number of the trophies.

U. S. Congress: "In recognition and appreciation of their ability, courage and success in navigating the air."

Ohio: "Presented to Wilbur Wright by an act of the General Assembly of the State of Ohio." (A similar medal to Orville)

Dayton: "A testimonial from the citizens of their home in recognition and appreciation of their success in navigating the air."

Aëro Club of America: "W. Wright, Sept. 21, 1908, Le Mans, France. O. Wright, Sept. 9, 1908, Fort Myer, Va., U. S. A."

Smithsonian Institution: "Langley Medal, Wilbur and Orville Wright. MCIX Aërodromics."

English: "Aëro Club of the United Kingdom awarded to Wilbur and Orville Wright for their pioneer work. 1908."

French: "The Academy of Sports. To Wilbur and Orville Wright, the two conquerors of the air."

English: "Presented by the Aëronautical Society of Great Britain to Wilbur and Orville Wright in recognition of their distinguished services to the science of aëronautics. 1908."

French: "Academy of Sciences. Wilbur Wright. 1909. *Caelum patet ibimus lac*." (A duplicate to Orville)

There were also a number of honorary degrees conferred by colleges and learned societies in various countries, including Germany and Austria.

Among all the medals and recognitions there was a

conspicuous absence of the only date which ultimate history will be able to preserve in her crowded calendar — December 17, 1903 — and no specific mention of what occurred on that day.

The brothers arrived at Fort Myer for the second government test in latter June. Father Wright went with them but found that at eighty years there was too much excitement for him and he returned home. If the members of congress were vague in their appraisal of the airplane creators, they were keen to see the machine perform and often adjourned committee sessions especially "to see the flying." President Taft visited the field several times. He found Katharine at the shed one day and identified himself with the words, "I met you at the White House." She answered that she well recalled the nation's chief executive. The brothers worked away on their plane with a special musical emphasis on "Traumerei," which was due to a piano player that had been thrust into their home by an enterprising concern for advertising purposes. They had found it impossible to dislodge the piano. Its *pièce de résistance* they sang, whistled and hummed from morning until night.

They needed music to keep their minds off the ordeal ahead. This was to be the first cross-country flight undertaken in America, and its hazards were great. The brothers accompanied army officers in an inspection of the route to Alexandria and back. The total distance was ten miles but the area was all hills and dales, rocks and woods, without a single landing place in case of trouble. Up to this time no one had ever flown over such rough country. Inventors and copyists alike had risen from smooth fields and had rarely strayed beyond their boundaries.

On the afternoon of July 30 the younger brother and his passenger, Lieutenant Benjamin D. Foulois — later a brigadier general — stepped aboard the plane for the decisive adventure. This was the spot where Orville had crashed less than a year before, sustaining serious injuries, while his companion, Lieutenant Selfridge, had been killed. The pilot and his present passenger well knew the peril but exercised their courage. Wilbur and Katharine, who were present, had more fear than they would admit.

President Taft, a rotund figure with grave face, stood watching the take-off. A great crowd on the military field buzzed with excitement, whispering about the previous accident.

"It's murder!" some declared. "This time both will get killed." . . . "Well, what can you expect of the military gang?"

Orville and his passenger were not laughing this time — perhaps a good omen. The plane became a dot over hills and ravines, then faded out of sight.

Wilbur stood like a statue, field glass to his eyes, a watch in hand. His agitated sister was beside him, biting her lips. He had closely estimated the time in which the plane should reappear. All over the country newspaper bulletins, scanned by awed multitudes, tolled off the minutes — "He's off! . . . One . . . Two . . . Three . . . Out of sight. . . . He should be reported now. . . . He is due. . . . He is overdue!"

The lean hawk face of Wilbur did not move a muscle to indicate his opinion or state of mind. But his forehead became beaded with sweat that rolled down his lined cheeks.

Charley Taylor, trusty mechanic and Sancho Panza to the Wrights, could not stand the strain as the overdue minutes accumulated, and wailed: "He's down! he's down!"

Katharine turned on him with a short sharp reprimand.

"How do *you* know he is down?" she demanded.

Wilbur silently dripped perspiration, his eyes fixed on the empty horizon. A cousin of the Wrights, Professor David W. Dennis, stood beside them.

At the end of four minutes Professor Dennis shouted: "There he is! There he is!"

Wilbur's face relaxed in a great content and Katharine's heart leaped with joy. A mighty cheer and tumult of motor horns arose from the parade grounds, as Orville and his companion came gliding home, and the acclaim was echoed by crowds in distant cities. The delay had been due to wind and a strayed balloon marker. But the plane made a record for passenger transport, fourteen minutes at forty-two miles an hour, and earned a bonus of five thousand dollars for its speed. President Taft congratulated the brothers on the spot.

Soon afterward Orville sailed for Germany with his sister so as to convince the hard-headed sceptics of that land that the air was navigable without aid of gas, a point which the Reich's high officials had not long before refused to concede. Wilbur stayed on this side to fly at the Hudson-Fulton celebration.

New York had its first sight of the airplane on September 29, 1909, when Wilbur rose from Governor's

(ABOVE) *President Taft bemedalling the Wrights with the "Wrong" Medals, at the White House, 1909. Katharine Wright stands beside her brother, Orville.*

(BELOW) *Victor Emmanuel, King of Italy, flanked by the Wright Brothers, at Rome, 1909. His Majesty was keenly interested in the Airplane and democratically cordial toward its Inventors.*

Island, circled it to the shrill salute of all harbor craft, landed and then rose again for a pioneer turn around the head of a well-known bronze lady. It is said that Liberty was flattered by the attention. Sirens screeched, handkerchiefs fluttered, skyscraper windows were black with dotheads of peering pygmies. These were the first flights made over American water. Bleriot had indeed crossed the English Channel two months before, which fostered the belief in some quarters that the French collaborated in the invention of the airplane. But Bleriot himself accorded pioneer honors to the men of Dayton.

The metropolis enjoyed its greatest treat on October 4, when Wilbur traced in the air part of the voyage made up a river by Henry Hudson in his ship the *Half Moon* three centuries before. A million spectators lined the shores and gasped at the sky craft skimming over ten miles of gray water and slate-hued battleships, assembled from the navies of the world. The route was to Grant's Tomb and back, some twenty miles done in about half an hour. A canoe was lashed under the machine. The inventors never used skis or built an amphibian. These are details as subordinate to the essentials of an airplane as a similar variety of ground contact parts in motored land vehicles.

On Wilbur's return from the river trip, he was told the press photographers wished to approach. He said:

"Why, yes, I guess it will be all right for them to come up. But I'll get out of the way."

He had planned to circle Manhattan Island on the same day, but the bursting of a cylinder head in his motor canceled the project.

"No more flights in New York," was his laconic comment.

Meanwhile Orville and Katharine, arriving in Berlin on their joint birthday, August 19, were received as personages of the first rank. The Esplanade Hotel begged the honor of lodging them in its imperial suite, free of charge. After looking over the brocaded walls and marble fittings, the guests agreed that the suite had not been mislabeled. It had dimensions. In fact, the bathroom might almost have served for a hangar, being not less than thirty feet in length. There was, too, a balcony decorated with some flowers, enough to stock a large florist shop.

The Teutonic mind is thoroughgoing. Two years before it had combated the existence of the airplane, despite its creators' pleas and citations of fact. Now the sceptics hailed Orville as a new Merlin, Faust, Loge and every other kind of a *kolossal wunderbar* magician. He was a superman. The populace played a game of reverential tag with his person, crowding around to touch the back of his coat or the edge of his sleeve. A handshake was enough to make an idolator faint.

At the first flight at Tempelhofer Field the crowd almost killed the inventor and his sister with pressing homage, so that afterward they were protected by a hollow square of Uhlans. As their car proceeded through Berlin streets with its clattering escort of cavalry, it was followed by a phalanx of young bicyclists who chanted: "Orevele Wright! Orevele Wright!" A quarter of a million throats bellowed *hoch* at the military field, sounding like a hurricane on a rocky coast.

A jaunty young man stepped from his car at the field. Shaking hands with Orville, he lifted his hat to Katharine with the words, "Is this your sister?"

The Crown Prince forthwith shook hands with Katharine, and then had the Americans meet the Crown Princess Cecilie.

The Kaiser's son quivered with excitement as the airplane roared, shot down its launching track, rose in the air, climbed and circled overhead. As the machine landed he gave vent to his impetuous emotions in terms like these:

"Wonderful! Magnificent! I'm just crazy about it. I'd like to fly with you, Mr. Wright. Will you take me up? Yes, right now!"

Orville did not care for the risk with such a passenger, especially on account of possible objections by his imperial sire, and having practiced the denial of royal pleas upon the King of Spain knew how to smile away the Crown Prince's desire.

The Emperor sent word he wished to meet the Americans at Tegel field on Sunday, August 29. Count Zeppelin was to be on the scene in his newest dirigible. A long-winded court preacher kept Wilhelm so long in Church that all at the field, including the gas-bag contingent hovering above, had to wait for hours. At last a string of tooting cars appeared. Officials became ramrods, goose-stepping soldiers cleared their throats to *hoch*. The War Lord greeted Orville in a friendly manner and conversed with him in fluent English. Katharine, tired of waiting, had wandered off and coolly disregarded the entreaty of a panting general, who had run after her, to return and meet the All Highest. What a woman! She never even asked Orville what he and Wilhelm said to each other on this occasion. Perhaps by this time she had a surfeit of monarchs. This was the fourth, not to mention a president.

Orville had a ride in the Zeppelin from Frankfort to Mannheim, and timing its speed by observation of telegraph poles, gleaned that its rate of travel was twenty-eight miles an hour instead of forty as was asserted.

At this time the Wright brothers were giving their greatest international show in simultaneous competition on both sides the Atlantic, Orville flying before the Kaiser and his hosts, Wilbur thrilling millions of uncrowned New Yorkers. Cables tossed the front page tidings back and forth daily. Brother was eclipsing brother. Wagers were placed on the record-smashing fraternal contest. It was thought to be an arranged affair, but in fact the happy rivalry was due to chance. It just happened on the day that Wilbur flew up the Hudson that Orville in Germany made a new passenger-carrying record of more than an hour and a half, with an altitude record above 1,600 feet.

The younger brother gave lessons in pilotage to Herr Keidel and Captain Paul Engelhardt of the German Wright company, which had been organized a few months before. The company included in its directorate the Krupps, Rathenaus and other.financiers of the first rank. As in the case of the French Wright company, the inventors realized more prestige than profit from the transaction.

The Crown Prince refused to be permanently smiled off from his desire to take an air ride. Telephone operator, maid and hotel proprietor had goose flesh and moaned in awe when the All Highest's son called up. Katharine had to answer the 'phone. Orville interviewed the Empress and diplomatically put the question whether it would be correct to give her eldest son a ride. She said she did not mind. So the Crown Prince was gratified with a brief flight, and he recompensed the inventor with a scarfpin with crown and the letter W set in diamonds.

Kaiser Wilhelm, as reward for a special flight in his presence at Potsdam, gave Orville an autographed photo of his imperially decorated self. Orville, with thanks, handed the picture to his sister.

"I see she has it already," laughed Wilhelm.

"Yes," replied Orville. "President Taft didn't even go through the formality of handing his picture to me. He handed it to her directly."

"That is where the American is more of a cavalier," observed the Kaiser.

Wilhelm showed in a somewhat lengthy chat that he understood the airplane and its future uses, and he gave full credit to the Wrights as the pioneers of the air, despite the current befogging of this issue in the European and especially the French press. He went into a discussion of the patent situation. He spoke of the military uses of the machine, and afterward commented on the ability of the airplane to maneuver quickly. The Kaiser also asked friendly personal questions, among them an inquiry about the inventor's father. Katharine felt that Wilhelm was as agreeable a monarch as she had met.

At this time there was a rival demonstration of

French copyists at the German capital. None could circle or make extended flights with the exception of Latham, who had an Antoinette monoplane equipped with the needful features of wing warping and a movable vertical rudder. He was thus able to fly over Berlin and thereby caused a furor. Orville beheld and smiled. . . .

It may be of interest to note here the aviation progress within the next two decades. Speed increased from less than fifty to three hundred fifty-seven miles an hour. Distance went from a circling jaunt over a smooth field of about a hundred miles to almost four thousand five hundred miles over land and sea. Duration extended from less than three hours to seventeen days — by expedient of refueling in midair. Altitude increased from a third of a mile to more than seven miles, topping earth's highest mountain by a wide margin. The passenger carrying capacity developed from one to one hundred sixty-nine persons!

Wilbur, who had spent the autumn teaching army officers to fly at College Park, Maryland, met his brother and sister on their return to New York from Europe on November 4. Here very shortly the Wright Company, a million-dollar corporation, was formed. Wilbur was president, Orville vice president and the directors included August Belmont, Theodore P. Shonts, Robert J. Collier, Andrew Freedman, Cornelius Vanderbilt, Russell A. Alger, E. J. Berwind, Allan A. Ryan, DeLancey Nicoll and Pliny W. Williamson. As counsel, Frederick P. Fish and Edmund Wetmore were retained. The brothers kept a controlling interest. There was a palatial New York office while the real office was at

(ABOVE) *The Kaiser and Kaiserin at Potsdam, 1909, with Orville Wright standing within Airplane. Wilhelm foresaw military value of the American Invention.*

(BELOW) *Reverent Germans doffing hats to the Yankee Vehicle in 1909. Two years before this, High Officials of the Reich feared to be humbugged by the Wrights' gasless Craft.*

Dayton in the little rooms above the old bicycle shop, reached by alley and wooden stairs.

It is easy to make sophisticated comment after the event and to suggest that the best arrangement for an inventor is to surrender with safeguards absolute control of his rights to a great corporation that will pay him a moderate royalty, attend to all matters of business, and prosecute infringement with ample expenditure and unflagging zeal.

A factory was built at Dayton to manufacture planes. Flying at exhibitions was the chief business in prospect and Roy Knabenshue, a man of dirigible balloon experience, was engaged as exhibition manager. It was arranged that Orville would supervise manufacture and the training of pilots while Wilbur took charge of legal matters.

A preliminary injunction in behalf of the Wright Company against the Herring-Curtiss Company and Glenn H. Curtiss was granted on January 3, 1910, by Judge John R. Hazel of the Federal District Court at Buffalo, New York. The ground for this action was infringement of the brothers' patent. The name heading the company enjoined was that of A. M. Herring, who has become somewhat familiar to the reader of this narrative. In his decision Judge Hazel said:

". . . the defendant Curtiss and the affiant Herring, both officers of the defendant corporation, obtained detailed information prior to the construction of the defendant's machine, as to experiments and pressure of wind on curved and flat planes and mode of maintaining equilibrium in flights, the former through correspondence passing between the patentees and the late

Lieut. Selfridge in January, 1908, and the latter from personal observation and investigation while at the camp of the patentees at Kitty Hawk, N. C., where the earlier Wright experimental flights were conducted, and subsequently both Curtiss and Herring practically admitted that in complainant's machine the problem of equilibrium appeared to have been solved. . . ."

His Honor also stated:

"It appears that the defendant Curtiss had notice of the success of the Wright machine and that a patent had been issued in 1906. Indeed no one [doubtless Judge Hazel meant, in the United States] interfered with the rights of the patentees by constructing machines similar to theirs until in July, 1908, when Curtiss exhibited a flying machine which he called the Junebug. He was immediately notified by the patentees that such machine with its movable surfaces at the tips or wings infringed the patent in suit, and he replied that he did not intend to publicly exhibit the machine for profit, but merely was engaged in exhibiting it for scientific purposes as a member of the Aërial Experiment Association. To this the patentee did not object. Subsequently, however, the machine with supplementary planes placed midway between the upper and lower aëroplanes was publicly exhibited by the defendant corporation and used by Curtiss in aërial flights for prizes and emoluments. It further appears that the defendants now threaten to continue such use for gain and profit and to engage in the manufacture and sale of such infringing machine."

A similar injunction in behalf of the Wright Company against Louis Paulhan, a French aviator temporarily in this country, was granted on February 17 of the same year by Judge Learned Hand at New York City. Judge Hand, who was later elevated to the Federal Circuit Court, distinguished himself by stemming the tide of public hysteria during the World War, and in this case indicated his impartiality by rebuking one of the Wright counsel for reference to the fact that Paulhan was an alien. The decision held, among other things, that it was an obvious evasion to disconnect the vertical rudder from the balancing ailerons and to operate the rudder separately but still as an auxiliary of the balancing process. Ailerons or flaps amounted to the same thing as a warp. It was noted that the defendant used Bleriot and Farman planes. It did not matter that the free rudder was used partly for steering and again as an aid to balance.

Judge Hand reviewed a multitude of prior claims or inventions, which were offered as anticipations of the Wrights' discovery. This review is summarized by the writer as follows:

D'Esterno: There was meager evidence as to the nature of this machine and "no proof that it was ever used or became more than a paper description."

Le Bris: "This is a description of the same kind which is too inadequate to understand or to give effect to."

Mouillard: "In no one of the nineteen claims is there anything which in any way even foreshadows the patent in suit."

Mattulath: "This was an abandoned patent," and there was no evidence to show that the Wrights "borrowed any ideas from Mattulath."

Zahm: He had an idea in 1894 to put slats in wings

but "It was at most only a speculative suggestion never reduced to practical form."

Ader: He thought a vertical rudder might be useful but regarded it as a "matter of preference." He had no idea of any connection between wings and his optional rudder.

"Bechtel; Crepar; Johnson; Stanley; Marriott; these are all for lateral planes to dirigible balloons. The whole problem is so entirely different when suspension is effected by a reservoir containing a lighter gas than air, that there is not the least resemblance between the patents and the patent in suit."

Boswell: "This is a device to be attached to a dirigible airship . . . and it is so wholly unlike the patent in suit both in structure and operation that I can see no similarity between them."

Davidson: "This is an English patent, and is not in the least like the patent in suit."

Lampson: "I cannot see any relevancy in this patent."

As the legal skirmish gradually developed toward the opening of battle on both sides the Atlantic, colleges bethought them to grant degrees to the men who had never gone beyond high school. Academic authorities looked up the word aërodynamics in the dictionary and wondered what titles would be suitable to bestow. The busy inventors found it difficult to keep track of the numerous honors. One day at a New York railroad station, homeward bound with brother and sister, Wilbur searched his waistcoat pockets for tickets. A bit of red ribbon fell on the floor. Katharine called his attention to it.

"Oh, yes, I forgot to tell you about that," said Wilbur, picking up the ribbon and handing it to his sister.

It was the ribbon of the Legion of Honor which the brothers had received that afternoon at the hands of the French consul.

Father Wright decided that in his eighty-second year it was time to test his sons' invention, and Orville obliged him at the home flying field. The Bishop noted the details on a photograph as follows:

"Milton Wright's flight, May 25, 1910. I arose to 350 feet. About 280 feet in the within picture."

Instead of being satisfied with the top altitude, which was somewhat better than the Bishop's estimate, the exhilarated passenger wished to exceed it and at the ceiling shouted to the pilot:

"Higher!"

Orville disregarded the paternal command through a sense of duty.

Never deigning to inform his son as to his final reactions on flight or his general opinion of the airplane as a vehicle, the Bishop afterward remarked to a neighbor:

"People look pretty small down there."

Charles D. Walcott, Secretary and virtual head of the Smithsonian Institution, wrote to Wilbur on March 7, 1910, saying that the National Museum would like to place a Wright machine or model on exhibition. Wilbur replied on March 26 expressing a desire to comply. He wrote: "We might construct a small model showing the general construction of the airplane, but with a dummy power plant. Or we can reconstruct the 1903 machine with which the first flights were made at Kitty Hawk. Most of the parts are still in existence. This machine would occupy a space 40 feet by 20 feet by 8 feet. Or a model showing the general design of the latter machine could be constructed."

To which the following reply terminated the correspondence:

Smithsonian Institution,
Washington, U. S. A.
April 11, 1910.

DEAR MR. WRIGHT:

Yours of March 26th came duly to hand, and the matter of the representation of the Wright airplane has been very carefully considered by Mr. George C. Maynard, who has charge of the Division of Technology in the National Museum. I told him to indicate what he would like for the exhibit, in order that the matter might be placed clearly before you and your brother. In his report he says:

The following objects illustrating the Wright inventions would make a very valuable addition to the aëronautical exhibits in the Museum:

1. A quarter-size model of the airplane used by Orville Wright at Fort Myer, Virginia, in September, 1908. Such a model equipped with a dummy power plant, as suggested by the Wrights, would be quite suitable.

2. If there are any radical differences between the machine referred to and the one used at Kitty Hawk, a second model of the latter machine would be very appropriate.

3. A full-size Wright airplane. Inasmuch as the machine used at Fort Myer has attracted such world-wide interest, that machine, if it can be repaired or reconstructed, would seem most suitable. If, however, the Wright brothers think the Kitty Hawk machine would answer the purpose better, their judgment might decide the question.

4. If the Wright brothers have an engine of an early

type used by them which could be placed in a floor case for close inspection that will be desirable.

The engine of the Langley Aërodrome is now on exhibition in a glass case and the original full-size machine is soon to be hung in one of the large halls. The three Langley quarter-size models are on exhibition. The natural plan would be to install the different Wright machines along with the Langley machines, making the exhibit illustrate two very important steps in the history of the aëronautical art.

The request of Mr. Maynard is rather a large one, but we will have to leave it to your discretion as to what you think it is practicable for you to do.

Sincerely yours,
CHARLES D. WALCOTT,
Secretary.

Mr. Wilbur Wright,
1127 West Third Street,
Dayton, Ohio.

The Wrights never replied to this letter. No doubt the fact that two Federal judges had so lately upheld their pioneer claims made them the more inclined to view the Smithsonian proposal with distrust. Indeed, was not the scientific group at the capital, who sought to pair Wright and Langley models, aiming to reverse the judicial decision as well as to negate historical truth? To be sure, the injunctions of Judges Hazel and Hand were dissolved by the Federal Circuit Court of Appeals on June 14, 1910, but the grounds were partly technical and there was no obstacle to a suit for infringement in the usual court procedure.

It was at this time also that the brothers were privately fortified by a letter from Lord Northcliffe, the foremost journalist of the period, who had aided in the weight-hauling launching ceremonies at Pau. The letter follows:

THE TIMES

26th May, 1910.

MY DEAR MISS WRIGHT:

I was very sorry to hear that anyone had said that I expressed surprise that your brothers did not enter for the various prizes that I have offered. I have never said anything of the kind. If they cared to enter for contests for their own amusement, one could possibly understand it; or, if they care to make exhibitions on national occasions, such as the Hudson-Fulton celebration, that also I could understand. But I have never made any statement other than that your brothers, the absolute inventors of all that is going on to-day in aviation, have by their natural instinct of American gentle folk and by the lofty nature of great minds, stood aside while others have exploited the fruits of their genius. That attitude is very well understood in England. . .

I have always two fears with regard to your brothers: firstly, that they will be robbed of the proper pecuniary reward of their many years of achievement under restraint; secondly, that dishonest men may (as in the case of the Dunlop tyre) so confuse the original issue that in the future there might be the same sort of doubt as exists to-day about the originator of the steamboat (which, as you know, Fulton was by no means the first to invent) the electric telegraph, the photograph and the bicycle. So far as England is concerned, I am resolved that that doubt shall never exist as to the aëroplane, and, on the occasion of the Manchester flight, I at once telegraphed to London from the Mediterranean, where I was, that in every reference to the flight credit to your brothers, as it was due, should be given in all my papers, editorially and in the reporting. . . .

I made a holiday trip in your West last autumn, and

hardly any of the newspapers would print what I said about Cook. Peary spent twenty-seven of the best years of his life getting to the North Pole, and got there, as assuredly as your brothers were the first persons to leave the earth in a mechanically propelled plane and to invent the means of controlling that plane. I did not find many Americans who realized what your brothers had done. I must except Mr. and Mrs. Roosevelt. Some seemed to regard it as a sort of vaudeville entertainment. . . .

[Apropos vaudeville, Lord Northcliffe wonders if Wilbur remembers acrobats, "Curzon brother and sisters", who applied for admission to his quarters at Pau, France, on the ground that "they were in the same line of business."]

I rejoice to hear two things; that your brothers are going on with their scientific work, and that there is a powerful body of men banded together to see that they are not robbed in order that rogues may be fattened. . . .

With our kind regards and respectful homage to you and your brothers.

Yours sincerely,
NORTHCLIFFE.

Miss K. Wright.

In June each brother received the degree of Doctor of Laws from Oberlin College and they accompanied their sister to her alma mater for the occasion. The site of the college is a town in Ohio not far from the city of Cleveland. The religious auspices were or used to be Congregational. Oberlin was the first of American colleges to admit women students and was also a pioneer, much antedating the Civil War, in the admission of Negroes. There were some two thousand students of both sexes at this time. Father Wright had sent Katharine here with some effort, on the theory that a woman especially needed an education in order to make a living.

At the alumni dinner public evidence was given of the close and sympathetic interest with which the brothers had followed Katharine's academic career. Indeed Wilbur's speech scandalized his sister by its references to undignified but humorous episodes of her undergraduate days which classmates were able to recognize. Wilbur released more intimate history of the same sort at the '98 class reunion, when Katharine was perhaps fortunately absent. Orville was also in touch with everything. It was recalled that he once amazed one of his sister's classmates, visiting in Dayton, by catching up the name mentioned and asking, "Which Whitney — the dark or the light Whitney?" It appears there was a blond and a brunette person of the same name.

Wilbur visited the South in the spring to find a training field for pilots and selected a site at Montgomery, Alabama, where the climate would permit activities throughout the year. His brother there instructed Brookins, Hoxsey and other candidates for the crew of Wright exhibition flyers. During the summer Brookins won a five thousand dollar prize awarded by a Chicago newspaper for a flight between the metropolis of the Middle West and Springfield, Illinois. Ex-President Roosevelt, who as chief executive had prodded the War Department to overcome its inertia and take action on the airplane which it had sent abroad, had an ascent with Hoxsey at St. Louis. There were exhibitions at Indianapolis, Asbury Park, Atlantic City and elsewhere.

There were domestic and foreign aviators with all kinds of machines in competition with the Wright flyers during this period. Such a situation did not improve the public understanding of the origin of the airplane. It intensified the confusion which already prevailed. Why did the inventors tolerate it and thus contribute to their own disadvantage? It was their policy, mistaken or otherwise, to coöperate with all and sundry in the promotion of an art yet in its infancy. They were pressing their rightful claims in a legal orderly way and felt that refusal to meet others in public events would be poor sportsmanship. If they had refused to coöperate, less flying would have been done and the cry of selfish monopoly would have been raised.

They did specifically reserve their legal rights when they agreed to a limited truce of court proceedings during certain of the public exhibitions. For example, the promoters of the St. Louis meet were licensed to operate provided, among other things, they advertised the fact "that all aviators and machines other than the Wright, which take part in this meet" were "under a special license granted by the Wright Company for this meet only." The latter company also agreed "to make no further charge against infringing machines" for the occasion. It was to supply five or more planes with pilots and was to receive half of the total gross receipts. The document, dated May 19, 1910, was subscribed by the Aëro Club of St. Louis through its president, A. B. Lambert. The meet was to be held October 8–18 of the same year.

The first international aviation meet in this country was held at Belmont Park, which is suburban to New

York City, in latter October, 1910. There were great crowds at this race-track field and the air was filled with the drone of varied machines that rose to seemingly dizzy altitudes and swooped perilously past the thrilled occupants of the grand stand. The air men of all nations seemed to be one happy family in a friendly contest. The press acclaimed the visitors as independent inventors and the public's hazy impression was confirmed that there were many fingers in the flying-machine pie. Indeed the variety of shapes and styles, not to mention color and decorations, infallibly suggested a diverse origin to the laity. A monoplane was one thing and a biplane another, one propeller was different from two, and a scalloped tail was quite unlike a square one. The French machines scored in beauty and grace, as the lady press writers stated. On the other hand the Wright double-deckers obtained most of the prizes and daily made ascents in winds which daunted the foreigners. There was a windy Sabbath when the Frenchmen discovered that one of the ten commandments coincided with the prohibition of the Beaufort scale. C. F. Bishop, President of the Aëro Club of America, called Wilbur by telephone at his New York hotel and held a conversation somewhat as follows:

"There is a great emergency down here, Mr. Wright. Twenty thousand people are inside and nobody wants to fly for them! Won't you kindly make an exception in your rule and let some of your men go up?"

"Can't do it, Bishop. Sorry."

The Wrights were never exponents of blue laws, and they had no thought of imposing on others their own preferences.

The First International Aviation Meet in America, Belmont Park, N. Y., 1910. The Wright Plane is at the top and various French Models are below. The origin of the Airplane was further befogged by such an apparently amicable rivalry between inventors and copyists.

Soon afterward Orville went abroad to look after matters of business, and while there learned with regret of the death of Ralph Johnston at a Denver field on November 17. Another Wright pilot, Hoxsey, who had taken up Ex-President Roosevelt, met his death in California on the last day of the year, at the same time that John V. Moisant, an independent aviator, was killed at New Orleans.

The brothers ever sought to prevent their pilots from taking undue risks and urged upon them the caution which they observed themselves. It did not matter what sensational feats others attempted, these flyers were commanded to remain within the limits of safety. Nor were the orders perfunctory. One day Wilbur arrived at Detroit without notice and bought himself a half-dollar seat at the field where his men were performing. Hoxsey and Johnston were in the air exhibiting their keen personal rivalry in a series of breathtaking maneuvers. Wilbur left a note of sharp rebuke for each star and quietly departed.

The reasonable prudence of the brothers, without which the airplane would not have been invented, was the occasion of a sneer by opposing counsel in an address to Judge Hazel: they went all the way from Dayton to Kitty Hawk to find "a feather bed to fall on." They had "a perfect genius for caution." Elsewhere counsel reflected a good portion of public sentiment of the time when he intimated that the chief use of the airplane was to "break the necks of hundreds."

To avoid confusion in legal matters it may be useful to state here that in effect there was only one lawsuit conducted by the Wrights in America — that against Curtiss or concerns bearing his name. Paulhan and Herring soon faded from the scene, although the latter's name was kept on the court documents. (The Herring-Curtiss Company early went into bankruptcy.) There were major legal conflicts in France and Germany, and a minor one in England. The other nations appeared as innocent onlookers, save that czarist Russia thriftily helped itself to the matter in issue without asking permission of any one.

Wilbur went to Europe in March, 1911, to testify in the French suit for infringement against eleven builders or users of planes. He proceeded to Germany and on April 23 paid a visit of respect to the widow of Otto Lilienthal, whose death by a gliding mishap in 1896 started the men of Dayton on the serious study which led to a triumph. The visitor told Frau Lilienthal of the inspirational debt that he and his brother owed to her husband, who had excelled all others of his time in his approach to the problem of flight. There was kindness and sympathy in the stranger's words, a note of homage in his attitude which he had scarcely shown in contacts with royalty. It was a timely tribute to a brave and noble German, compatriot of Wilbur's maternal grandfather; for the inventor had but another year to live.

There had been an effort in France to maintain that Santos-Dumont, who made his first flight in November, 1906, was the world's pioneer in aviation. The date proved to be too recent and the name of Clement Ader, who built a machine toward the end of the nineteenth century, was brought forward as a substitute. The

French Minister of War had a secret official report on a government trial of the Ader machine and had declined to publish it at the request of the Wrights. But now patriotism on the part of plane builders demanded and compelled the publication of the secret report. This showed that the device had never left the ground; it had lifted part of its own weight as indicated by the "lightening of its tracks." The government would not pay for further experiment.

Wilbur saw this machine on two occasions in its place of rest, the Musée des Arts et Metiers at Paris. Once the court adjourned to look it over and again Wilbur, with the permission of the curator, climbed a ladder and studied the apparatus at his leisure. He noted that there was a hand wheel which, being turned thirty or forty times, moved the wings four to five inches!

The American inventor used the word "preposterous" — a word of unusual strength for him — in summing up his estimate of the Ader machine, which closely imitated animal or bird physiology, including a "multitude of pieces, cords, ligaments and so on . . . for which no use is disclosed. . . . It disregards all principles of machine design in a slavish attempt to imitate nature. Various parts are included merely because bats or birds possess such parts."

The case was tried before the Third Tribunal of The Seine with three judges and a so-called Substitute or State's attorney of technical knowledge, who advised the court and gave a separate opinion in advance. Of him Wilbur said:

"He gave us bushels of brightly colored husks but the kernels went to the infringers."

The Substitute awarded the Wrights credit for their invention but unfortunately they had lost title through the early disclosures made by Octave Chanute in Europe and by Wilbur in his two addresses on gliding before the Western Society of Engineers at Chicago. Besides, they had patented the machine before it was practical, unable to make turns. Further, the patent only provided for a joint mechanical operation of wings and vertical rudder, overlooking the possibility of separate hand-control of the rudder as discovered by copyists. Finally, however, there were no prior inventors who anticipated the Americans. These were indeed "brightly colored husks" of compliment!

A month later, in the spring of 1911, the tribunal of three judges rendered a decision which supported much of the Substitute's opinion but held that "any means" in the Wright patent included human as well as mechanical operation of wings and vertical rudder. However, the disconnection of wing and rudder ropes was not an evasion but an improvement under the patent. The last point was decisive and most alarming to the defense. It gave them in turn the bright husk of an ingenious improvement but suggested a basic debt payable to the Americans. Bleriot, the largest builder of aircraft, wished to concede the patent and settle with the Wrights. He signed a preliminary agreement to this end. But there was an outburst of patriotism on the part of other manufacturers and an appeal was made to a higher court. The patriotic group was led by Esnault-Pelterie, who was next to Ferber in early experiment. One can hardly refrain from repeating here an earlier tribute to the courage of those Frenchmen who first hopped with a mere simulacrum of the airplane. One of these, the early Voisin, was cited by a defense counsel in the suit in America as triumphant evidence that an air vehicle required practically nothing but a steering rudder which also gave it balance.

For the last two years of his life Wilbur's time was largely absorbed by litigation and it became an increasing burden to him. The case was highly complicated and technical from the legal viewpoint. It was a delightful challenge to a host of erudite lawyers in three countries, as fascinating as a mysterious new disease to a congress of doctors. Almost no one knew anything about the subject but every one soon qualified by a course of reading. Few reckoned that the reading matter was almost void of information.

James W. See, a mechanical engineer of high standing, who was one of the chief witnesses for the Wrights in the American suit, said to opposing counsel:

". . . I propose right now to take a little time and send along with the record a justification of my ignorance in case this cross-examination runs very far into lines about which neither you nor I know anything with certainty. The art of practical flying is a new art, born yesterday, so to speak. Before the birth of this practical art there was an imposing bibliography of the science, much of which had been accepted as gospel. . . . Now . . . grave errors have been discovered and, greatest of all, it has been proven that we are greatly in the dark."

The dusty archives of patent offices in every land

were searched for patents of the remotest applicability to flight, whether pertaining to gliders, balloons, marine vessels or to pure fantasies of hallucinated inventors. Words and phrases were twisted to show that a glimmering surmise was a valid anticipation of the brothers' actual achievement. Suddenly the gloomy record of failure in an obscure necromantic field became a brilliant scene of triumph in prior art which only culminated in a lucky accident at Kitty Hawk. In truth the Wright machine as patented was a poor thing at best; it would "stagger over the face of the country like a drunken sailor." On the other hand, Pilcher and Lilienthal had produced "successful, practical gliding machines." — although both were killed by them.

The angle of incidence was bandied about the courtrooms, declaimed and conjugated in three languages. Lift and drift were used in threatening tones, while relative wind and torque sounded as defamatory epithets. Judges brushed up their trigonometry and met counsel halfway with remarks on cosines of given angles. Experts were produced after some effort, ranging from very youthful flyers to a scientist who sounded Wilbur carefully as to how long his services would be required and who finally demurred at supporting a patent "monopoly" against the public interest.

Thanks to their early reading, the brothers were familiar with the antiquarian lore of flight, knew it better than their antagonists, and could often cancel in a few words a laborious hypothesis founded on dusty legend.

A new science and a new art had arisen in the world.

It is no wonder that even upright judges and honest lawyers had their heads turned and groped in a cimmerian forest of bewilderment. They could not understand that a new law of nature had been incorporated in a vehicle. One miracle called for another. The attitude was like that of the French commission at Dayton. There should be all kinds of new treasure in the aërodynamic mine and many ways to recover it. The sky was open for any one to enter with another and perhaps better style of carriage.

One of the American judges in this case could well have said of it what he did in regard to another scientific issue before him:

"I ought to have gone to Massachusetts Tech. instead of to a law school."

There was some alleviation in the fact that a jury trial was avoided and twelve good men and true did not have to struggle with a question that baffled bench and bar.

Wilbur used his great knowledge and rare memory in a way that amazed when it did not discomfit his adversaries. He revealed himself as a born teacher, able to clarify and illuminate the most complex problems. He excelled his brother in this gift. He knew the theory of the airplane as well as its practice, and lectured upon both at length in depositions for judicial use. At the injunction hearing before Judge Hand, he chanced to arrive in court at a moment when one of his own counsel was puzzled over a certain point. Wilbur asked permission to lighten the obscurity. He walked to a blackboard on the wall and, with chalk and a bit of string, drew some diagrams.

"If it hadn't been for Wright and his old string," remarked Clarence J. Shearn, defense attorney and later a justice of the State Supreme Court, "we would have won the case."

Apropos expert and other eyewitness testimony, the inventor in a deposition cited the following instance of lack of observation: In going left on a bicycle, most persons said they turned the handle bars left. Was this correct? It seemed to be, yet in fact it was necessary first to turn the front wheel slightly to the right. Aviators were inclined to similar errors of observation. They did not know what happened in the air. After thirteen years' experience, Wilbur had found that "the best guide to accurate observation is a correct understanding of the physical laws involved." He was continually emphasizing the physical laws, going back to them to explain complicated phenomena, reiterating the Newtonian first principles like a pedagogue with a dull class. The brothers both had anchored their minds to basic truths, and they clung to them with almost fanatic tenacity.

It would be strange if Wilbur's memory, though it was like a photographic plate, had never failed when taxed with recalling a thousand details of an experience equal to several average lifetimes. Thus, according to his brother in later years, he was mistaken in regard to certain observations made upon the flight of pigeons. Again he appeared to err in saying that no free glides with the warping device in operation were made in 1900, the first year at Kitty Hawk. Aside from these matters, any pettifogging lawyer could find ammunition in parts of Wilbur's early writing, as in 1901,

when, on the threshold of first-hand discovery with his
brother, he credited the air tables of Langley, Lilienthal,
Chanute and the rest as having "a good degree of
accuracy."

CHAPTER XII

When Wilbur returned from Europe in August, 1911, he learned that his brother had planned a vacation camping trip to Kitty Hawk with a program of renewing the pioneer sport with a glider. It would be play combined with a moderate flavor of science. He said enviously:

"I'd go too if I didn't have fifty law-suits."

There were also other matters to look after, as a meet in Chicago; and Cal Rodgers was practicing at Dayton in preparation for the cross continental flight for which a prize of fifty thousand dollars had been offered.

The camping party consisted of Orville, his brother Lorin, the latter's ten-year-old son Horace (Buster to his fond uncle and family), and Alexander Ogilvie, an English friend of the inventors who had crossed the ocean upon invitation to join the excursion. There was care-free solitude for a few days beside the Atlantic and then the pressmen arrived. However, they did not greatly interfere with pastime or experiment. There was a new glider which was considerable of a refinement beyond the last machine of this type which the brothers had practiced with here nine years before. The pilot found its control much easier because of improved construction and perhaps more because of his expertness in handling and his knowledge of favorable rising air currents. He had learned much of the birds' secret of soaring. He recalled an experience at Montgomery, Alabama, where heated air rose above dark plowed ground and wafted his plane upwards during a period of five minutes or more, despite the use of all engine power to descend.

There was a fifty-mile gale sweeping inland over Kill Devil Hill, birthplace of the airplane, when Orville rose in his glider. He soared into the teeth of the wind which daunted wild fowl and caused ships to take in sail. He moved the great pinions in easy mastery of angry gusts. Over the top of the hill, advancing and retreating before the thunderous margin of the ocean, Orville hovered for a period of nine and three quarters minutes. The best previous performance by the Wrights in flight without a motor had been about one minute, while the nearest approach to that record by any other human being before them had been some thirty seconds, achieved by Lilienthal. The structure of the German's glider required a speed of not less than thirty feet a second and the distance given for his longest flight thus limited his time in the air to about half a minute.

Orville's performance stood as a world's record for a number of years. It was marvelous for its time although now far eclipsed. The Germans, banned from building power craft by the treaty of Versailles after the World War, proved the uses of adversity by leading all nations in the art of motorless flight. They have glided fourteen hours solo, nine with a passenger, and have soared nonstop a circuit of three hundred miles. A fascinating new era seems to be opening. It is in order that landscapes should be mapped with their invisible columns of support for the future traveler, winging his way across valleys and along the sides of mountain chains. He may find a convenient if somewhat leisurely daytime route for going from one end of the country to the other. Like a marine sailing vessel with auxiliary power, he may have a tiny motor to cover the gaps between the regions favorable to gliding.

Despite his aptness in teaching and exposition, Wilbur detested the legal conflict with its hair-splitting quibbles and ritualistic absurdities. The devious methods and endless delays bore him down. He worried and fretted. He often declared that he would rather lose the case than have it drag on. He could not see that there was anything constructive or useful in litigation. He did not belong to the breed of talkers. Moreover, he felt the injustice of the proceedings done in the name of equity; perhaps more keenly than Orville because of his immediate contact with the harassing details. After a session with the lawyers, Wilbur would "come home white." The effect of the same ordeal upon Orville afterward was to make him ill for two days. But on the whole the younger brother had more philosophy or resignation, which he thus expressed:

"We have fared a good deal better than most inventors. Most inventors get nothing, either credit or money."

It is probable that Wilbur suffered more because the struggle impaired his health and his nervous system. He was tired out while yet in his prime. He complained little, even to those nearest to him. They gathered what was in his mind by incidental expressions rather than direct statements. For example, he said in his latter days that when he was through with law-suits, he wished to devote the rest of his life to obtaining justice for inventors. His own predicament aroused his sympathy for the other creators and benefactors.

The brothers used to agree on the statement:

"In the days of the invention it was all fun and no worry, but when we succeeded it was all worry and no fun."

They had foreseen a painful ordeal in the marketing of their discovery and had early sought to leave the repugnant arena of business and to retire to the laboratory of their dreams. They were scientists and had no interest in the arts of barter and trade. The world forced business and law-suits upon two of its most gifted creators. If it was wasteful of genius for England to give Robert Burns employment at gaging whiskey barrels, it was no less shortsighted of America to give the Wrights the task of combating law-suits and of becoming business men.

During the preceding fall and winter, Wilbur had been away from home for long weeks, squandering time and vitality in courtrooms and lawyers' offices, but in the spring of 1912 he had a brief respite with his family. There was a project to build a new house. A site not far from the old homestead was chosen but Katharine persuaded Wilbur to approve a more desirable location in a high suburb of Dayton. Orville, learning of the change, said, "Nonsense!" Wilbur then saw it was nonsense, but the sister as mistress of the house had the final decision. The four members of the family visited the site in Oakwood village, about two miles south of Dayton, on Thursday, May 2. A knoll upon the seventeen-acre wooded tract was christened Hawthorn Hill, the very spot where the future dwelling would stand. It was a splendid bit of wilderness, flanked by a public park in a state of natural beauty. The redbuds, which are native ornamental shrubs or small trees, were in magnificent bloom.

Each person told what he wanted in the new house. Father Wright was to have a large room that would be cool in hot weather without recourse to an ingenious expedient which his sons had devised in the old home. Wilbur had always said:

"All I want is a bathroom for myself."

But his wish was not gratified. He never saw the new dwelling. The little group separated, Orville and his father returning home in an old two-seat roadster, Wilbur and his sister by street car. Then the brothers proceeded to their flying field, which was still a cow pasture, to test some of the half dozen machines ordered by the United States Government.

On the return from the field the next afternoon, Orville noticed that his brother was very quiet. It was the servant's day out and Katharine, who prepared supper, noted that Wilbur did not eat much. He was at his office the next morning and after luncheon at home said, "Guess I'll lie down awhile. Don't feel very good." But soon he said to his sister, "Guess I'll go out to the field." Katharine saw that he was feverish and would not permit him to go. Doctor D. B. Conklin was sent for in the late afternoon and he ordered the patient to bed.

It was nearly a week after the first symptoms before the case was diagnosed as typhoid fever. Wilbur knew by Wednesday, the eighth, that he had a serious ailment, having surreptitiously learned his temperature by means of a clinical thermometer. On the Sunday before he fell ill he had said to his brother:

"We're going to lose the . . . case."

"Nonsense!" Orville had replied.

Wilbur became very nervous and excitable. He was again in the courtroom, outlining history to lawyers and judges, explaining and explaining, but neither the crystal clarity of his exposition nor the merit of his case had any effect. He labored for hours over interminable details in a New York courtroom and then hastened to another on the banks of the Seine to resume the contest against finespun technicalities.

There were soon two nurses in attendance. A fortnight after the first onset, Orville's presence in Washington was urgent in connection with the government business. The physician assured him that he might safely take the trip and he left on the sixteenth without telling his brother. Wilbur asked for him the next morning and on learning where he had gone, became excited and worried, although assured that Orville would be back immediately.

Wilbur had said not long before that he would like to devote the rest of his life to helping inventors. Now in his last illness his fevered mind doubtless reviewed the long roll of buffeted and baffled creators to whom our civilization owes a debt.

He thought of the American pioneer whose cotton gin enriched the South and indeed made the young republic prosperous, an invention appropriated by burglary as well as by the usual infringement. Eli Whitney stated that he had no recompense for his epochal benefaction. He was hard put to prove in a Southern court that his machine was in use at the moment when the noise of three gins at work within fifty yards reached the entrance of the courthouse. (The sick man smiles wryly. Justice deaf as well as blind!) Whitney well understood a universal principle, later elaborated and termed economic determinism. . . . "I should have had no difficulty in causing my rights to be respected if it had been less valuable. . . ." (How true! Exactly as in the case of the airplane.) After years of legal fencing, South Carolina awarded the inventor fifty thousand dollars and the other cotton States gave paper promises which were not redeemed. (Probably the lawyers got the fifty thousand dollars, since Whitney declared he had no profit at all from his machine.)

There was another American whose discovery revolutionized modern life. After years of starvation and a term in debtor's prison, Charles Goodyear patented his rubber-vulcanizing process. It was infringed right and left. He went abroad to fight for his rights (somewhat like two brothers of Dayton half a century later); lost . . . pawned his wife's jewels in order to pay for a passage home . . . died some years afterward, leaving a *minus* estate — debts, in short — of $200,000. A little help would have been appreciated by a man in his position. There might be another Goodyear, alive and struggling, whom one could help. He could be pulled right out of his hole and set upon his feet. (What

a thirst this fever gives! A mountain lake of icy water
. . . sparkling atop the Pyrenees . . . water!)

Lord Northcliffe hauled on the derrick weight at
Pau when the King of England — no, that's not the
point at all — Northcliffe wrote he feared "that dishonest men may (as in the case of the Dunlop tyre)
so confuse the original issue." Dunlop was evidently
another one.

They say that Westinghouse, the air-brake man,
has become sort of a figurehead. . . . A chap named
George E. Whitney is credited with starting two flour-
ishing automobile businesses on the basis of his patent,
but he is not listed in Bradstreet. . . . Christopher
Latham Sholes was an American who spent all his
money and mortgaged his home . . . (nothing original
in that; anyhow Number 7 Hawthorn Street was mortgaged too) . . . then sold his typewriter invention for
twelve thousand dollars cash . . . and lived to see his
machine in world-wide use.

Used to be a high school at Richmond, Indiana. A
lot of kite-making and flying there too — Orville sold
some to the local boys. And a turning lathe with marble
ball bearings that made more noise than a cyclone. . . .
What's the connection? . . . Oh, yes, C. Francis Jen-
kins, a local boy, gave a demonstration there of his
machine for putting moving pictures on a screen. Others
contributed something but he was the first practical
one and all this new industry or art is founded on
his work. You don't see him listed among the million-
aires.

Yes, there are plenty of struggling inventors trying
to keep their heads above water. (Water! Just a lake

full of the coldest to drink!) . . . It would be fine to
help them. The biggest investment in the world is to
help others. . . . They need help. . . . It will be a
good thing to spend the rest of one's life that way. . . .
If it is — not — too late. . . .

On the night of Friday, the seventeenth, Wilbur almost had convulsions and after recovering a little told
the doctor:

"It was just nerves, I guess."

A hypodermic injection was given and the patient
was never ‚again conscious — save for an instant —
remaining in a stupor. Besides Doctor L. Spitler, the
family physician, there was consultation with Doctor
Forscheimer, a specialist of Cincinnati. The two local
doctors came twice a day, one of them also calling at
night. The eldest brother, Reuchlin, arrived from his
home in Kansas on May 24. Two days later on Sunday morning Wilbur's temperature was lower. It was
the first hopeful sign in ten days. Orville at breakfast
said:

"I'll have another cup of coffee on that."

Katharine had her first brief outing in a fortnight,
but on her return from the walk, she saw that her
brother was worse.

It was impossible to escape from poignant memories
and lacerating suggestions anywhere within or without the little frame homestead. At meals one recalled
that under the gaslight in this room an intense, flashing-
eyed young man had twisted a pasteboard box
before the astonished gaze of his younger brother. Here
a helicopter toy had spun to the ceiling while two little
boys exclaimed in rapture. Within a step was the newel

post carved by Orville and the stairs built by the brothers. Wilbur had leaned over the newel post at the first landing, talking with father and sister on the night of triumphant return from Kitty Hawk.

Perhaps there would be escape outdoors. But no. On this lawn, green under the gentle sunshine, a brisk young man hummed, whistled and sang as he laid out cloth for wings, and then ran up the seams upon a sewing machine. Even the street reminded of things nevermore to be — it was his daily route to shop and office, with every trifling detail on the way faithfully recorded on the sensitive film of his mind.

On Tuesday night the family was called together but there was a revival through stimulants. On Wednesday morning Wilbur, though unable to speak, smiled at Orville in a fleeting return to consciousness, and was better until overtaken by a chill. Again that evening the family was called together, but the patient rallied. The next morning at a quarter past three o'clock on May 30, with the father, three brothers and sister at his bedside, Wilbur died. His age was forty-five years and forty-four days.

President Taft had sent a telegram which arrived when Wilbur was unconscious. Now messages came from many parts of this country and from foreign lands. The King of Spain cabled: "The Queen and I send deepest sympathy to you and your sister." Another cable read: "Deepest sympathy dear Katharine and Orville Wright. Very great grief in England at world's loss. Lord and Lady Northcliffe." On Saturday, June 1, all church bells in Dayton tolled. The remains were in state in the First Presbyterian Church from morning until time for the service at three o'clock in the afternoon, and thousands of people walked past the coffin. A special train from New York had brought Robert J. Collier, the publisher — with members of the Aëro Club of America, and other friends. There was no music and the entire funeral service lasted some twenty minutes. Reverend Doctor Maurice E. Wilson, pastor of the church, read scriptural passages and an outline of Wilbur's career, chiefly told in dates, as written by Reuchlin. A member of the United Brethren Church whom Wilbur had always liked came from his home in Huntington, Indiana, and read Luther's hymn, "A Mighty Fortress is Our Lord." The interment was in a local cemetery.

Wilbur left an estate which would seem large if we did not consider the fact that it was in good part capital in a hazardous new industry and all of it subject to a heavy deduction by the costs of law-suits, present and future, perhaps an endless drain. Moreover the total estimate of two hundred and seventy-seven thousand dollars, as submitted to the probate court by Orville as executor, included the problematical value of patent rights. Half of the total inventory was stock in the Wright Company; no value was assigned to similar stock in foreign companies. There were bequests of fifty thousand dollars each to the two elder brothers and the sister; a remembrance of a thousand dollars to the father, and the balance went to Orville as residuary legatee. If it be maintained that Wilbur died in comfortable circumstances, the fact remains that he believed otherwise and suffered all the torments

Wilbur Wright in his prime. His most characteristic photograph and his usual costume, whether for flying or meeting kings.

of one who is in a precarious position as he leaves
this world. He did not know that either fortune or
name would long survive him.

Orville became president of the Wright Company,
and the exhibition business was discontinued. In
August the inventor and his sister visited the East
with two nieces and on the return trip Orville saw
Niagara Falls for the first time. In the autumn Griffith
Brewer, an English friend and early admirer of the
Wrights, was a guest for several weeks. After a brief
visit in England, Orville and Katharine were in Berlin,
where they had gone for the trial of the patent suit
before the German Supreme Court in February,
1913, when they learned of a favorable decision
in the similar case before the American Federal
Court.

The German patent office had originally granted a
patent, then had reversed itself after a long interval
and canceled the document on the ground of prior
disclosure of its contents by Wilbur Wright and Octave
Chanute. Now the supreme court found that while the
Americans were the originators of wing warping they
had, to the "great regret" of the court, lost title to
that discovery because of the disclosures mentioned.
However, the inventors still owned their combination
of warping with a vertical rudder. It may be said in
passing that the ground of disclosures cited had an
air of extreme legal casuistry in a land where high officials of the army disbelieved in the existence of the
airplane as late as the year 1907. In any case the disclosure principle would seem to exonerate a pickpocket

if his victim made a gesture which published the location of his purse.

From Berlin the travelers went to Paris for a week and Orville chanced to walk into a session of a French High Court when, without his previous knowledge, his case was under consideration. He assisted the lawyers in their arguments. The court sustained the previous decision of the Third Tribunal of the Seine and indeed improved upon it from the standpoint of the American inventors, stating that the disconnection of rudder from wing warping was not an improvement but part of the basic principle claimed by the Wrights. This seemed to be another great victory. It was in truth a formal triumph, for the court allowed the defense plea to have a board of experts resurvey the ground. This meant two years' delay and the chief defense lawyer assured the inventor that a legal rearguard action could be easily continued until the expiration of the French patent in 1917. Orville decided to withdraw from the fray.

The American decision for the Wrights was given on February 21, 1913. It was a decree on final hearing, rendered by Judge John R. Hazel in the Federal District Court at Buffalo, New York, in the equity suit by the Wright Company against the Herring-Curtiss Company and Glenn H. Curtiss. The lawyers for the complainant were H. A. Toulmin, Frederick P. Fish and Edmund Wetmore, and for the defendants Emerson R. Newell and J. Edgar Bull. Of the dozen and a half claims in the patent, the vital ones numbered 3, 7, 14 and 15 were held to be infringed.

After discussing the state of prior art and dismissing

a few more miscellaneous patents retrieved from dusty archives in addition to those previously considered in the injunction proceedings, Judge Hazel said:

". . . the patentees, by their method of securing the equilibrium of the planes, made an important advance in an embryonic art. They were not the first to conceive the idea of using monoplane or biplane surfaces . . . or to use vertical tails or rudders for steering, or to place horizontal rudders. . . . The prior separate use of such elements is freely admitted by the patentees; but they assert, rightly, I think, that the patented combination was a new combination, performing a new and novel result. . . . Having attained success where others failed, they may rightly be considered pioneer inventors in the aëroplane art . . . the patentees . . . are entitled to a liberal construction of their claims. . . .

"The defendants urge that the patentees' invention is without practical utility, that the flat planes described in the specification were never used. . . . But the patentees did not limit themselves to the precise details of construction. . . . Defendants further contend that the patent is silent regarding the use of a motor, and that therefore it was never intended to pass beyond the gliding machine stage; but this is incorrect, as the specification expressly alludes to flying either by the application of mechanical power or gravity. Moreover, the use of motors in aërial machinery was not a new idea, and was never regarded as a knotty problem. . . .

"This brings me to the final question of whether or not there is in defendants' machine a tendency to spin or swerve, which is checked or counteracted by the operation of its vertical rudder. . . . If I am correct in my interpretation of claim 3 . . . the ailerons of defendants' construction and the manner of using them are within its scope. The witness Curtiss frankly testified that the purpose thereof is to preserve the lateral balance. . . . Such concession supports the asserted infringement of the claim under consideration. There is, however, other testimony showing the specific manner in which the result is attained. The witnesses for complainant have sworn that in defendants' construction the aviator to restore lateral balance causes the ailerons to be lowered or raised, thus increasing the angle of incidence of one while decreasing that of the other, by inclining his body and moving his seat towards the high wing. It is true that the vertical rudder is not connected so as to coact with the ailerons . . . but each is controlled separately. . . .

"The testimony of witnesses who have flown the defendants' aëroplane and swear that the rear rudder is not in fact used for recovering lateral balance . . . would ordinarily be entitled to greater weight . . . were it not that there is cogent evidence tending to modify or qualify their denials of the use of the vertical rudder except for steering. Willard concedes that the rear rudder is turned to the high side to gain additional restoring power. . . . In the Curtiss letter in evidence it is substantially admitted that the rear rudder is turned toward the high side at times *to assist in balancing* the machine by steering or turning. The testimony of Lieutenant Milling of the United States Signal Corps . . . strongly supports the claim that the defendants employed the vertical rudder for the dual purpose of steering and recovering balance under certain conditions. . . .

"The defendants are believed to have appropriated the substance of claim 7, and to have infringed claim 14, inasmuch as, in addition to the essential elements of the Wright patent . . . they also employ . . . a horizontal rudder. . . . Claim 15 contains the essential elements, and specifies the location of a vertical rudder at the rear of the machine and a horizontal rudder at the front thereof. The defendants have embodied in their aëroplane the various elements of the claims in suit. While it is true, . . . that the defendants have constructed their machine somewhat differently from complainant's, and do not at all times and on all occasions operate the same on the Wright principle, yet the changes they have made in their construction relate to the form only."

While ordering a decree with costs in favor of the Wright Company, Judge Hazel, "because of the importance of the litigation", allowed "a supersedeas . . . upon condition that an appeal be diligently prosecuted."

The decision would have caused rejoicing, perhaps even a celebration, had Wilbur been alive. He had laid the ground work for it.

Orville and Katharine returned from abroad after an absence of five weeks and were at home six days before the Miami River flooded a large part of Dayton on March 25. It was three weeks before the airplane factory could be opened and the inventor spent much time exploring in the mud within the Hawthorn Street house, finding veritable historical treasures. He

saved diaries and records, the loss of which would have
been irreparable. The new house on Hawthorn Hill,
at a safe elevation above flood menace, had been under
way since the previous August. Its construction was
a useful anodyne. Brother and sister oversaw every detail of building and made trips to various cities to
obtain furnishings. In midsummer of this year Grover
Cleveland Loening, a young collegian, was employed
to do odd jobs at the airplane factory and remained a
year. There was a visit in the fall by Griffith Brewer
and Alexander Ogilvie: the pair of friendly Englishmen vainly sought to get Orville to take a vacation
with them at Kitty Hawk. No doubt a vacation would
have been helpful. The inventor was beginning to have
symptoms of neuritis with pain localized at the leg
fracture sustained at Fort Myer, and at intervals in
the future he was seriously affected by it. In the summer of the following year Mr. Brewer spent two and
a half months with the Wrights in their new home with
the intention of writing a history of the airplane, but
despite the assistance of his host he did not proceed
far with the project.

The Federal Circuit Court of Appeals, by Judges
Lacombe, Coxe and Ward, gave decision on January
13, 1914, affirming the previous interlocutory decree
of Judge Hazel. The tribunal of appeals said:

"As we are in full accord with the reasoning by
which [Judges Hazel and Hand] reached the conclusions that the patent in suit is a valid one, that the
patentees may fairly be considered pioneers in the
practical art of flying with heavier-than-air machines,
and that the claims should have a liberal interpretation,

it seems unnecessary to add anything to what has been already written. That the third claim, when liberally construed has been infringed, seems too plain for argument. . . . Such use of the rudder constitutes infringement, and a machine that infringes part of the time is an infringement, although it may at other times be so operated as not to infringe . . . the decree is affirmed, with costs."

The reader may prefer to have the last chapter of the legal story told here without regard to its sequence in the general narrative. A Wright lawyer had overlooked in the previous litigation one claim which seemed to afford the defendants a means of continuing at least part of their activities. Therefore a new suit was commenced on November 17, 1914, by the Wright Company against the Curtiss Aëroplane Company. Within the next year the inventor sold his patent rights and retired from business. The new owners of the Wright Company discontinued the suit on August 20, 1917, at a time when this country was involved in the World War and the United States Government commanded a patent truce among all manufacturers of aircraft.

The British Government, being sued in 1914 on Orville's behalf by a group of his English friends, made settlement in October of that year by paying the inventor seventy-five thousand dollars for past, present and future use of the airplane.

It thus appears that Wilbur and Orville Wright were generally vindicated as creators of the airplane by the courts of America, France and Germany, and the Government of England. The international victory was diminished in effect by technical points. It did not dispel to any appreciable extent the public fog which enveloped aviation. And the battle of the professors now began, to reverse judicial opinion and to minimize as far as possible the accomplishment of the Wrights.

In early 1914, soon after the Federal Circuit Court of Appeals had decided for the Wrights against Curtiss, the remains of the Langley flying machine which had been wrecked in the Potomac River in 1903 were taken from the government museum at Washington and sent to Hammondsport, New York, to receive a test at the hands of Glenn H. Curtiss. If this machine could fly, that fact would tend to discredit the Wrights as pioneers. Doctor A. F. Zahm, who had appeared as an expert witness for Curtiss in the previous litigation, was appointed to represent the Smithsonian Institution as official observer at the Hammondsport tests. A payment of two thousand dollars to Mr. Curtiss for his work was made by the Smithsonian but not, according to the press, until three years later. The entire proceedings took place under the authority of Doctor Charles D. Walcott, then Secretary of the Smithsonian Institution, who had earlier suggested to the Wrights that their airplane should be exhibited beside the Langley device.

A later administration of the Smithsonian admitted injustice to the Wrights in this affair with its developments. Meanwhile it may be observed that the Langley machine, after it had been considerably altered and refurbished, and equipped with a new motor and propeller, made some short hops or skips over the waters of a small lake. This proved no more and no less than a similar accomplishment with a box kite simulacrum of the airplane in France. Orville Wright made an affidavit for court use upon the Hammondsport test, pointing out the alterations which had been made in the Langley machine. Among these changes was a strengthening of parts, which seems to a layman innocent and even laudable, but which in fact amended Langley's incorrect understanding of aërodynamic facts. Orville's affidavit refers to the original Langley machine as follows:

"The failure of the Langley machine was due to faulty design and not to a mere accident in launching. The machine was not a practical one for the following reasons:

I. It was dynamically inefficient.

II. It was structurally weak.

III. It lacked adequate means for obtaining equilibrium.

IV. It lacked practical means for launching.

V. It lacked practical means for landing.

"The Langley machine introduced no new system of equilibrium. Langley adopted the Penaud tail for fore and aft equilibrium, and the dihedral angle for lateral balance. Neither of these systems is adequate to the needs of a practical flying machine."

The Smithsonian Annual Report for 1914 said that a miracle had occurred in the resurrection of a museum relic, using these terms:

"Owing to a defect in the launching apparatus, the two attempts to fly the large machine during Dr. Langley's life proved futile, but in June last, without modi-

fication, successful flights were made at Hammondsport, N. Y."

A later administration of the Smithsonian recanted
the foregoing statement thus:

"Certainly this was not literally true."

CHAPTER XIII

The new house on Hawthorn Hill was occupied at the end of April, 1914. It was built of light colored brick in Southern colonial architecture with two large fluted pillars, painted white, flanking the front entrance and extending to a roof of moderate pitch. A pair of lesser pillars guarded the doorway, above which a little balustrade gave the effect of a classic balcony. There were ample open porches with tile floors, on three sides of the mansion.

A winding private road led to the house from the street, not far, yet made sufficiently distant by graceful screens of elms and maples, native and planted shrubs. Velvet areas of lawn sloped away and disappeared amid the shadowy trees and thickets. The estate had no fences or signs of minatory intent, no gate-keeper's lodge and not even a watchman to patrol the grounds. There was small effort to alter the natural wildness of the tract. In accordance with Orville Wright's early principles, there was no garden, ornamental or practical. Nature supplied flowers and the market had vegetables.

The guest entering this house found himself in a spacious rectangular hall with stairs at the rear, a dining room at the left and on the right a passage ornamented with Louis Carvin's bronze — "The Muse of aviation showing to the first bird-men the secrets of flying" — a work of beauty with incidental portrait-figures of the Wrights. One looked in vain for other personal mementos. There were enough, as a visitor remarked, to decorate an entire room in the manner of Andrew Carnegie. But the inventor kept his multitude of medals in a box and rarely produced them. The passage led to the living room, a generous apartment with small brick fireplace, Orient rugs, tapestry chairs selected by personal visitation to Grand Rapids, alabaster light bowls likewise obtained in New York, and French style doors in mahogany leading to the favorite main porch. The tone of the room was of subdued pastel effect. A piano was added as an afterthought for the benefit of musical guests. The bedrooms, each with bath, were on the second floor with only an attic space above.

The main water supply was a problem, solved by use of cisterns which stored rain water. There was a period of halcyon days in the excellent and comfortable mansion, although Katharine once said, with moist eyes:

"We were happier down in Hawthorn Street."

At such moments there was emptiness in the wide rooms with polished floors, the foreign rugs were less than homely domestic weaves, and the most costly silk-covered divan appeared of trifling value beside a crude armchair which a swift-fingered youth had once built and carved for his ailing mother.

It was well there were minor difficulties and adjustments to divert the mind, as the doors in a new house. A little ceremony of making the rounds to lock doors was nightly participated in by host and guests at the retiring hour. The French-style mahogany doors usually could not be forced into place and after a formal struggle, were left unlocked. It would not do to have them cut down, since after seasoning they would fit properly.

Father Wright enjoyed the peace and comfort of the new habitation. He spoke a short grace at every meal; took daily walks about the grounds and even in the street, despite approach to his ninth decade; corresponded with church friends, and did not fail to enlarge his useful diary although "some days there's not much to write." He ruminated upon the past with judicious calm appraisal, was never garrulous or inclined to volunteer reminiscence without some little prompting. There was no pride manifest in him. He would discuss incidents with his son and stanchly dispute, if necessary, the minutiæ of bygone matters, including the day of the week and the hue of a cat. If the Bishop had any cross toward the end of his pilgrimage it was the lack of coffee, deemed injurious to his health by the tender solicitude of his daughter.

The fare at table was ample and appetizing, served with deft ceremony by the husband of "faithful Carrie" — the only domestics. When these had their usual Sunday evening off, the family and guests invaded the kitchen and sat there for an improvised supper selected from the ice-box. Buster, the favored nephew, might be present at Sunday dinner, gently quizzed and teased by uncle and aunt as to his future vocation of ornithology. No church was attended. It has been stated earlier that guests were few and the Wrights rarely went abroad for any social or recreative purpose.

Pets in the mansion were few and impermanent. A

vagabond cat might be entertained at the kitchen for a time. At one period there was an immense dog of somewhat indeterminate lineage and mournful eyes; the lumbering animal developed rheumatism and was never much comfort to anybody. The real pets were at liberty in the thickets and groves around the place, making the woodland ring with their music from early spring until winter. There was a favorite wren whose dwelling was almost within hand reach in a tree in front of the house. Visits were paid to it by the inventor and his sister after breakfast. It seemed that the little singer gave them a special recital. Sometimes Orville used a field glass to study distant and rare birds.

There were at least two score species of habitual visitors. One kind of bird required no glass for its observation. Indeed it was so pert and impudent as to perch upon the bronze screen of the inventor's bedroom window at daybreak and tap noisily on the woodwork, shattering slumber. The man within would approach the window and cry "Shoo!" The vexatious bird was the flicker or golden-winged woodpecker, handsome enough in its motley of red and black crescents, with areas of gold and white, but given to "the peculiar and silly habit of boring out a number of superfluous holes for nests," even in buildings. It is barely possible that the flicker was an agent of the entire bird tribe inflicting a mild revenge upon the man who flew but disclaimed any debt whatever to the birds.

On summer evenings when crickets sang in the grass, fireflies made zigzag trails and the whippoorwill echoed in the distance, the unlighted main porch was the family rendezvous. There was a low-voiced but cheerful re-telling of anecdotes, such as the famous exploit of Wilbur and the glass of jelly *en route* to Kitty Hawk. He was spoken of as one departed but yet not absent. There was a jolly anecdote of "the watermelon reporter." During the Fort Myer flights in 1909, on a torrid day, a pressman marched across the dusty field, bearing half a watermelon to the inventors' tent, and he said:

"We can't seem to get anything out of you. Thought we'd try to put something into you."

The reporter was Charles Van Loan, who afterward attained a reputation as a humorist.

When gliding experiments were spoken of, some one might recall that Wilbur, writing to a friend in Germany, not long before his passing, had said:

"The birds can fly without a motor — why can't man?"

The Wrights were by nature peace-loving, the antithesis of everything connoted by pugnacity and militarism. Although they early saw the military use of the airplane and indeed negotiated with the war departments of several governments to that end, they doubtless believed that their invention would play the part of aërial scout rather than become an engine of death and destruction. Probably the scouting rôle did not seem to them a direct implication in the process of fighting.

There is negative evidence as to the Quakerish attitude of the brothers, whose harmless and innocent vehicle was for a time converted by the ironical fates to a savage inhuman purpose. This evidence is their record of silent avoidance of the military topic. They refrained from military sales talk in favor of their machine. They never sought to exploit the emotion of patriotism or to suggest that national security required a multitude of martial wings.

Wilbur died before the lethal capacity of the airplane was demonstrated.

There is a bit of positive evidence as to Orville's reaction in this matter. Shortly before the outbreak of the World War the press noted that England was experimentally dropping oranges from an airplane to the deck of a vessel, so as to find whether the bombing of ships would be feasible. At this time Professor J. A. Huffman, later Dean of the School of Theology in Marion College, Indiana, happened to be a tenant and neighbor of the inventor. Professor Huffman took the press cutting to his landlord, asking his opinion as to war and the airplane, and states that Orville made comment as follows:

"Up to the present time the wars of the world have been fought largely by the common people, while those who were responsible for declaring war have remained at home. The airplane will change all this. As a result of the use of the airplane, the palaces of kings and rulers will no longer be safe, but will be in danger of being blown up by bombshells dropped upon them from airplanes. I believe," concluded the inventor with an optimism that at least was sincere, "that the airplane will help to put an end to war, for when the men who make war find their own lives in danger, they will be less likely to decree war."

As Nobel, the inventor of dynamite, was a humanitarian who established prizes to advance science and promote international peace, so the Wrights, inventors of a craft with baleful potencies, were essentially devoted to the welfare of mankind. Dynamite and the airplane will be used in the world's peaceful progress long ages after war has been outlawed and forgotten.

Sometimes a group of children invaded a high open part of the estate at Hawthorn Hill to fly kites. If Orville happened to be about he would hasten to join them and would zestfully assist in tying strings, making suggestions of improvement and generally promoting the success of the enterprise. For a little while he was happy as any youngster and indeed seemed to have returned to the gay absorbed period of kite making and flying during the family sojourn in Richmond, Indiana.

When the world did not know in 1904 that the airplane existed, its creators thought of making it automatically stable in flight, and four years later they patented certain basic principles to that end. Wilbur did not devote much attention to the problem, and his main contribution was the idea of a vane to secure fore-and-aft balance. A non-automatic inclinometer to show the pilot the fore-and-aft angle of his machine was early devised.

Now Orville resumed study of the whole subject in his new private laboratory located in a business section of Dayton, to which he drove daily in his roadster. There were conveniences and refinements of equipment that would have seemed incredible in the days of the alley shop behind the bicycle store. Instead of the pioneer wind tunnel made of odds and ends, there was an imposing glassy-varnished pipe of generous dimension and room length, to fill which with rushing air would almost tax the puffing cheeks of Aeolus. It was better in every way than the original wind tunnel. At the same time it could not surpass the crude device by which man for the first time discovered the true laws of the air in motion.

The problem of automatic stability is tantalizing, and deceptive in its promise of easy solution. There was an early attempt by those who developed the gyroscope to win through by this means, but a device suitable for marine vessels will not serve in the air. An ordinary pendulum works too fast or too slow in regard to side tilting of a plane. In the Wright system a pendulum was connected with an electric battery which operated a clutch on the wing controls. The actual power to warp wings, or move equivalent ailerons, was given by a propeller moved by the windstream. The latter was an improvement following the use of compressed air as source of power.

The automatic fore-and-aft control was similar to the lateral, except that there was a vane instead of a pendulum. The vane could be set at any desired flying angle and if the plane departed from that angle it would be immediately brought back to it by suitable movement of the horizontal rudder actuated by propeller power.

Orville found that the automatic equipment enabled him to fly for several minutes with hands off the controls. The plane kept within half a degree of its required angle fore-and-aft. While this was better than the average pilot's performance, it was not accurate

enough for the inventor. Besides, the electrical part of
the mechanism did not always prove reliable. There
was more work to be done. While the basic features of
the whole apparatus had been patented, it appeared
that the completed combination would lack legal protection. On this point the inventor, having had world-
wide experience, said with calm philosophy:

"What's the use of patenting them?"

It was enough that the idea interested him and the
work was worth doing. It might be considered scientific
play, like much of the brothers' early activity. There
was a similar mingling of sport with science when Orville mounted an airplane engine and propeller upon a
boat to be used on vacation trips to Canada. There were
other vacations, as an automobile trip to the far West,
not to mention visits to New York and other cities.

By this time all airplanes had become somewhat
standardized in appearance. The Wright machine had
had wheel control instead of levers since 1910. The
landing gear combined skids and wheels, and the
launching derrick was no more. A single propeller was
placed in front of some machines. The old front elevator was placed in the rear and the fuselage was
modified, especially for use on water. The warping was
reduced from a helicoidal twist of the entire wing to
a conical warp of the rear margin, a triangular section
a dozen feet in length with a width of two or three feet
at the tip and an extreme motion up or down of some
eighteen inches.

In October, 1915, Orville Wright realized the
early dream of the brothers to retire from business.
He sold his controlling interest in the Wright Company

to a syndicate of New York financiers, including William B. Thompson, Albert H. Wiggin and T. Frank Manville. Various estimates of the price were given in the press, ranging from six hundred and seventy-five thousand dollars to a million and a half dollars. The inventor was quoted as saying:

"I sold in order to devote my time to research work. The cares of modern business little encouraged the tastes of one who feels that his work is not done. I will devote the balance of my life to scientific research."

The Wright Company manufactured planes for some years, underwent a change of ownership and finally confined itself to the exclusive production of aircraft engines.

Bishop Milton Wright died on April 3, 1917, at the age of eighty-eight years and nearly five months. He had outlived his father by seventeen years and his wife by three decades. The mansion on Hawthorn Hill was emptier than it had been before.

The Smithsonian Institution now began to display the reconstructed Langley machine under a series of labels which had progressive evolution in the course of years. The first label, as applied in 1918, read:

THE ORIGINAL, FULL-SIZE,
LANGLEY FLYING MACHINE, 1903

At some "later" time, the precise date not being given by the authorities concerned, "this label was amplified to read as follows:"

ORIGINAL LANGLEY
FLYING MACHINE, 1903

THE FIRST MAN-CARRYING AEROPLANE IN THE HIS-
TORY OF THE WORLD CAPABLE OF SUSTAINED FREE
FLIGHT. INVENTED, BUILT, AND TESTED OVER THE POTO-
MAC RIVER BY SAMUEL PIERPONT LANGLEY IN 1903.
SUCCESSFULLY FLOWN AT HAMMONDSPORT, N. Y., JUNE
2, 1914. DIMENSIONS: 55 FEET LONG, 48 FEET WIDE;
SUSTAINING WING SURFACE 1,040 SQUARE FEET.

In early 1925 the American press buzzed with the
news that the pioneer Kitty Hawk airplane was to be
sent to an English museum. The New York *World* on
May 3 published a statement by Orville Wright in part
as follows:

"I stated . . . that I was sending the machine to
the Science Museum at South Kensington, London, because I did not dare to intrust it to the only suitable
national museum in America, in view of the fact that
that institution has allowed the historic relics of the
Langley machine of 1903 to go out of the institution
into the hands of private parties to be mutilated for
private purposes; that the machine now hanging in
the institution is, much of it, new material and some
of it of different construction from the original, and
that the card attached to the machine is not true of the
original machine or of the restored one."

After reviewing the circumstances of the Hammondsport test of the Langley machine, the inventor
continued:

"Our machine is now wholly in its original form and
almost wholly of its original material. I would not
wish to leave to the discretion of the management of
any museum the right to make any change in the de-

sign of it for any purpose whatever. If one half of the changes made in the Langley machine were to be made in our machine it could easily be proved not 'capable of sustained free flight.' No one could possibly regret more than I do that our machine must go into a foreign museum. It is not safe where it is. It suffered in one flood and has always been liable to fire. Excepting the national museum or the Smithsonian, I know of none in this country so suitable for such an exhibit as the Science Museum at South Kensington, London."

President Coolidge politely hoped that the pioneer airplane would not be exiled but diplomatically refrained from taking part in a war of the professors. Various domestic museums offered hospitality. There was talk of congressional investigation of the national museum and also of a Federal law that would forbid the exportation of an American trophy, such as the Kitty Hawk plane. Secretary Walcott of the Smithsonian Institution gave to the press his version of the Langley affair and sympathetically deplored that "any fancied grievance with an individual" should cause the loss to America of "the original machine that first carried a man in flight. . . ."

As a result of the commotion the inventor held in abeyance his project to find a foreign resting place for the ancestral vehicle of the air. Two years later he presented to the Royal Scottish Museum in Glasgow an airplane engine practically identical with one of those used by the brothers in the early period of their discovery. This was a little gift, yet more than any that went to a home museum. One who has read the Northcliffe letter and the statement of the British Government's relatively fair attitude toward the Wrights will understand the little gift and the reason why England seemed to Orville Wright a desirable haven for the original airplane.

Instead of executing retreat from an untenable position, the professors at Washington decided to make a new offensive with a fresh label on the Langley machine. Secretary Walcott appointed a commission of two men, Joseph S. Ames, Professor of Physics in Johns Hopkins University, and D. W. Taylor, a retired rear-admiral, to advise upon history and labels. They found that while the Wrights did fly first of all men, Langley was a Moses within "sight of the same goal." He at least saw "the promised land." His machine was "capable of sustained flight" and only missed it by a launching accident.

Accordingly Secretary Walcott, in October, 1925, ordered the following legend, Label Number III, affixed to a museum specimen:

LANGLEY AERODROME

THE ORIGINAL LANGLEY FLYING MACHINE OF 1903, RESTORED

IN THE OPINION OF MANY COMPETENT TO JUDGE, THIS WAS THE FIRST HEAVIER-THAN-AIR CRAFT IN THE HISTORY OF THE WORLD CAPABLE OF SUSTAINED FREE FLIGHT UNDER ITS OWN POWER, CARRYING A MAN.

THIS AIRCRAFT SLIGHTLY ANTEDATED THE MACHINE DESIGNED AND BUILT BY WILBUR AND ORVILLE WRIGHT, WHICH, ON DECEMBER 17, 1903, WAS THE FIRST IN THE

HISTORY OF THE WORLD TO ACCOMPLISH SUSTAINED
FREE FLIGHT UNDER ITS OWN POWER, CARRYING A MAN.

A lengthy statement elaborating the foregoing legend
as to Langley and his machine, and displayed beneath
it, is omitted. The complete inscription, like its predecessors, was in due time officially withdrawn and canceled.

The injustice of man is mitigated in effect by the
understanding of its motives and compulsions, while
the blows of fate appear as stark irrational cruelty.
Thus the deeds of individuals almost become as pin-
pricks beside the pain inflicted by life, without ascer-
tainable reason, upon the personages of our narrative.

"There has been such an upheaval in our world —
Orville's and mine," Katharine wrote to a friend, an-
nouncing her marriage, which occurred on November
20, 1926.

Her husband was Henry J. Haskell, formerly a fellow student at Oberlin College, then an editor of the
Kansas City *Star*. The newspaper was one of the most
influential in the Middle West and attained a national
importance when Theodore Roosevelt, retired from the
presidency, became a contributing editor. Mr. Haskell
had been a family friend for thirty years. No doubt
romance had blossomed in the college period, had been
cherished through adverse circumstances and at last
found expression.

Katharine had to fulfill her life, although her action
spelled an upheaval and there was an "inevitable
cloud" in the thought of separation from a lifetime

companion, now left alone in a mansion upon a hill. She was happy and at the same moment sad. There was a little consolation that "faithful Carrie" was in charge, ordering the routine of material comfort with entire competence.

Friends rejoiced with Katharine in her happiness while they sympathized with the loneliness and hurt of a brother whose dearest support had been removed. She had been a source of light and cheer, a personality of normal balance and gayety, one who had made the home a refuge in the darkest hour, who had laughed away tribulation as unimportant adventure upon life's highway.

As if fate — let those who will, say providence — had not inflicted sufficient hardship, the happiness of Katharine was as a candle that flickers out in a puff of air. She died in her new home at Kansas City of pneumonia on March 3, 1929. Her husband had become editor of the *Star* within a few preceding months and within the week his joint ownership, with associates, of the newspaper had been confirmed by the Supreme Court of the United States.

Her brothers, Orville and Lorin, were at her bedside at the last.

A friend wrote of Katharine:

"No spirit could be happier than hers, and she leaves all who knew her a memory that is in itself solacing. Her character was beautiful. She served the world to great advantage, as well as the circle of those about her."

There are lines written by Elizabeth Barrett Browning which seem to apply:

If I leave all for thee, wilt thou exchange
And be all to me? Shall I never miss
Home-talk and blessing and the common kiss
That comes to each in turn, nor count it strange,
When I look up, to drop on a new range
Of walls and floors, another home than this?

.   .   .   .

And a voice said in mastery, while I strove, —
"Guess now who holds thee?" —
        "Death," I said. But, there,
The silver answer rang, — "Not Death, but Love."

After holding it in abeyance for three years, Orville
Wright fulfilled his intention to send the pioneer airplane to the English museum, in February, 1928. The
American press buzzed anew and published many articles and statements. The inventor had an interchange
of views with the new and somewhat conciliatory head
of the Smithsonian Institution, Doctor C. S. Abbot.
The latter offered a compromise, saying that he would
change the label on the Langley machine to a noncom-
mittal formula and would apply to the Kitty Hawk
plane, if it were retrieved for the national museum, an
inscription that would meet the approval of its joint
creator. Secretary Abbot proposed a bargain. He did
not think that "anybody would wish us to recant
falsely." If the inventor would concede that the professors at Washington had been sincere in their claims for
the Langley machine, those claims would be withdrawn,
"not in confession of error, but in a gesture of goodwill
for the honor of America. . . ." The friends of Langley
would then transfer public allegiance to the Wrights and
would "let Langley's fame stand on its merits. . . ."

Orville Wright reviewed the whole controversy in an

article which he contributed to the *United States Air Services* magazine, and he later indicated elsewhere that the Smithsonian proffer did not appeal to him.

A press cable from London, dated March 20, said the pioneer airplane "proved a great attraction to the King and Queen of England to-day. The plane, which landed on English soil February 21, was the center of interest in the new buildings of the Science Museum at South Kensington, which were opened by the King. After the formalities, the sovereigns had their first view of the machine. They inspected it carefully. . . ."

The goad of kingly interest has ever been required to persuade the American democracy to a belated and spasmodic recognition of the Wrights. There was now the usual effect. Our leading magazines, which had been indifferent if not hostile toward the origin of the airplane, now displayed a lively interest in the subject and published articles upon it. One of the magazines appeared in the guise of a long-standing champion of the Wrights, berated the officials at Washington and patriotically demanded the return of the American trophy to its native land.

On September 29 of this year Secretary Abbot of the Smithsonian published an official document, "The Relations Between The Smithsonian Institution and The Wright Brothers." This was a review and a qualified apology to the inventors. Injustice was admitted. "I acknowledge with regret that the summary of the proceedings given at an earlier page of the Smithsonian Annual Report for 1910 (pp. 22–23) is misleading." This referred to an occasion when Wilbur Wright's actual words were supplemented with an interpolated extract of a private letter from the Wright brothers, giving the effect that they acknowledged a considerable debt to Professor Langley. The official proceeded: "I concede to Mr. Wright that it lacked of consideration to put the tests of the Langley plane into the hands of his opponent, Mr. Curtiss." It was not improper to make the tests. "But I feel that it was a pity that Manly, Doctor Langley's colleague, could not have been the man chosen to make them."

Secretary Abbot furthermore confessed: "The claims published by the Smithsonian relating to the 1914 experiments at Hammondsport were sweeping." That a flight had been made "without modification" of the machine "was not literally true. . . ." Of course the official who wrote the statement "believed this to be true." Secretary Abbot here attenuated apology by asserting that the effects of the now admitted changes were of a pro-and-con speculative nature. The professors might still argue that they were right. "It must ever be a matter of opinion."

"In concluding this account," declared Secretary Abbot, "I express, on behalf of the Smithsonian Institution, regret:

"1. That any loose or inaccurate statements should have been promulgated by it which might be interpreted to Mr. Wright's disadvantage.

"2. That it should have contributed by the quotation on page 23 of the Smithsonian Annual Report of 1910 to the impression that the success of the Wright brothers was due to anything but their own research, genius, sacrifice, and perseverance.

"3. That the experiments of 1914 should have been

conducted and described in a way to give offense to Mr. Orville Wright and his friends."

There was a renewed invitation to the inventor to deposit the Kitty Hawk plane in the national museum. "Finally, as a further gesture of good-will, I am willing to let Langley's fame rest on its merits, and have directed that the labels on the Langley Aerodrome shall be so modified as to tell nothing but facts, without additions of opinion as to the accomplishments of Langley."

Accordingly Label Number IV — the fourth in a decade or an average of one new label every thirty months — was affixed as follows:

LANGLEY AERODROME
THE ORIGINAL SAMUEL PIERPONT LANGLEY
FLYING MACHINE OF 1903, RESTORED
DEPOSITED BY
THE SMITHSONIAN INSTITUTION

Orville Wright did not respond to the olive branch. Others may feel that the Smithsonian humbled itself enough and that even scientists should have the privilege of keeping their private opinions, however misguided, as long as their public conduct is correct. The opinions of the professors, having no factual or provable basis, are bound to be dissipated in time. Meanwhile it is more important that the general public should have the outline of truth.

The twenty-fifth anniversary of flight by the Wright brothers was celebrated in mid-December, 1928, in connection with the International Civil Aëronautics conference at Washington, D.C. Delegates from many lands attended. Brazil declined to send a delegate on the ground that her favorite son, Santos-Dumont, was an air pioneer. It appears he is the last of the foreign claimants. At one time the leading nations each had one or more candidates for pioneer honors.

A number of the foreign delegates arrived in Dayton by air, visited the laboratories at the government Wright Field, placed a wreath on the tomb of Wilbur Wright and called at the home of the surviving brother. Orville Wright was present at a public meeting where he received a scroll from his fellow citizens and was lauded in addresses by Lord Thomson, England's former Minister of Air; Ahmed Mouehtar Bey, Turkish Ambassador to the United States; William P. Mac-Cracken, Assistant Secretary of Commerce for Aëronautics. There were unofficial tributes from General Italo Balbo of Italy, who said, "It is known to all peoples that Dayton is the home of the airplane"; Pierre E. Flandin, Vice President of the French Chamber of Deputies; and from Lieutenant Colonel P. Amara, who said that his country, Siam, was also becoming airminded.

The chief ceremony at Washington occurred on December 12, at the opening of the aëronautical conference with one hundred and twenty-five delegates present from thirty-nine countries. Colonel Lindbergh and other celebrities were in the assemblage. Orville Wright, the guest of honor, was conspicuously absent because his train was four hours late. At the announcement, "a subdued ripple of laughter swept over the gathering. . . ." The program did not wait, although the world formerly waited more than four hours for the arrival of a new means of transport.

President Coolidge made an address lauding the Wrights with a meed of careful credit to their predecessors. The roll began with Pegasus, Dædalus and Icarus. The "authentic record" of a flying pigeon made by Archytas, a Greek, some three centuries before the Christian era, was cited. Leonardo da Vinci came next, and the period of hot air balloons received attention. The work of Santos-Dumont and of Zeppelin with dirigible balloons was recalled. Disregarding the opinions of judges who had studied the record of prior art and had declared the independent paternity of the airplane, President Coolidge continued:

"In the meantime, beginning with Cayley, Englishman and 'father of aërodynamics,' who died in 1857, and continuing down through Henson and Stringfellow, Maxim, Ader, Lilienthal and Langley (of Washington), scientists were gradually, with gliders and other devices, working out the problem of a heavier-than-air machine."

Having achieved these reservations in behalf of the academic true believers, the address continued in a vein of almost complete eulogy:

"With genius, indomitable perseverance and a will to overcome obstacles, the Wrights, mindful of what had gone before, applied themselves to the solution of the problem. They experimented at Kitty Hawk for three seasons; and in the fourth, on December 17, 1903, success crowned their efforts."

President Coolidge noted the fact that in 1908 a Wright plane "was bought by the War Department, our government being the first to utilize this new device," omitting to mention that the same government through its War Department rejected the inventors' offer of a monopoly of the airplane in 1905. There was a suitable peroration.

Some of the phrases of the presidential address have a reminiscent aroma which at length may be identified with the musty air of an institution founded by a Briton named James Smithson. It would seem that the Post Office Department took advice from the same source when it issued for the twenty-fifth anniversary a new postage stamp, showing a picture of the Wright plane of 1908 instead of a picture of the Kitty Hawk machine that inaugurated aviation five years earlier. Perhaps the same influence led an American scientist, discussing aërodynamic theory before the delegates, to cite some twenty-nine contributors to that theory while forgetting to mention the brothers who in effect created aërodynamics.

No flying was done at the Kitty Hawk rites for lack of a landing field, it was stated, although the first airplane had no trouble landing there and modern machines circle the globe, heedless of terrain.

Congress voted the Distinguished Flying Cross to the living inventor and to his departed brother. The trophy was appropriate to the half-dozen gallant pilots, domestic and foreign, to whom it had previously been awarded. It harmonized with the earlier medals and the new postage stamps.

During the ceremonies here, Frenchmen across the sea gathered to lay a wreath upon the monument to Wilbur Wright at Le Mans, where he gave the Old

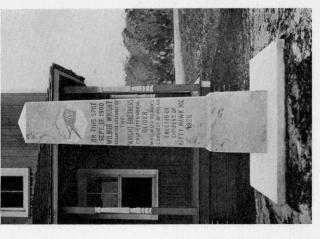

Orville Wright at Kitty Hawk, N. C., December 17, 1928, revisits the scene of great achievement during the celebration of the Twenty-fifth Anniversary of Flight. Besides the Memorials here shown, the foundation of a Government Monument was laid upon Kill Devil Hill. England and France joined America in Tribute to the Conquerors of the Air.

World its first view of the New World's discovery. In England, on the eve of December 17, a banquet table was set for one hundred persons in the Science Museum, London, beneath the uplifted wings of the machine in which man conquered the air at Kitty Hawk. Prominent persons spoke, the Wrights were toasted, a cable from the surviving brother was read. A scene such as that may have disconcerting elements to an American, however much he may appreciate English courtesy.

If Orville Wright felt that suitable amends had been made here, he did not signify it by recalling the virgin aircraft from its exile. He spoke no word at any of the triple ceremonies which he attended at Dayton, Washington and Kitty Hawk.

A frail age-weary figure, none of his kin beside him, stood in a peopled solitude by a monument newly erected by the citizens of Kitty Hawk to mark the spot where two nimble, hopeful young men began to assemble their first glider a generation before. . . . Halvers on everything, Wilbur — the skimpy as well as the good! Share and share alike. Three piles of hickory nuts on the barn floor — nobody can touch anybody else's except —

Some of the folk standing near by had a ghostly familiarity.

Why, of course, Postmaster Tate! Boarded at his house. Wilbur used his wife's sewing machine and his little girls had sateen dresses out of the glider wings! Glad to see you, Postmaster. But who are these three men? Why, they're the stout lads tanned by sun and salt water, who came over from the government coastguard station on a bleak winter day and helped to launch the power machine. Daniels, Dough and Etheridge. Boys, you look fine! That was a great day, wasn't it? Let's see, a couple of chaps are missing. Brinkley, a lumber buyer. And where's Johnny Moore? He was only sixteen years old and I guess that roaring engine scared him a mite. . . .

Secretary of War Davis spoke and there was oratory by Senator Bingham and Congressman Lindsay Warren.

Man shall fly like a mighty swan.

Saw the heavens fill with commerce, argo-
   sies of magic sails,
Pilots of the purple twilight, dropping down
   with costly bales:

Ahoy, Sir Walter Raleigh, tell Queen Bess —

Orville Wright did not seem to hear or heed the words of suave eulogy. His eyes roamed over the desert of sand with its curved wind-made hills ideal for gliding — wonderful sport! How is the wind to-day? — across the waters of Albemarle Sound and toward the surging ocean where the eagles used to steal the prey of fishhawks, diving like lightning from the blue, keenly watched by two young men who planned with a Promethean presumption to steal from the eagles their dominion of the sky.

The cornerstone was laid for a government memorial to the Wrights upon Kill Devil Hill.

THE END